T0344376

'Don't expect to be motivated every day to get out there and make things happen. You won't be. Don't count on motivation. Count on Discipline.'
Jocko Willink, retired U.S. Navy SEAL officer

'This is a tremendous resource for every security professional and organization whose goal is to improve their cybersecurity posture. The evidence-based cybersecurity approach ties the criticality of understanding human behavior with the technical aspects of cyber-crime. A true data centric treasure trove of valuable knowledge.'
– *Kausar Kenning, Executive Director, Cyber Security, Morgan Stanley*

'Despite its technical nature, the evidence base supporting cybersecurity as a field of practice remains flimsy, at best. Some have even compared cybersecurity to "medieval witchcraft"'. This timely and essential book provides a much needed and comprehensive overview of the available evidence and of the knowledge gaps that persist, also charting the path ahead for a more scientific approach to the design, implementation, and evaluation of cybersecurity measures.'
– *Dr. Benoît Dupont, Professor of Criminology, University of Montreal, Canada, and Canada Research Chair in Cybersecurity*

'Dr. Pomerleau does a masterful job of deep diving into the realm of contemporary Cybersecurity. Beyond recounting the historical evolution of Cybersecurity, Pomerleau astutely weaves together a traditional IT risk management system approach with a multi-faceted humanistic approach (with ethical, sociological, psychological, and criminal elements) to present a comprehensive how-to guide for evidence-based Cybersecurity analysis.'
– *Dr. David L. Lowery, Full Professor of Homeland Security & Public Administration, Northcentral University*

Evidence-Based
Cybersecurity

Security, Audit and Leadership Series

Series Editor: Dan Swanson, Dan Swanson and Associates, Ltd.,
Winnipeg, Manitoba, Canada.

The *Security, Audit and Leadership Series* publishes leading-edge books on critical subjects facing security and audit executives as well as business leaders. Key topics addressed include Leadership, Cybersecurity, Security Leadership, Privacy, Strategic Risk Management, Auditing IT, Audit Management and Leadership

Rising from the Mailroom to the Boardroom: Unique Insights for Governance, Risk, Compliance and Audit Leaders
Bruce Turner

Operational Auditing: Principles and Techniques for a Changing World (Second Edition)
Hernan Murdock

CyRM^{SM}: Mastering the Management of Cybersecurity
David X Martin

The Complete Guide for CISA Examination Preparation
Richard E. Cascarino

Blockchain for Cybersecurity and Privacy: Architectures, Challenges, and Applications
Yassine Maleh, Mohammad Shojafar, Mamoun Alazab, Imed Romdhani

The Cybersecurity Body of Knowledge: The ACM/IEEE/AIS/IFIP Recommendations for a Complete Curriculum in Cybersecurity
Daniel Shoemaker, Anne Kohnke, Ken Sigler

For more information about this series, please visit: https://www.routledge.com/Internal-Audit-and-IT-Audit/book-series/CRCINTAUDITA

Evidence-Based Cybersecurity

Foundations, Research, and Practice

Pierre-Luc Pomerleau
David Maimon

CRC Press

Taylor & Francis Group
Boca Raton London New York

CRC Press is an imprint of the
Taylor & Francis Group, an **informa** business

First edition published 2022
by CRC Press
6000 Broken Sound Parkway NW, Suite 300, Boca Raton, FL 33487-2742

and by CRC Press
4 Park Square, Milton Park, Abingdon, Oxon, OX14 4RN

CRC Press is an imprint of Taylor & Francis Group, LLC

© 2022 Pierre-Luc Pomerleau and David Maimon

Library of Congress Cataloging-in-Publication Data
Names: Pomerleau, Pierre-Luc, author. | Maimon, David, 1978- author.
Title: Evidence-based cybersecurity : foundations, research, and practice / Pierre-Luc Pomerleau, David Maimon.
Description: First edition. | Boca Raton, FL : CRC Press, 2022. | Series: Internal audit and IT audit | Includes bibliographical references and index. | Identifiers: LCCN 2021060090 (print) | LCCN 2021060091 (ebook) | ISBN 9781032062761 (hbk) | ISBN 9781032062785 (pbk) | ISBN 9781003201519 (ebk)
Subjects: LCSH: Computer security. | Comptuter networks--Security measures. | Computer crimes--Prevention.
Classification: LCC QA76.9.A25 P5968 2022 (print) | LCC QA76.9.A25 (ebook) | DDC 005.8--dc23/eng/20220201
LC record available at https://lccn.loc.gov/2021060090
LC ebook record available at https://lccn.loc.gov/2021060091

ISBN: 9781032062761 (hbk)
ISBN: 9781032062785 (pbk)
ISBN: 9781003201519 (ebk)

DOI: 10.1201/9781003201519

Typeset in Sabon
by KnowledgeWorks Global Ltd.

To all cybersecurity professionals and researchers
working tirelessly to make the world a safer place.

Contents

Foreword

Many cybersecurity books share potentially useful perspectives on methodologies, tools, and innovative insights. That said, as a cybersecurity practitioner for over 20 years, I still find it overwhelming to determine how best to evolve my security program while keeping costs in line. Are the dollars I am investing truly improving my security posture? Are the solutions performing in my environment the way the vendors promised they would?

A few years ago, for instance, my goal was to find a better way to quantify the effectiveness of security investments. I attended one of the first meetings of the Evidence-Based Cybersecurity research group, a collegiate program led by Dr. David Maimon. To hear cybersecurity discussed in terms of criminology, darknet data analysis, and the motivations/patterns of cybercriminals was enlightening. That meeting is also where I met Dr. Pierre-Luc Pomerleau, this book's coauthor. He had flown from Canada to Atlanta for this session and was the head of a financial institution's security team. We had very similar lightbulb moments during David's presentations, and we exchanged ideas that resonated in the space of evidence-based cybersecurity.

Academic theory can seem distant from real-world security applications, but I soon learned that evidence-based cybersecurity merges the best of both worlds. A strong security program has well-defined people, technology, and processes to maximize investments and minimize business risks. (Don't be fooled – we will never reduce risks to zero.) While cybercrime may seem like you are always fighting bots, there are humans behind the tactics, techniques, and procedures driving those threats. There is very little research on the psychology on cybercriminals and why they do what they do. Understanding cybercriminals helps you target better investments in your environment.

Fifteen years ago, threats were more likely a nation-state or highly financed, tech-savvy groups. Technology today allows anyone, anywhere to be a potential threat. One cannot protect an environment without understanding the underlying technology, how it is interconnected, and what the crown jewels of your business are. If vital records got out in the public domain, for instance, how would this impact your brand and customer trust?

Once you have a high-level understanding of your environment, you then need in-depth visibility into its events, operations, and activity. There are a myriad of security tools, managed services, and consultants that can guide you through these decisions. But how do you measure their effectiveness? This is where an unbiased, evidence-based research approach can measure a solution's effectiveness by price point. We all wish we had a $1B security budget, but the reality is we must protect our organizations with what we have. Empirical evidence allows security practitioners to map their risks, develop a realistic roadmap, and produce an investment timeline with full transparency on what risks the organization must accept.

As security practitioners, it often feels like we are always reactionary and always three steps behind the bad guys (which we are). But we are starting to see more and more solutions that produce earlier insights into developing threats, or at least awareness of a breach/compromise before it becomes public. Next-generation endpoint detection and response (EDR) solutions are helping us evolve to get ahead of the threats. Machine learning and artificial learning accelerate the identification and remediation of malicious behavior. Research is needed to place these tools in real-world honeypot environments, to see how they perform and reduce risk. The more we know about how cybercriminals respond when they encounter these tools, the better we can meet their attacks.

What I love about this book is the combination of real-world research in active security programs. This adds to our collective body of knowledge and matures our security practices. Pierre-Luc and David are growing this research and advancing important insights to protect our organizations and lower our risk. If you want to learn about this revolutionary, evidence-based approach, this book is for you.

Max Garcia

About the authors

Pierre-Luc Pomerleau is a Partner at VIDOCQ. His role consists of assisting VIDOCQ's clients in growing their business and innovating while managing their risks and protecting their assets. He does so by bringing years of experience and deep expertise in cybercrime, investigation, fraud prevention, anti-money laundering, physical security, business administration, technology, and risk management. Before joining VIDOCQ, he was Vice President at National Bank of Canada, managing the Financial Crime and Corporate Security division, including data analytics and innovation.

Dr. Pomerleau holds a PhD in Business Administration with a specialization in Homeland Security from Northcentral University (USA), an MBA from the University of Sherbrooke (Canada), and a bachelor's degree in criminology from the University of Montreal (Canada). He holds various security and financial crime professional certifications such as the CPP, PSP, PCI, CFE, CAMS, CCCI, & CFCI certifications. In addition to his role with VIDOCQ, Dr. Pomerleau is currently an adjunct in cybersecurity at Polytechnique Montreal. From 2020 to 2021, he was a postdoctoral researcher and a research associate in cybercrime at Georgia State University (USA). In 2020, he co-authored the book *Countering Cyber Threats to Financial Institutions: A Private and Public Partnership Approach to Critical Infrastructure*. From 2015 to 2018, he was the President of the Association of Certified Fraud Examiner Montreal Chapter. In October 2016, he was awarded an honorary diploma by the University of Montreal School of Criminology for his exemplary contribution to the advancement of society.

David Maimon is an Associate Professor in the Department of Criminal Justice and Criminology at Georgia State University (GSU) and the director of the Evidence-Based Cybersecurity research group (see ebcs.gsu.edu). Dr. Maimon is also Chief Science Officer at VIDOCQ. He received his PhD in Sociology from the Ohio State University in 2009. Prior to joining GSU, Dr. Maimon held academic position in the Department of Criminology and Criminal Justice in the University of Maryland and the Department of Sociology in the University of Miami. In 2015, he was awarded the 'Young Scholar Award' from the 'White-Collar Crime Research Consortium of the National White-Collar Crime Center' for his cybercrime research. Throughout his career, he has raised more than $3 million to conduct Evidence-Based Cybersecurity research. Since joining GSU, Dr. Maimon has established the Evidence-Based Cybersecurity research group, where he and his researchers seek to produce and review multi- and interdisciplinary empirical evidence about the effectiveness of cybersecurity tools and policies. The group and its unique approach to cybersecurity education and research have been acknowledged on popular media platforms (https://edtechmagazine.com/higher/article/2020/09/training-next-generation-cyber-professionals). Moreover, the group's close relationships with cybersecurity professionals in several industries and law enforcement agencies have led to the adoption of the Evidence-Based Cybersecurity approach by several organizations. Dr. Maimon teaches the course 'Intro to Evidence-Based Cybersecurity' at the undergraduate level and 'Evidence-Based Cybersecurity' at the graduate level.

Acknowledgment

We would like to thank Dr. John Acker (Acker Editing & Consulting) for working with us in editing this manuscript.

Chapter 1

The case for an evidence-based approach to cybersecurity

Cyber-dependent crimes, such as hacking or distributing malicious software, are crimes that could not exist without computer technology and the Internet (McGuire & Dowling, 2013). Although the actual frequency of these crimes against individuals and organizations is still unknown, it is obvious that they are costly and disruptive to their victims and our larger society. Take for example the cyberattack on Colonial Pipeline on 29 April 2021. According to media reports, a group of hackers known as 'DarkSide' infiltrated the networks of Colonial Pipeline by exploiting a virtual private network account that was no longer in use at the time of the attack. A little over a week after the initial infiltration, a ransom note appeared on the company's computers, demanding a cryptocurrency payment. The hackers had stolen nearly 100 gigabytes of data from Colonial Pipeline computers and threatened to leak it if the ransom wasn't paid.

The employee who discovered the note notified an operations supervisor, who immediately began the process of shutting down the pipeline. Colonial Pipeline paid the hackers a US$4.4 million ransom shortly after the hack. However, they did not reopen their pipeline until their in-house security experts and a team of cybersecurity consultants were able to conclusively determine that the attack had been contained. This resulted in a sudden fuel shortage across the eastern half of the United States (Englund & Nakashima, 2021). This attack is only one of many ransomware attacks in the past few years: according to the Identity Theft Resource Center (2021), 18% of the 878 cyberattacks reported in 2020 were ransomware attacks. Reports from all around the globe document governmental and private organizations being held hostage by ransomware, and many agree to pay the ransom solely to avoid the cost of extended downtime of the organizations. The average ransom costs alone increased from US$115,123 in 2019 to US$312,493 in 2020 (Unit 42, 2021).

Other forms of cybercrime are equally disruptive. Verizon (2021) documented a total of 5,258 confirmed data breaches occurring in 16 different industries and four world regions, just in 2021. Many of these breaches resulted in damages to both the hacked companies and their customers. For example, the luxury department store chain Neiman Marcus disclosed in

DOI: 10.1201/9781003201519-1

September 2021 that the personal information of 4.6 million of its customers was compromised during a 2020 data breach of the company's servers. Some of the compromised information included customer names, addresses, contact information, usernames, and passwords for Neiman Marcus online accounts, and credit card numbers and expiration dates (Sharma, 2021). Hacked customer databases are often uploaded onto darknet platforms for online offenders to use in their ever-ongoing online fraud operations.

Meanwhile, Distributed Denial of Service (DDoS) attacks, spamming, and malware campaigns are constantly growing in both intensity and volume. Voice over IP (VoIP) providers are common victims of DDoS attacks. One major attack, on VoIP.ms, started on 16 September 2021, targeting their domain name system (DNS) name servers and other infrastructure to disrupt telephony services. This resulted in customers being unable to make or receive calls (McKeever, 2021).

In this climate of ever-evolving transnational crime, numerous cybersecurity companies offer a wide range of services to reduce individuals' and organizations' cybercrime risk. Starting with application and endpoint security solutions, going through network security tools, and ending in risk assessment and threat intelligence products, these cybersecurity companies promise to strengthen their customers' cybersecurity infrastructure and reduce the probability of cybercrime victimization. A recent cost assessment by Proven Data reveals how pricy these services may get. For example, firewall protection (including product cost, installation fees, and monthly/yearly subscription) is expected to cost between US$1,500 and US$15,000, depending on the size of the client network and the client's security needs.

For other services, most businesses pay US$3–$6 per user per month for quality email protection, between US$3 and $5 per user per month for basic antivirus on their workstations, and another US$5–$8 per server per month. The average cost for endpoint detection response ranges between US$5 and $8 per user per month and US$9–$18 per server per month, and the cost for two-factor authentication can be US$0–$10 per user per month. Finally, the cost for a vulnerability assessment ranges between US$1,500 and $6,000 for a network with 1–3 servers and between US$5,000 and $10,000 for a network with 5–8 servers, while the pricing for network monitoring can range between $100 and $500 per month for a small-sized network and US$500–$2,000 per month for a medium-sized network (Proven Data, 2021). Unfortunately, our knowledge regarding the effectiveness of these services and tools is limited. Therefore, it is impossible to tell how successful they are in preventing and mitigating cyberattacks. These circumstances led Anderson and Moore (2006) to describe cybersecurity as a 'market for lemons.'

Akerlof (1970) coined the term 'market for lemons' to describe a market failure in which the quality of goods traded in a market is devalued in the presence of information asymmetry between buyers and sellers. In his classic example, Akerlof described a situation in which potential buyers of a used car have less information about the car than the seller does, simply because the seller knows the history of the car they are offering for sale. Under such market conditions, the buyer agrees to pay a fixed price that averages the price of a defective car ('lemon') and a good car ('peach') car. According to Akerlof, the quality of the cars traded in this market can degrade, leaving only lemons in the market. Sellers know whether the car they're selling is a peach or a lemon, but selling the peaches at a lower rate (due to the lemon prices bringing the average down) would cause them to lose money. Thus, they will withdraw the peaches from the market. This reduces the average willingness-to-pay of buyers even further, drives prices down, and may even result in the collapse of the market.

A similar information asymmetry exists in the cybersecurity market, where cybersecurity consumers have less information about security products and services than cybersecurity vendors do. In fact, some vendors don't even have enough information to defend the security products they sell. In this kind of market, consumers are not willing to pay high prices for cybersecurity products, so instead they 'gamble' on the security of their organizations with the deployment of cheaper products. If vendors of high-quality cybersecurity products cannot meet production costs for an average market size, they may exit the cybersecurity market altogether, leaving behind a market dominated by low-quality cybersecurity products.

One of the solutions for a market for lemons is changing the information asymmetry between consumers and vendors. For example, using Akerlof's (1970) example of a used-car market, buyers can become more informed about the quality of the used car they are considering by hiring a mechanic who can inspect the car on their behalf. Such inspections will reduce the information asymmetry but may be costly in their own right. A similar change in the information asymmetry regarding the effectiveness of cybersecurity products and tools is desirable within the cybersecurity ecosystem. To drive this change, we propose using the evidence-based approach to guide practitioners' and scholars' efforts to generate empirical evidence around cybersecurity tools and policies. This book aims to explain the basic tenets of the evidence-based approach in cybersecurity and demonstrate its relevance for guiding consumers' decisions before, during, and after they implement security technologies.

THE EVIDENCE-BASED APPROACH

The evidence-based approach establishes best practices and effective policymaking by moving beyond decision-makers' political, financial, or social background, as well as their personal experience, when deciding which professional practices and policies to implement. Instead, this approach adopts tools and policies based on scientific findings. Scientific evidence should support the ongoing, methodical quest to differentiate between unsystematic 'experiences' or 'common sense' and systematic facts observed by testing research hypotheses using rigorous research designs.

Accordingly, rigorous scientific research designs including field experiments, longitudinal surveys, and observations should be deployed to generate evidence that could identify best practices and policies. In addition to strengthening the research process, a crucial component of the evidence-based approach is translating research findings into a format that is accessible and easy to digest for professionals in the field. The overarching goal of this approach is to give practitioners easy access to relevant scientific research, which in turn they can use to address problems and issues in their respective personal and organizational contexts.

The usefulness of the evidence-based approach has been demonstrated in a variety of fields and through numerous evaluative programs. Below, we discuss three poignant cases in which the implementation of evidence-based practices – in the fields of medicine, policing, and education – resulted in significant improvements in the human condition.

EVIDENCE-BASED MEDICINE

Polio was once one of the most feared diseases in the US. Also known as poliovirus or PV, polio is a disease resulting from lower motor neuron damage, characterized by flaccid paralysis (Baicus, 2012). Polio outbreaks became frequent and severe, especially in the US and Europe, at the beginning of the 20th century. By the late 1940s, the Centers for Disease Control and Prevention reported that polio was disabling an average of 35,000 people a year in the US alone (CDC, 2021). Most of the victims of this disease were children. Many parents were terrified for their children's health and kept them isolated in fear that they would catch the disease.

A charitable organization founded in the late 1930s, the National Foundation for Infantile Paralysis (NFIP), took it upon itself to fund research in aim to eradicate polio. Over a period of 20 years, the NFIP launched a massive information campaign and funded several attempts to develop a polio vaccine. However, it wasn't until 1953 that Jonas Salk and his team revealed findings from a series of lab experiments they had performed – first with monkeys and later with a small group of children – that suggested an effective polio vaccine (Baicus, 2012). Still, to prove the effectiveness of the vaccine, a larger experiment was needed. What followed was an unprecedented clinical field trial which sparked the evidence-based medicine movement and eradicated polio in the US.

The clinical trial started on 23 April 1954 and involved more than 1.8 million American subjects. A total of 650,000 of the participants (all children) were assigned to receive either Salk's polio vaccine or a placebo, while the rest of the sample (1.2 million children) received no vaccine and served as a control group. Out of a total sample of more than 1.8 million children, a total of 1,013 developed polio during the study period. In total, 585 of these cases were observed in the control group and 428 cases were observed in the placebo group. No confirmed polio cases were observed in the treatment group. Moreover, the vaccine proved safe with only negligible negative reactions: only 0.4% of the vaccinated children suffered minor reactions to the vaccine. These conclusive findings unleashed a massive vaccination effort – and since its conclusion, the US has been polio-free. This example demonstrates how implementing evidence-based principles in the context of medicine helped support the eradication of a major disease and improve the quality of life for generations to come.

EVIDENCE-BASED POLICING

The US experienced a dramatic increase in violent crime rates from the early 1970s through the early 1990s, reaching 758 violent crime incidents per 100,000 in habitants during the peak years of 1990–1992 (Kelling & Sousa, 2001; Uniform Crime Report, 1995). Facing public demand to restore safety in the streets (Weisburd & Braga, 2006), many police departments underwent rigorous evaluations from a group of economists, criminologists, and public policy scholars. These scholars exposed the ineffectiveness of certain police efforts in reducing crime (Greenwood et al., 1975; Kelling et al., 1974; Levine, 1975; Wellford, 1974).

For example, Levine (1975) and Welford (1974) assessed the relationships between the size of police workforces and crime rates. These scholars reported that an increase in the police workforce did not translate to reductions in robbery and murder rates. Similarly, Kelling et al. (1974) showed that random preventive patrols along municipal streets did not reduce crime, while Spelman and Brown (1984) noted that rapid response to calls for service rarely resulted in criminal arrests. Finally, Greenwood et al. (1975) found that routine follow-up investigations by police detectives rarely resulted in solving cases. These and other studies convinced police professionals to change many traditional policing practices and opened the door to closer collaborations between criminologists and police professionals (Weisburd & Braga, 2006).

In one of those early collaborations, Sherman et al. (1989) discovered that criminals tended to concentrate in a small number of locations, which were identified as 'hot spots' of crime (Sherman et al., 1989). Building on this finding, which has since been replicated in cities around the world (Weisburd, 2015), Sherman and Weisburd (1995) replicated the patrol experiment of Kelling et al. (1974) but focused their attention on hot spots of crime. They found that increasing the number of police patrols in the experimental hot spot locations resulted in fewer crime calls and less disorder than in the control hot spots where patrol rates were not changed (Sherman & Weisburd, 1995). Subsequent assessments suggest that adopting 'hot spot' policing practices was one of the key factors responsible for the sharp decline in US violent crime. This and other similar encouraging studies pushed police departments around the country to adopt an evidence-based approach when exploring ways to diversify their policing tool kits and prevent crime more effectively, in both urban and rural areas (Braga et al., 2019).

EVIDENCE-BASED LEARNING

US education has shown a persistent disparity in academic achievement between minority or disadvantaged students and their white counterparts. This disparity, known as the racial achievement gap, does not exist early in life. For example, Fryer and Levitt (2013) showed that at the age of nine months, there are no observable cognitive differences between black and white babies. However, differences seem to arise at two years of age and are noticeable at kindergarten age (Fryer & Levitt, 2004). The achievement gap grows in every subject and at every grade level (Neal, 2006). Over the years, many policy interventions have attempted to close this gap, including early childhood interventions (Anderson, 2008), placement of disadvantaged students in better schools (Angrist & Lang, 2004; Hastings et al., 2006), mandatory summer school (Jacob & Lefgren, 2004), and even merit pay for principals, teachers, and students. None of these attempts resulted in a change in the racial achievement gap.

The discouraging findings from a long list of empirical program assessments sparked a lively debate among scholars, policymakers, and practitioners about whether schools alone can close the achievement gap (Dobbie & Fryer, 2011). Advocates of the school-centered approach referred to anecdotes from outside the US, in which poor children were placed in superior schools and were able to outperform their average counterparts in US schools (Chenoweth, 2007). In contrast, proponents of the community-focused approach suggested that teachers and educational materials cannot bridge the achievement gap alone, since some of the issues that hamper poor students' success originate outside of the classroom (Fryer & Levitt, 2004). Therefore, in addition to the in-school efforts, they recommended tailoring constructive out-of-school time for underperforming students, which may lead to better and more focused instruction in school. Adopting the more comprehensive approach, The Harlem Children's Zone (HCZ) (https://hcz.org/) in central Harlem took upon the challenge of closing the achievement gap.

In brief, the HCZ is a 97-block area in central Harlem, New York, that integrates the work of charter schools with a web of community services designed to ensure a positive and supportive social environment outside of school, from birth to college graduation (Dobbie & Fryer, 2011). This unique project started in 1970 as a group of after-school programs, truancy, and anti-violence programs, but was reformed in the 1990s into a single project designed to address all of the issues that poor children face. HCZ offers a number of community-focused programs (which serve over 8,000 youth and 5,000 adults) and school-focused programs (which serve 1,300 students who attend the HCZ public charter schools).

Analyses of student demographics and outcomes from HCZ files and the New York City Department of Education (NYCDOE) show that the HCZ has been effective at increasing the achievement of the poorest minority children (Dobbie & Fryer, 2011). Specifically, Dobbie and Fryer (2011) reported that HCZ students who are enrolled in the sixth grade gain more than four-fifths of a standard deviation in math and between one-quarter and one-third of a standard deviation in English Language Arts (ELA) by eighth grade. These findings suggest a strong enough effect to close the racial achievement gap in mathematics and reduce it by about half in ELA. Moreover, students in the HCZ elementary school gain approximately four-fifths to one-and-a-half of a standard deviation in both math and ELA by third grade, closing the racial achievement gap in both subjects (Dobbie & Fryer, 2011). The proven success of the comprehensive approach taken by HCZ in New York in closing the achievement gap (i.e., bringing in both in and out of school efforts) led to replications of the program in many cities across the US (including Albany, Allentown, Atlanta, Boston, Camden, Charlotte, Detroit, Hartford, Indianola, Jacksonville, Kansas City, Los Angeles, Miami, Newark, New Orleans, Orlando, Philadelphia, Pittsburgh, Richmond, Rochester, San Francisco, Santa Fe, Savannah, and Washington DC), as well as in several countries around the world (including Israel, Netherlands, Uganda, and South Africa).

THE CASE FOR EVIDENCE-BASED CYBERSECURITY

Haskins (2018) identifies three key contributors to the recent rise of the evidence-based movement in guiding best practices and policies. First, the social sciences have matured and advanced sufficiently to allow the production of evidence that could prove useful for policy formulation. Specifically, behavioral scientists acknowledged the value of experimental research designs as the gold standard of rigorous academic research and learned how to conduct experiments under real-world conditions. This led to the deployment of a wide range of field experiments, whose findings resulted in more accurate assessments of programs designed to reduce social problems such as gaps in school achievement, violent crime, or teen pregnancy. Second, local governments have now accumulated a critical mass of evidence-based programs which demonstrated significant desired impacts. Finally, Haskins (2018) argues that many more policymakers believe that they can use empirical evidence, generated by evaluations of best practices and policies, to develop and provide political support for promising or demonstrably effective policies.

Building on the success of the evidence-based movement in other fields of study, we will argue in this book that in order for the cybersecurity field to more successfully defend against cybercrime, it is necessary to understand what works and what does not work when protecting cyberspace. Specifically, we call for the deployment of rigorous scientific research designs to identify and test the most effective ways to:

1. Identify online threats and vulnerabilities and educate targets of cybercrime.
2. Guide policy development and guardians' efforts to secure cyberspace.
3. Improve the design and configuration of computing environments to effectively mitigate the consequences of cybercrime events.
4. Translate research findings into a format that is accessible and easy to digest for cybersecurity professionals in the field.

To lay the groundwork for the evidence-based cybersecurity approach, chapter 2 and chapter 3 present some background about relevant technical and human issues that manifest themselves in cybersecurity. We will explain how computers and computer networks work, demonstrate the necessity of cybersecurity, and then highlight the need to understand human behavior in cyberspace while drawing on scientific knowledge from the social sciences. In chapter 4, we explain the criminological, sociological, psychological, ethical, and biological models that are relevant to better understand cybercrime and cybercriminals. From there, we will explain in chapter 5 the necessity of adopting scientific approaches and methods while producing evidence regarding the effectiveness of cybersecurity tools and policies. This chapter draws on insights from the previous chapters to clearly outline the pillars of the evidence-based cybersecurity approach. Chapters 6, 7, and 8 of the book review the relevance of evidence-based cybersecurity in assessing endpoint security, network security, Internet of Things (IoT), data and website security, data privacy, training and awareness. Chapter 9 presents a case study we conducted while drawing on the evidence-based approach to assess the effectiveness of online threat intelligence in guiding financial institutions' incident response to customers' accounts takeover incidents. We believe that this case study could be used as a template by other financial institutions when assessing the effectiveness of their cybersecurity tools and policies. The final chapter (chapter 10) concludes with thoughts about the consequences of failure to embrace the evidence-based cybersecurity approach both for the cybersecurity discipline and the private industry. Finally, we provide our perspective regarding the future of evidence-based cybersecurity.

REFERENCES

Akerlof, G. A. (1970). The market for 'lemons': Quality uncertainty and the market mechanism. *Quarterly Journal of Economics, 84*(3), 488–500.
Anderson, M. L. (2008). Multiple inference and gender differences in the effects of early intervention: A reevaluation of the Abecedarian, Perry preschool, and early training projects. *Journal of the American Statistical Association, 103*(484), 1481–1495.

Anderson, R., & Moore, T. (2006). The economics of information security. *Science*, *314*(5799), 610–613.

Angrist, J., & Lang, K. (2004). How important are peer effects? Evidence from Boston's Metco program. *American Economic Review*, *94*, 1613–1634.

Baicus, A. (2012). History of polio vaccination. *World Journal of Virology*, *1*(4), 108–114.

Braga, A. A., Turchan, B., Papachristos, A. V., & Hureau, D. M. (2019). Hot spots policing of small geographic areas effects on crime. *Campbell Systematic Reviews*, *15*(3), e1046.

CDC (2021). https://www.cdc.gov/polio/index.htm

Chenoweth, K. (2007). *It's being done: Academic success in unexpected schools.* Harvard Education Press.

Dobbie, W., & Fryer, R. G. Jr (2011). Are high-quality schools enough to increase achievement among the poor? Evidence from the Harlem Children's Zone. *American Economic Journal: Applied Economics*, *3*(3), 158–187.

Englund, W., & Nakashima, E. (2021). *Panic buying strikes southeastern United States as shuttered pipeline resumes operations.* The Washington Post. https://www.washingtonpost.com/business/2021/05/12/gas-shortage-colonial-pipeline-live-updates

Fryer, R., & Levitt, S. (2004). Understanding the Black–White test score gap in the first two years of school. *The Review of Economics and Statistics*, *86*(2), 447–464.

Fryer, R., & Levitt, S. (2013). Testing for racial differences in the mental ability of young children. *American Economic Review*, *103*(2), 981–1005.

Greenwood, P. W., Chaiken, J. M., Petersilia, J. R., Prusoff, L. L., Castro, R. P., Kellen, K., & Wildhorn, S. (1975). *The criminal investigation process: Volume III: Observations and analysis.* RAND Corporation.

Haskins, R. (2018). Evidence-based policy: The movement, the goals, the issues, the promise. *The ANNALS of the American Academy of Political and Social Science*, *678*(1), 8–37. https://doi.org/10.1177/0002716218770642

Hastings, J., Kane, T., & Staiger, D. (2006). Gender and performance: Evidence from school assignment by randomized lottery. *American Economic Review*, *96*(2), 232–236.

Identity Theft Resource Center. (2021). *2020 in review: Data breach report.* https://notified.idtheftcenter.org/s/2020-data-breach-report

Jacob, B., & Lefgren, L. (2004). Remedial education and student achievement: A regression- discontinuity analysis. *Review of Economics and Statistics*, *86*(1), 226–244.

Kelling, G. L., Pate, T., Dieckman, D., & Brown, C. E. (1974). *The Kansas City preventive patrol experiment.* Police Foundation.

Kelling, G. L., & Sousa, W. H. (2001). Do police matter?: An analysis of the impact of New York city's police reforms. CCI Center for Civic Innovation at the Manhattan Institute.

Levine, J. P. (1975). The ineffectiveness of adding police to prevent crime. *Public Policy*, *23*(4), 523–545.

McGuire, M., & Dowling, S. (2013). *Cyber crime: A review of the evidence.* Home Office.

McKeever, G. (2021). *DDoS attacks on VoIP and the urgent need for DDoS protection.* https://securityboulevard.com/2021/10/ddos-attacks-on-voip-and-the-urgent-need-for-ddos-protection/

Neal, D. (2006). Why has black-white skill convergence stopped. In E. Hanushek, & F. Welch (Eds.), *Handbook of economics of education* (pp. 511–576). Elsevier.

Proven Data. (2021). *How much does cyber security cost? Common cyber security expenses & fees.* https://www.provendatarecovery.com/blog/cyber-security-cost-expenses-fees/

Sharma, A. (2021). *Neiman Marcus data breach impacts 4.6 million customers.* https://arstechnica.com/information-technology/2021/10/neiman-marcus-data-breach-impacts-4-6-million-customers/

Sherman, L. W., Gartin, P. R., & Buerger, M. E. (1989). Hot spots of predatory crime: Routine activities and the criminology of place. *Criminology, 27*(1), 27–56.

Sherman, L. W., & Weisburd, D. (1995). General deterrent effects of police patrol in crime "hot spots": A randomized, controlled trial. *Justice Quarterly, 12*(4), 625–648.

Spelman, W., & Brown, D. K. (1984). *Calling the police: Citizen reporting of serious crime.* US Department of Justice, National Institute of Justice.

Uniform Crime Report. (1995). *Crime in the United States 1995.* https://ucr.fbi.gov/crime-in-the-u.s/1995

Unit 42. (2021). *2020 ransom demands averaged $847,000. Don't be next.* https://start.paloaltonetworks.com/unit-42-ransomware-threat-report

Verizon. (2021). *2021 Verizon Data Breach Investigations Report.* https://www.verizon.com/business/solutions/secure-your-business/business-security-tips/

Weisburd, D. (2015). The law of crime concentration and the criminology of place. *Criminology, 53*(2), 133–157.

Weisburd, D., & Braga, A. (Eds.). (2006). *Police innovation: Contrasting perspectives.* Cambridge University Press.

Wellford, C. R. (1974). Crime and the police: A multivariate analysis. *Criminology, 12*(2), 195–213.

Chapter 2

Computers, computer networks, the Internet, and cybersecurity

INTRODUCTION: COMPUTERS AND COMPUTER NETWORKS

Most computer users know how to browse the Internet, conduct online transactions, develop and store documents and presentations, and use various applications. However, when it comes to understanding how computer networks communicate and what needs to be done to secure computers and their communications, only a small percentage of the population can claim to be an expert.

Computer networks connect nodes (connection points) like computers, routers, and switches using cables, fiber optics, or wireless signals (IBM Cloud Education, 2019). These connections allow devices in a network to share information and resources (IBM Cloud Education, 2019), using specific protocols that allow communication and define how communications are sent and received. Each device on a network uses an Internet protocol or IP address – a unique numerical or hexadecimal identifier – so the network can identify a given device and let other devices recognize it (IBM Cloud Education, 2019).

This section provides an overview of the most important network protocols. Overall, there are hundreds of communication protocols, each defining rules for different machines exchanging information. These rules can set the syntax, semantics, and error detection for each data packet – the unit of data that is routed between an origin and a destination on the Internet – to successfully transmit data between multiple computers, servers, and/or networks (Infosec, 2017). The parties involved in the communication process have to agree to pass the data from one entity to another. To make this possible, the different hardware, software, and other devices used in a communication chain must coordinate issues ranging from interoperability and multi-vendor support to logical addressing (Infosec, 2017).

In the 1980s, computers were added to the Internet at an exponential rate. These computers were primarily being used by governments, academics, and research organizations (Bourgeois, 2014). Much to engineers' surprise, the Internet's early popularity was driven not by research applications but

DOI: 10.1201/9781003201519-2

by electronic mail (Bourgeois, 2014). Unfortunately, these early computers were not using a single protocol to communicate effectively with each other. This problem was solved by the invention of the transmission control protocol/Internet protocol (TCP/IP; Bourgeois, 2014). The TCP/IP model developed by the US Department of Defense is the industry standard today, with almost 40 years of history. Comprising dozens of individual protocols, TCP/IP was designed to allow networks running on different protocols to have an intermediary protocol, like a common language, that would enable them to communicate. It is also platform-independent and based on open standards, which we will explain more in the next section (Harris, 2013).

In other words, as long as the network supported TCP/IP, computers could communicate with all of the other systems running TCP/IP. Consequently, TCP/IP rapidly became the standard protocol. As Bourgeois (2014) mentioned, this breakthrough popularized the term *Internet*, which means 'an interconnected network of networks' communicating with each other. Today, all operating systems support and operate with TCP/IP protocols. Therefore, the TCP/IP protocol combination is known as the *language* allowing us to communicate on the Internet. Still, it is a vulnerable protocol, easy to hack because it was created for ease of use rather than security (Harris, 2013). As the Internet user population continues to grow enormously, secure communication becomes even more important, which is why security is now so important in everything we do with computers.

Computer security is an information security concept relying on three principles, often abbreviated to CIA: *confidentiality*, *integrity*, and *availability*. Confidentiality refers to preventing unauthorized disclosure of data and resources and is the most well-known concept among the CIA triad. In today's age of technology, computer users are relatively well aware of what confidentiality is and the importance of protecting confidential information. Integrity prevents the unauthorized modification of data and resources, thus ensuring we have access to the original information. For example, integrity could show a company's leaders that the financial data used to create financial statements has not been manipulated. Similarly, the concept of availability protects data and resources, as well as users' access to them (Harris, 2013). Online banking, for example, requires the bank to provide confidentiality, integrity, and availability. It must keep our transactions and personal information confidential, use data integrity to ensure that our financial records are accurate, and provide consistent access via the online banking platform, 24/7.

As users connected to more and more websites for business and personal purposes, especially using mobile devices, it became clear that the original CIA triad was not enough to secure communications and manage network identities. Accordingly, two other concepts entered computer security: *authentication* and *authorization*. Authentication is the process of recognizing a user's identity before allowing access to a device, process, or online platform, so that the user can demonstrate he or she is allowed to access it (Death, 2017). On the other hand, authorization tracks which permissions or access levels are granted to a given user, allowing him or her to connect to, use, and access a specific application, file, or online computer system.

THE OPEN SYSTEM INTERCONNECTION (OSI) MODEL AND THE COMMUNICATION PROCESS

On a more technical level, we can explain network and telecommunication systems' functions using the 'seven layers' model, also known as the Open System Interconnection or OSI model. This conceptual framework, as defined in 1984 and published as international standard ISO/IEC 7498-1, should still be relied upon today. It is a practical and widely accepted way of explaining how a network works. The seven layers are: (1) the physical layer, (2) the data-link layer, (3) the network layer, (4) the transport layer, (5) the session layer, (6) the presentation layer, and (7) the application layer (Tipton & Hernandez, 2013). For example, when an application transmits data over the network, the data enters at the top layer (7), the application layer. It will move down to each level until it is finally transmitted over the network at layer 1, the physical layer (Tipton & Hernandez, 2013).

More precisely, the application layer (7) is what most users see, as it is closest to the end user. It receives information directly from users and displays incoming data to the user. The presentation layer (6) represents the independent area of data representation at the application layer, as the application prepares or translates data for network formatting. Next, when two devices, computers, or servers need to 'speak' with one another, a session needs to be created, so this activity is done at the session layer (5). The transport layer (4) coordinates the data being transferred between end systems and hosts – things like how much data to send, at what rate, and where it needs to be sent.

Moving down through the OSI framework, the network layer (3) is the router functionality; this layer is responsible for packet forwarding, including sending packets through different routers. The data link layer (2) provides node-to-node data transfers (those between two directly connected devices) and handles error correction from the physical layer. Finally, the physical layer (1) includes the system's electrical and physical characteristics – everything from the cable type, radio frequency link, and bits and bytes to the layout of pins, voltages, and other physical requirements (Shaw, 2020).

Understanding this framework helps network managers narrow down problems, such as a loose physical connection or an incompatibility with an application. For example, when a networking problem occurs, network security professionals tend to go directly to the physical layer to verify that all of the cables are correctly connected, or the power plug hasn't been pulled from the router, switch, or even the computer itself (Harris, 2013; Shaw, 2020, Tipton & Hernandez, 2013). The OSI framework also helps computer programs develop applications that work well with the other relevant layers, while it lets vendors help customers understand which layer a product works with or whether it works 'across the stack' of all seven layers (Shaw, 2020).

To be sure, cybersecurity professionals should understand each of these layers, so they can better analyze potential cyber-threats to the computer systems they want to defend. Although this framework is far from being perfect, it teaches potential cybersecurity professionals how the entire computer ecosystem communicates, including potential vulnerabilities, intrusion points between two OSI layers in a communication process interacting with various internal systems (i.e., legacy systems, supervisory control, and data acquisition – SCADA), as well as how different organizations and system types may change their defense priorities (Sandberg & Hunter, 2017).

THE IMPORTANCE OF CYBERSECURITY

Cybersecurity is the practice of protecting systems, networks, and programs from digital attacks and threats that may affect any organization using computers and technology, which is now almost every organization worldwide. In 2020, approximately 5 billion people accessed the Internet worldwide (Internet World Stats, 2020). Most of them did so without proper security training and protection, which means individual Internet users represent a significant point of weakness in cybersecurity. Establishing adequate cybersecurity measures for both individual users and organizations is vital to preventing cyberattacks and adverse consequences from cyber-threats. Cyberattacks usually aim to access, modify, or destroy sensitive information, extorting money from users, and stealing critical assets (known as 'crown jewels') from organizations. Similarly, a cyber-threat is the possibility of a malicious attempt to damage or disrupt a computer system or network (Pomerleau, 2019; Secureworks, 2017). For instance, an active cyber-threat to financial institutions worldwide is hackers using social engineering techniques and spear-phishing emails to lure banking employees into breaching their employer's network security (Pomerleau, 2019; United States District Court for the Central District of California, 2018).

Stevens (2018) defined cybersecurity as 'a means not only of protecting and defending society and its essential information infrastructures, but also a way of prosecuting national and international policies through information-technological means' (p. 1). Cybersecurity represents a complex configuration of actors, organizations, and institutions working together to ensure our cyber-infrastructure's security (Choucri, 2012; Collier, 2018; Pomerleau, 2019). More specifically, cybersecurity management is a shared responsibility, through interrelated and inter-twined intra- and inter-industry relationships among governments, law enforcement, security agencies, the military, and the private sector – which owns and operates most of the critical infrastructures – as well as its citizens (Stevens, 2016). Thus, cybersecurity is essential as it encompasses every sphere of our physical, online, and connected lives.

It allows us to protect sensitive information, personally identifiable information or identifiers (i.e., Social Security numbers, passport information), intellectual property, health information, governments' and private organizations' data, the electronic devices we use, and other aspects of our society's critical infrastructures.

Until very recently, the security of computers and the Internet was left to the market. This approach might have been satisfactory when the world's population associated relatively few risks with computers and the Internet. Private organizations offered security for their products and services. Meanwhile, governments worldwide tried to provide some governance by enacting privacy laws to protect customers' personal data, even while recognizing that their new laws, rules, and regulations could hardly keep up with technological evolution. In line with this situation, Schneier (2018) wrote that people tended to see security mostly as a privacy matter using bits and bytes.

Nowadays, however, most people know that it is possible to become victims of hacking, identity theft, and fraud through any Internet-connected computer. With more organizational data breaches every day, it is hard to believe that anyone will avoid cyber victimization. The population shows signs of habituation to this form of crime, as being a data breach victim is now, unfortunately, the new normal. Most citizens understand the impact, how much it may cost them, and the time it might take to rectify the situation or reestablish their identity if they become victims.

Although we should not minimize the impact of hacking, fraud, online scams, or identity theft – all very unpleasant situations leading to victimization – they are not catastrophic (Schneier, 2018). With so many tools, accessories, and devices connected to the Internet – including pacemakers, the city's power grid, electrical and mechanical components, cars, and home appliances such as our microwave, stove, air conditioner, thermostat, refrigerator, water dispenser, and even garage door – cybersecurity is imperative to protect our homes and families. Connecting more devices to the Internet generates new significant threats to property and most importantly to human life (Schneier, 2018). People used to say that online crime's psychological impact was less important than crimes committed in the physical world, but future online crime might just as easily impact us physically, undoubtedly a game-changer.

In today's reality of omnipresent interconnected devices, an everyday individual can easily be the victim of a crime enabled through one of their Internet of Things (IoT) devices, an idea once reserved for dystopian fiction. By hacking a smart home, for instance, a hacker could lock residents inside, rapidly increase the interior temperature, then use embedded speakers to broadcast a ransom demand – payable in virtual currency – to release the data he has encrypted on the victim's laptop. Goodman (2016) and Schneier (2018) presented many similar IoT-based scenarios, and today's society is simply not equipped to handle them. For instance, when a citizen reports such crimes, how will law enforcement respond? Will local police have the necessary technical skills to assist and respond quickly enough to defuse the situation? How will they investigate these crimes? These are the questions that many security professionals and cybersecurity scholars reflect on today.

IoT threats are one of the many reasons why we need to increase our cybersecurity capabilities and awareness. This can be done by learning what works and what does not work, reducing the vulnerabilities in existing and future technologies, and making sure our citizens know what companies to trust with their own cybersecurity. One of the first steps is adopting laws and enforcing regulations that promote a 'secure by design' mentality. For example, the US IoT Cybersecurity Improvement Act of 2020 sets minimum security standards on Internet-connected devices sold by US vendors to the Federal government (McDowell, 2021). This standard should also apply to purchases by the general population: civilians should know what they are buying, the risks associated with these devices, and how to recognize and respond to the cyber-threats they face while using various computing devices connected to the Internet. Put differently, only by better understanding the current state of cybersecurity, including the technological, business, political, societal, and criminal risks of using the Internet and new technologies, will society be able to create growth economically and socially.

THE CYBERSECURITY ECOSYSTEM

As systemic risk grows, organizations can no longer solely rely on their internal prevention and detection capabilities to ensure cybersecurity and resilience. Since organizations are increasingly interdependent through integrated technologies, collaborative processes, systems, and outsourcing, the broader ecosystem's stability and security matter critically. In this digital era, in other words, the cybersecurity ecosystem is more important than ever. Implementing effective cybersecurity measures is particularly challenging today because there are more devices than people and cybercriminals are becoming more innovative. Since most individuals use multiple computers or devices with embedded computers (e.g., smartphones and tablets), the number of potential attack venues and potential targets for hackers is expanding rapidly.

Moreover, organizations need a better understanding of the supply chains in which they operate, including third-party and even fourth-party risks to their operations (Huang et al., 2018). Organizations might outsource some security functions, but they cannot outsource risks. Failure to ensure resilience and security may affect other divisions within the enterprise, organizations within the same industry, and even other businesses in the ecosystem with increasingly harmful consequences, since the sources of risks are often hidden (World Economic Forum, 2020).

Having a holistic approach to cybersecurity management is now imperative, allowing security professionals to build up a defense against and response to cyber-threats. Organizations cannot fight cybercrime by themselves: they need to involve their employees, other organizations within the same industry, and essential stakeholders such as cybersecurity and technology vendors, law enforcement professionals, and regulators. Failure to manage operational risks, including both internal and external threats, may lead to considerable reputational damage, loss of clients, and regulatory fines.

To manage cybersecurity, organizations need to invest in training and improving awareness, so their employees will understand and comply with basic data security principles – such as choosing strong passwords, being wary of attachments in email, or backing up data in a secure folder on the company's network. Organizations must also establish a framework with documented procedures and processes for dealing with both attempted and successful cyberattacks. For example, the National Institute of Standards and Technology (NIST) cybersecurity framework explains how organizations can identify attacks, protect systems, detect and respond to threats, and recover from successful attacks.

Computer security tools are vital for organizations and individuals to protect themselves from cyberattacks. Some of these tools are endpoint detection and response tools for computers, laptops, and the ever-growing list of mobile devices connected to the corporate network. To monitor logs and mitigate potential data theft, organizations can rely on security information event managers (SIEM), data loss prevention (DLP), intrusion prevention, and detection systems. Other standard technologies used to protect organizations include next-generation firewalls, user behavior analytics (UBA), domain name system (DNS) filtering, malware protection, antivirus software, and email security solutions. Overall, an organization's people, processes, and technology must complement one another to effectively defend against cyber-threats.

Risks associated with *people* may include insider threats, individuals who have legitimate access to critical assets and privileges based on a position of trust within the organization (Catrantzos, 2012; Pomerleau & Auger-Perreault, 2020). These risks can arise from employees, consultants, interns, or vendors at any level in the organization who have contractual access to the organization's data, systems, or premises. Also, risks may arise when individuals in the company are targeted by subterfuge and cyberattacks, such as phishing or spear-phishing attacks, social engineering, tactics against employees, online extortion, ransomware, deepfakes (fake videos or audio recordings that look and sound just like the real thing), artificial intelligence, or machine learning poisoning. All of these tactics can lead to exfiltration, disruption of data, and interruption of normal business. Other risks posed by people could be associated with remote workforces (increasingly common due to the COVID-19 pandemic), unethical behaviors during layoffs leading to data theft, or limited staff availability for critical tasks that require supervision.

Cyber-incidents most often happen because internal *processes* and controls were inexistent or inadequate to protect against an attack. For instance, procedures were not followed, there was a lack of consistency or alignment between the company's requirements and some line of business processes, or due to the weight of the business climate, some controls were not added because they were considered too expensive after completing a risk assessment (Grant Thornthon, 2020).

For the risks associated with *the use of technology*, outdated and unpatched technology is still unfortunately common within organizations. A recent example arose in the cyberattack against Equifax in 2017. The organization failed to patch a vulnerability discovered in Apache Struts, an open-source development framework for Java applications, leading to unauthorized access of 143 million consumers' personal information (Fruhlinger, 2020). When technologies are implemented rapidly to support the workforce, organizations rarely deploy the appropriate technology, controls, and protocols required for monitoring, which could lead to data loss or vulnerabilities in legacy systems exploited by attackers. Unfortunately, this situation is only one of many potentially devastating cybersecurity risks. This is why a scalable unified threat management system should be in place, allowing organizations to evolve equally with business needs, automate integrations across security products, and accelerate essential security operations functions: detection, investigation, and remediation. No organization is fully protected against all cyber-threats; it is only a matter of when they will be attacked.

Organizations and cybersecurity security professionals must combat a vast array of cyber-threats, so they should prepare for a long list of potential threat scenarios. While the attackers only need one successful attempt to penetrate the infrastructure, cybersecurity professionals must work full-time to prevent numerous attempts against the organization's critical assets. Professionals can use 'known unknown' scenarios (i.e., the things we know that we don't know) and 'unknown unknown' scenarios (i.e., things that we don't know we don't know) to make inferences about future 'known known scenarios' (i.e., things that we know we know) (Perera & Higgins, 2017; Pomerleau, 2019).

CYBERSECURITY DOCTRINES, PRACTICES, AND POLICIES

Over multiple successive generations, advancements in technology and accelerating machine networking have led to considerable changes in social interactions. These social advances have significant security implications, as the increase in digital connectivity is an opportunity to alter power distribution (Valeriano & Maness, 2018). Security is now at the center of the social contract between people and the state (Stevens, 2016). Unfortunately, the escalation of cyberattacks over the years demonstrates that the current approach to managing cybersecurity is not effective. This is a significant problem since market dynamics foster a non-collaborative approach. Building robustness into digital devices is very expensive and some producers may sacrifice robustness in exchange for higher profitability, so cybersecurity costs are unevenly distributed (Taddeo, 2019).

Recently, a series of doctrines have been advocated to enhance cybersecurity: *prevention, risk management,* and *deterrence through accountability* (Mulligan & Schneider, 2011). These doctrines are essential to understand some of the intricacies of cybersecurity, as it is not possible to comprehend cybersecurity only through technical analysis. These doctrines also provide a framework in which to consider several technical and policy solutions essential for managing cybersecurity.

The main objective of the *doctrine of prevention* is to create systems that are completely free of vulnerabilities, making it practically impossible to attack them. It is improbable that such a state is possible since absolute cybersecurity does not exist, but it is worthwhile to reduce vulnerabilities as much as possible (Mulligan & Schneider, 2011). In cybersecurity, attacks do evolve. Even though a system may be deemed highly secure today, it will not necessarily be safe tomorrow. Testing may only confirm the presence vulnerabilities, not their absence, as the exhaustive testing necessary would not be an economical or a sustainable solution (Mulligan & Schneider, 2011).

The *doctrine of risk management* is a little more modest because it relates to managing risk rather than eliminating it. Specifically, this doctrine argues that mitigating risk and investing in security should reduce expected losses as it is impossible to have zero cybersecurity risks (Mulligan & Schneider, 2011). In adopting this doctrine, one understands that not all vulnerabilities are equal. It is preferable to focus primarily on reducing the probability of the most critical perceived threats and the most expansive system compromises (Mulligan & Schneider, 2011).

However, it is often challenging to make a risk calculation in cybersecurity. There is a lack of information about potential vulnerabilities, infrequent incidents, and potential losses attributed to these incidents. The unknown impact of an incident and the probability of a vulnerability being exploited make it challenging to evaluate cybersecurity. Most risk management professionals still have difficulty evaluating extremely low-probability events (Mulligan & Schneider, 2011). For example, consider a cyberattack against the organization in which hackers take advantage of an unknown system vulnerability to encrypt all the information in a system (i.e., ransomware), paralyzing the business operations of the organization for days. Suppose such an incident never happened to the organization in the past or to similar companies within the same industry or similar industries (e.g., transportation and telecommunications) and that the organization is not aware of any system vulnerability that could be exploited by cybercriminals. In this situation, some risk managers may believe this risk has a low probability of occurrence, even though its impact would be significant. It is difficult for people to estimate the consequences of such low-probability events, and the cost may vary tremendously from one incident to another (Mulligan & Schneider, 2011). For this reason, operational risk management is an art, not a science.

It is also challenging to fully understand the risks associated with an organization's relationships with third parties. A single cyber-incident could force the company to close its operations. It is no small task to identify the actual value of the confidentiality of the information, the integrity of the data, the direct costs associated with recovering from a cyber-incident, and the indirect costs for customers who have had their personal information stolen or compromised (Mulligan & Schneider, 2011). Thus, it can be difficult to evaluate the benefits of investing in cybersecurity. Neither security professionals nor companies can fully understand and control their vulnerabilities through investments in detection (Mulligan & Schneider, 2011). Although breach notification laws exist and can be viewed as a risk management intervention, these laws focus on a narrow set of breaches. Thus, cybersecurity investments are artificially skewed since organizations are still investing significant sums of money in managing risks that are not fully understood (Mulligan & Schneider, 2011).

The *doctrine of deterrence through accountability* treats cyberattacks as crimes and focuses primarily on identifying and prosecuting the perpetrators of attacks (Mulligan & Schneider, 2011). According to this doctrine, deterrence, or the inhibition of criminal behavior by fear of punishment, is a crime prevention strategy that can be utilized to increase criminals' chances of being deterred by the probability of being found and prosecuted. However, in cyberspace, attribution of attacks is a complicated issue. For example, individuals, organized crime groups, and even nation-state actors can easily hide their identity through computer technology, use false identities, rely upon various proxies to conceal their tracks or location, or have another party commit the attack on their behalf (Lin, 2016). These tactics can cast reasonable doubt on the attacker's identity, an obstacle to effective prosecution. The victim of a cyber-incident may also be in a different country than the suspect, which renders it very complicated for law enforcement to prosecute the hacker. Legislations vary from one country to another, and at least two law enforcement agencies would need to collaborate to arrest the hacker and bring him to justice. Consequently, compared with the physical world, the threat of punishment for committing cyberattacks is not necessarily effective against global cyber-threats (Mulligan & Schneider, 2011).

Mulligan and Schneider (2011) proposed another doctrine for dealing with cybersecurity: the *doctrine of public cybersecurity*. This model seeks to produce cybersecurity while managing the public's potential insecurity about balancing individual rights and public welfare (Mulligan & Schneider, 2011). For Mulligan and Schneider (2011), cybersecurity should be perceived as a public good and in the public interest, much like public health efforts (Taddeo, 2019). These efforts, they point out, seek to produce a healthy population with a lower prevalence of disease (Mulligan & Schneider, 2011). To do so, various agencies are mandated to engage in a broad set of activities such as (1) public education (minimizing exposure and facilitating early detection), (2) researching and using various methods of prevention and treatment (antidotes and vaccines), and (3) identifying and managing the disease and the individuals affected (facilitating isolation and quarantine) (Mulligan & Schneider, 2011). This last step is accomplished by having proper mechanisms in place for surveillance, information gathering and sharing, analysis, mandatory reporting, testing, and screening, to identify public health threats that may affect the whole population and require compulsory treatment (Mulligan & Schneider, 2011).

Following the example of public health laws, the state should offer frameworks to protect the entire population against cybersecurity risks (Mulligan & Schneider, 2011). For instance, public health requires each child to be vaccinated for the greater good (e.g., herd immunity) of the community, although some children might have side effects. Over the years, public health, disease detection, and prevention mechanisms became accepted as logical ways to protect the population. Various public health strategies led to a 'societal perception of health from a primarily private concern to a concern of the collective' (Mulligan & Schneider, 2011, p. 76). By carefully analyzing the public cybersecurity doctrine, this analogy should inspire decision-makers, leaders, and cybersecurity practitioners. Since *public cybersecurity* does not focus on restitution, it does not punish victims of diseases, and just like in public health, prevention is preferred to recovery (Mulligan & Schneider, 2011).

Instead of focusing solely on technical measures to manage cyberthreats, cybersecurity should be perceived as a social component of our lives. Cybersecurity is not merely a list of tools, processes, and systems that both organizations and governments should utilize in their business's normal course. Valeriano and Maness (2018) argued that too much emphasis has been put on technology's consequences instead of understanding technology as a domain, its coercive potential, and its usage by various actors. Cybersecurity should be perceived as a *public good* that must be framed as a collective action problem for public and private actors (McCarthy, 2018).

Cybersecurity management thus requires the collaboration of both public and private sectors to ensure an acceptable level of system robustness (Taddeo, 2019). The public sector should establish standards, certifications, and procedural testing and oversight to ensure an adequate security level is maintained. In contrast, the private sector should be responsible and accountable for designing robust systems and services for users (Taddeo, 2019). A public good is something that one can consume without reducing its availability to others and from which no one is excluded (Stevens et al., 2019). But referring to cybersecurity as a public good does not mean that cybersecurity should be free for everybody or that governments should be paying the costs. As Taddeo (2019) argues,

Just like street-lights and national defence—both involve costs, while allowing all citizens of a state to access them and maintain them through their taxes—cybersecurity can function as a non-rivalrous, non-excludable good, if its costs are shared equitably among the relevant stakeholders. (p. 351)

Cybersecurity was not taken into consideration at the beginning of the Internet. With the creation of new generations of computers and software, organizations are now obliged to deal with legacy systems, obsolete infrastructure, and unsecure systems that did not keep up with technology's rapid pace. Therefore, policymakers should use legislation to create incentives for system developers, operators, and users to consider the good of others and the good of the society as a whole when it comes to cybersecurity (Mulligan & Schneider, 2011). Just as public health laws help prevent disease through vaccination or monitoring the food and water supply chain, incentive structures, laws, and new innovative methods should be used to increase cybersecurity (Mulligan & Schneider, 2011).

Privacy is as paramount in public health as it should be in cybersecurity. For instance, collecting data about someone's health has similar privacy concerns to collecting Internet network traffic: it all depends on how we secure the data, how it is stored, how long we keep it, and who has access to it (Mulligan & Schneider, 2011). Education could also play a critical role; software developers should build systems with fewer vulnerabilities, and practitioners should work more often with universities (Mulligan & Schneider, 2011). New legislation and mandatory standards could become another vehicle to improve cybersecurity by forcing system producers and purchasers to make the necessary investments in cybersecurity (Taddeo, 2019). More importantly, it would influence proper security behaviors, reduce poor coding practices (which allow hackers to exploit vulnerabilities), formulate limits on liability for damages, and support research identifying connections between security development processes and good security outcomes (Mulligan & Schneider, 2011).

We should also start to change our paradigms and see cybersecurity as a social problem, one we can address with policies and not just technology (Pomerleau, 2021). As of today, on the world stage, cybersecurity does not have a mandatory standard or any obligations for organizations to respect specific laws to ensure the security of the infrastructure they manage. Other than the voluntary NIST framework, there are no other frameworks that require organizations to make sure security controls are in place and working, detection systems are effective, and critical data is encrypted with robust encryption mechanisms (Pomerleau, 2021). Moreover, there is no regulatory body for developing IT systems, software development, and coding. The IoT Cybersecurity Improvement Act mentioned above, which regulates Internet-connected devices sold by vendors to the US government, is one recent example of what will be required for all aspects of cybersecurity in the future. However, cybersecurity management is broader that IoT technology. Hopefully, a *public cybersecurity doctrine* (Mulligan & Schneider, 2011) will soon be adopted to influence the public policy discourse about cybersecurity, pushing for reasonable goals and encouraging public action.

CURRENT PRACTICES, TOOLS, AND POLICIES
TO SECURE CYBER INFRASTRUCTURES

Current cybersecurity practices and policies to secure cyber infrastructures leave much to be desired. Chief executive officers and board members of numerous organizations, policymakers, and government leaders are astutely aware of the critical importance of potential losses from cyberattacks (Huang et al., 2018; O'Donnell & Nesbitt, 2016; Pomerleau, 2019; Pomerleau & Lowery, 2020). Based on investment forecasts and market estimates for the coming years, companies will continue to make astronomical investments in cybersecurity. By 2023, enterprises are predicted to spend US$12.6 billion on cloud security tools and US$24.6 billion on infrastructure protection per year, and the global cybersecurity market should be worth US$270 billion by 2026 (Columbus, 2020). As Schneier (2018) pointed out, if required security standards (beyond the currently voluntary NIST framework) existed, governments and organizations could test products and services against these standards to differentiate the efficacy of each through scoring criteria or ratings. Currently, there is an absence of universally accepted metrics and performance standards to measure security controls and policies (Maimon, 2020). Some think tanks are evaluating cybersecurity products, but the methodology they use is not always known or made public. It focuses primarily on surveys. Their reports are also so expensive that only a few clients can afford the license to access them.

Moreover, both the government and the private sector are interested in the provision of cybersecurity, but so far public-private partnerships have not worked effectively (Bures, 2013; Carr, 2016; Pomerleau, 2019; Pomerleau & Lowery, 2020). Specifically, these partnerships have been ineffective in monitoring, detecting, and reacting to cyber-threats (Bures, 2013; Dunn-Cavelty & Suter, 2009). The provision of security is a function of the state, but most of the cybersecurity of critical infrastructures is maintained by the private sector (McCarthy, 2018). Thus, in the event of a significant cyberattack on critical infrastructure, it would be natural for the government to request authority and responsibility for the matter (Carr, 2016). However, due to the fragmentation in the provision of security, the state cannot take a traditional standing as a primary security provider when it comes to cybersecurity matters related to critical infrastructures. Organizations must be able to defend themselves on their own (Collier, 2018).

As of today, there is no scientific method to analyze a detection system's efficacy or help cybersecurity leaders estimate just how secure their systems are. Developing such a method would offer a basis for assessing the added value from specific investments (products and systems) made in support of cybersecurity. Organizations invest in many security systems and products, but no one can comprehensively compare their efficacy. If Product A costs $10 million while Product B costs $14 million, how can cybersecurity professionals explain the differences in value to protect the organization? Will the additional $4 million make a significant difference? Will Product B better protect against a specific cyber-threat or reduce the number of alerts that the organization will generate, thus decreasing costs compared to system A? Without objective standards to evaluate such products, organizations, IT managers, and business executives are more often influenced by powerful marketing strategies, extremely talented salespeople, and the argument that a single cybersecurity incident could bring the organization to its knees.

While worst-case scenarios might have a considerable impact on the organization's business operations, this argument is not backed by facts nor scientific research. There is no evidence demonstrating that investments made in cybersecurity lead to a return on investment for the organizations or that these investments were proportionate to the organization's risks and genuinely served to counter cyber-threats. Unfortunately, there is nothing available to cybersecurity professionals like the Underwriters Laboratories (UL), a checklist to confirm that a product is safe or that the manufacturer of a product followed a strict set of safety rules in building it, to protect the organization (Schneier, 2018). Even though such a cybersecurity checklist would confirm the product is secure today, it would need to be updated regularly as cyber-threats evolve rapidly.

Also, system evaluations derived entirely from empirical observations do not themselves justify investments. Because companies are not providing access to their systems, scholars do not have access to real operational data to test security systems and measure if they are worth what companies are paying. In the actual state of cybersecurity operations, the absence of detected system compromises may indicate three possible scenarios: (a) investments made to harden the systems worked, (b) attacks have not been attempted, or (c) cybersecurity professionals did not yet identify the point of compromise (e.g., individual responsible for the theft of confidential information) (Mulligan & Schneider, 2011). Thus, it is impossible to know whether or not prior security investments were well targeted, an unfortunate situation that forces security professionals to justify investments based solely on non-events (Mulligan & Schneider, 2011).

Since organizations and cybersecurity leaders invest enormously in cyber detection systems but cannot measure the systems' efficacy or system outputs to address cybersecurity risks, many cybersecurity operations are doomed to create enormous quantities of alerts. Usually, these alerts need to be worked by security operations center (SOC) employees. Generating phenomenal amounts of alerts without detecting any confirmed security incidents cases often leads cybersecurity employees to work alerts with a very high false-positive ratio instead of working on real cyber-incidents, leading to what some call 'alert fatigue' (Wafula, 2021). For this reason, the evidence-based cybersecurity research approach should be prioritized, in order to objectively assess standardized tools and policies used to achieve security goals, to manage cybersecurity incidents, and to investigate cybercrimes against both governments and private organizations (Maimon, 2020; Maimon et al., 2014; Maimon et al., 2019; Testa et al., 2017; Wilson et al., 2015).

Mulligan and Schneider (2011) claimed that today's software-procurement market does not provide incentives that would prompt developers to adequately incur the additional expenses to protect the software they sell to consumers and organizations. This statement was also supported by Mikolic-Torreira et al. (2016), in a Rand Corporation report describing a framework for exploring cybersecurity policy options. Moreover, buyers are unable to predict the costs of a system's vulnerability to cyberattack. Without ways to measure a system's security, these buyers have no way to rationalize paying higher prices (Mulligan & Schneider, 2011).

To counter the evolving cyber-threat, we need a better understanding of how computers work and communicate through the Internet. Increasing users' security awareness is also key in managing cyber-threats effectively. The cybersecurity ecosystem is complicated. However, by looking at each component – people, processes, and technology – or through the problem analysis triangle – a place, a malicious actor, a victim, and a guardian – it is possible to understand how certain actors can attack places and victims by taking advantage of vulnerabilities in the cyber ecosystem. Like their public health counterparts, cybersecurity professionals have devoted decades of experience, expertise, and insight to these questions (Manky, 2020). Still, cybersecurity is not as mature as other sciences. Cybersecurity is a social problem, and we will need all cybersecurity professionals, decision-makers, academics, and end users to come together to tackle this societal issue.

REFERENCES

Bourgeois, T. D. (2014). *Information systems for business and beyond*. Saylor Foundation.

Bures, O. (2013). Public-private partnerships in the fight against terrorism? *Crime, Law & Social Change*, 60(4), 429–455. https://doi.org/10.1007/s10611-013-9457-7

Carr, M. (2016). Public-private partnerships in national cyber-security strategies. *International Affairs*, 92(1), 43–62. https://doi.org/10.1111/1468-2346.12504

Catrantzos, N. (2012). *Managing the insider threat: No dark corner*. Taylor & Francis.

Choucri, N. (2012). *Cyberpolitics in international relations*. MIT Press.

Collier, J. (2018). Cybersecurity assemblages: A framework for understanding the dynamic and contested nature of security provision. *Politics & Governance*, 6(2), 13–21. https://doi.org/10.17645/pag.v6i2.1324

Columbus, L. (2020). *2020 roundup of cybersecurity forecast and market estimates*. https://www.forbes.com/sites/louiscolumbus/2020/04/05/2020-roundup-of-cybersecurity-forecasts-and-market-estimates/?sh=2c047e88381d

Death, D. (2017). *Information security handbook*. https://www.packtpub.com/product/information-security-handbook/9781788478830

Dunn-Cavelty, M., & Suter, M. (2009). Public-private partnerships are no silver bullet: An expanded governance model for critical infrastructure protection. *International Journal of Critical Infrastructure Protection*, 2, 179–187. https://doi.org/10.1016/j.ijcip.2009.08.006

Fruhlinger, J. (2020). *Equifax data breach FAQ: What happened, who was affected, what was the impact?* https://www.csoonline.com/article/3444488/equifax-data-breach-faq-what-happened-who-was-affected-what-was-the-impact.html

Goodman, M. (2016). *Future crimes: How our radical dependence on technology threatens us all.* https://www.amazon.ca/-/fr/Marc-Goodman/dp/0385682581/ref=sr_1_1?__mk_fr_CA=%C3%85M%C3%85%C5%BD%C3%95%C3%91&dchild=1&keywords=future+crimes&qid=1605266904&s=books&sr=1-1

Grant Thornthon. (2020). *Internal audit and cyber risks.* https://www.grantthornton.com/library/articles/advisory/2020/internal-audit-cyber-risk.aspx

Harris, S. (2013). *CISSP all-in-one exam guide.* https://www.amazon.com/CISSP-All-One-Exam-Guide/dp/0071781749/

Huang, K., Siegel, M., & Madnick, S. (2018). Systematically understanding the cyber attack business: A survey. *ACM Computing Survey, 51*(4), 1–36. https://doi.org/10.1145/3199674

IBM Cloud Education. (2019). *Networking.* https://www.ibm.com/cloud/learn/networking-a-complete-guide#:~:text=where%20to%20go.-,How%20do%20they%20work%3F,communications%20are%20sent%20and%20received

Infosec. (2017). *CISSP domain 4: Communications and network security; What you need to know for the exam.* https://resources.infosecinstitute.com/certification/communications-and-network-security/

Internet World Stats. (2020). *Internet usage statistics: The Internet big picture.* https://www.internetworldstats.com/stats.htm

Lin, H. (2016). *Attribution of malicious cyber incidents: From soup to nuts.* Aegis Paper Series No.1607. https://www.hoover.org/sites/default/files/research/docs/lin_webready.pdf

Maimon, D. (2020). Relevance of evidence-based cybersecurity in guiding the financial sector's efforts in fighting cybercrime. In P. L. Pomerleau, & D. L. Lowery (Eds.), *Countering cyber threats to financial institutions; A private and public partnership approach to critical infrastructure protection* (pp. 9–28). Palgrave Macmillan. https://doi.org/10.1007/978-3-030-54054-8_2

Maimon, D., Alper, M., Sobesto, B., & Cukier, M. (2014). Restrictive deterrent effects of a warning banner in an attacked computer system. *Criminology, 52*(1), 33–59. https://doi.org/10.1111/1745-9125.12028

Maimon, D., Testa, A., Sobesto, B., Cukier, M., & Wuling, R. (2019). Predictably deterrable? The case of system trespassers. In G. Wang, J. Feng, M. Bhuiyan, & R. Lu (Eds.), *Security, privacy, and anonymity in computation, communication, and storage* (pp. 317–330). Springer.

Manky, D. (2020). *This is the partnership we need to fight global cybercrime.* https://www.weforum.org/agenda/2020/10/the-partnership-we-need-to-fight-global-cybercrime/

McCarthy, R. D. (2018). *Privatizing political authority: Cybersecurity, public-private partnerships, and the reproduction of liberal political order.* https://www.cogitatiopress.com/politicsandgovernance/article/viewFile/1335/1335

McDowell, B. (2021). *Cybersecurity alert: IoT security bill is signed into law.* https://www.lexology.com/library/detail.aspx?g=b7ce4b27-ba92-4d11-b276-e2e3f596dfac

Mikolic-Torreira, I., Henry, R., Snyder, D., Beaghley, S., Pettyjohn, L. S., Harting, S., Westerman, E., Shlapak, A. D., Bishop, M., Oberholtzer, J., Skrabala, L., & Weinbaum, C. (2016). *A framework for exploring cybersecurity policy options.* RAND Corporation. https://www.rand.org/pubs/research_reports/RR1700.html

Mulligan, D., & Schneider, F. (2011). Doctrine for cybersecurity. *Daedalus, 140*(4), 70–92. http://www.jstor.org/stable/23046915

O'Donnell, B., & Nesbitt, R. (2016). *Cyber risk and security in Canada.* https://globalriskinstitute.org/publications/cyber-risk-security-canada/

Perera, T., & Higgins, D. (2017). *Theoretical overview of knowns, unknowns, and unknowable risks to property decision makings.* https://www.researchgate.net/publication/320943325_Theoretical_Overview_of_Known_Unknown_and_Unknowable_Risks_for_Property_Decision_Makings

Pomerleau, P. L. (2019). *Countering the cyber threats against financial institutions in Canada: A qualitative study of a private and public partnership approach to critical infrastructure protection (Order No. 27540959).* ProQuest Dissertations & Theses Global (2320957957). https://about.proquest.com/products-services/pqdtglobal.html

Pomerleau, P. L. (2021). *La cybersécurité: Un bien public!* https://www.revuegestion.ca/serie-cybersecurite-et-travail-a-distance-la-cybersecurite-un-bien-public

Pomerleau, P. L., & Auger-Perreault, M. (2020). Fraud risk management: Using fraud analytics to combat external and insider threats. In L. R. Shapiro, & M. H. Maras (Eds.), *Encyclopedia of security and emergency management* (pp. 1–9). Springer. https://link.springer.com/referenceworkentry/10.1007/978-3-319-69891-5_296-1

Pomerleau, P. L., & Lowery, D. (2020). *Countering the cyber-threats to financial institutions.* Springer. https://link.springer.com/book/10.1007/978-3-030-54054-8

Sandberg, C., & Hunter, B. (2017). Cyber security primer for legacy process plant operation. In *Petroleum and Chemical Industry Technical Conference (PCIC), Calgary* (pp. 97–102), https://doi.org/10.1109/PCICON.2017.8188728

Schneier, B. (2018). *Click here to kill everybody: Security and survival in a hyper-connected world.* https://www.amazon.ca/-/fr/Bruce-Schneier/dp/0393608883

Secureworks. (2017). *Cyber threat basics, types of threats, intelligence & best practices.* https://www.secureworks.com/blog/cyber-threat-basics

Shaw, K. (2020). *The OSI model explained and how to easily remember its 7 layers.* https://www.networkworld.com/article/3239677/the-osi-model-explained-and-how-to-easily-remember-its-7-layers.html

Stevens, T. (2016). *Cyber security and the politics of time.* https://www.amazon.ca/Cyber-Security-Politics-Time-Stevens/dp/1107109426

Stevens, T. (2018). Global cybersecurity: New directions in theory and methods. *Politics and Governance, 6*(2), pp. 1–4. https://doi-org.proxy1.ncu.edu/10.17645/pag.v6i2.1569

Stevens, T., O'Brien, K., Overill, R., Wilkinson, B., Pildegovičs, T., & Hill, S. (2019). *UK active cyber defence: A public good for the private sector.* https://www.kcl.ac.uk/policy-institute/assets/uk-active-cyber-defence.pdf

Taddeo, M. (2019). Is cybersecurity a public good? *Minds & Machines, 29*(3), 349–354. https://doi.org/10.1007/s11023-019-09507-5

Testa, A., Maimon, D., Sobesto, B., & Cukier, M. (2017). Illegal roaming and file manipulation on target computers: Assessing the effect of sanction threats on system trespassers' online behaviors. *Criminology and Public Policy, 16*(3), 687–726. https://doi.org/10.1111/1745-9133.12312

Tipton, F. H., & Hernandez, S. (2013). *Official ISC2 guide to the CISSP CBK.* https://www.bookdepository.com/Official-ISC-2-Guide-CISSP-CBK-Third-Edition-Steven-Hernandez/9781466569768

United States District Court for the Central District of California. (2018). *United States v. Park Jin HYOK, also known as ("aka") "Jin Hyok Park", aka "Pak Jin Hek"*. https://www.justice.gov/usao-cdca/press-release/file/1091951/download

Valeriano, B., & Maness, C., R. (2018). International relations theory and cyber security: Threat, conflict, and ethics in an emergent domain. In C. Brown, & R. Eckersley (Eds.), *The Oxford handbook of international political theory. Oxford handbooks online* (pp. 259–272). https://www.oxfordhandbooks.com/view/10.1093/oxfordhb/9780198746928.001.0001/oxfordhb-9780198746928-e-19

Wafula, I. (2021). *6 strategies to reduce cybersecurity alert fatigue in your SOC.* https://www.microsoft.com/security/blog/2021/02/17/6-strategies-to-reduce-cybersecurity-alert-fatigue-in-your-soc/

Wilson, T., Maimon, D., Sobesto, B., & Cukier, M. (2015). The effect of a surveillance banner in an attacked computer system: Additional evidence for the relevance of restrictive deterrence in cyberspace. *Journal of Research in Crime and Delinquency, 52*(6), 829–855. https://journals.sagepub.com/doi/abs/10.1177/0022427815587761

World Economic Forum. (2020). *Future series: Cybersecurity, emerging technology and systemic risk.* https://www.weforum.org/reports/future-series-cybersecurity-emerging-technology-and-systemic-risk

Chapter 3

Human behavior in cyberspace

INTRODUCTION: CYBERCRIME AND CYBERSPACE

Many people still assume that cybercrimes are always perpetrated through technical means requiring technological systems (Leukfeldt & Holt, 2020). While this is partially true for specific types of crime, most cybercrimes are committed by human beings – networks of cybercriminals with nefarious motivations – who act within cyberspace to take advantage of people's and organizations' vulnerabilities. Most crimes committed through cyberspace are not separate from crimes in the physical world.

The current literature on cybercrime offers various definitions of criminal activities conducted through cyberspace. Lusthaus (2018) defined cybercrime as 'the use of computers or other electronic devices via information systems such as organizational networks or the Internet to facilitate illegal behaviors' (p. 8). Many scholars differentiate *cyber-dependent* crimes – crimes occurring due to the existence of technology (e.g., denial of service and hacking) – from *cyber-enabled* crimes or crimes facilitated through the use of the technology (e.g., online fraud, social engineering, phishing, business email compromise, and online stalking and harassment) (Powell et al., 2020; Wall, 2007; Weulen Kranenbarg, 2020). Mcguire (2020) offered a third category in his typology of cybercrime: *cyber-assisted crimes*. In these crimes, computers play more incidental roles, such as facilitating criminal communications or conspiracy. However, there is still a gray area between cyber-enabled and cyber-assisted crimes (Mcguire, 2020).

Since many authors did not agree on the tripartite definition of cybercrime – (a) cyber-dependent, (b) cyber-enabled, and (c) cyber-assisted – other models sought to explain cybercrime through more complex interactions between humans and technology (Leukfeldt, 2017; Mcguire, 2020; Nurse, 2018). Mcguire (2020) suggested that cybercrime can be explained in terms of (1) *actions* through typologies of cybercriminal acts that follow general taxonomies and (2) *situations* through interaction spaces (environmental) or spatial contexts. Mcguire (2020) also recommended avoiding using the prefix *cyber* to differentiate crimes associated with technology and cyberspace, as labeling an otherwise traditional crime 'cyber-theft' or 'cyber-violence' does nothing to help form a comprehensive definition of *cyber*crimes.

DOI: 10.1201/9781003201519-3

Today, many crimes can be cyber-enabled as we rely on technology in our daily lives. A wide array of online crimes and frauds are among the criminal activities that have become part of our digitally transformed living habits, in which the human factor plays a critical role (Ribaux & Souvignet, 2020). We are always connected to the Internet through our electronic devices and to a network of physical objects – things – embedded with sensors, software, and other technologies, all interacting with each other to connect and exchange data over the Internet. As Furnell (2017) pointed out, deciding whether a crime is enabled by or dependent on technology is often a matter of the tools used to commit the crime rather than the crime itself. The Internet is a new tool for cybercriminals, one that allows for a *greater reach* when committing crimes previously limited in their causal range (Mcguire, 2020). For example, there is no spatial limit or geographical boundary for a phishing email – a criminal may use a physical computer located in Canada to try and steal personal information (e.g., banking credentials) from potential victims in Australia. Thus, a crime common in the physical world – theft of data – can now be committed in cyberspace using phishing as a technological modus operandi. Attacks using emails are still attacks on people, not on technology.

Wall (2007) proposed three categories of cybercrime: (1) crime in the device, (2) crime using the device, and (3) crimes against the device (as cited in Nurse, 2018). The Department of Justice (DOJ) in the US relies on similar categories, distinguishing between crimes in which the computer is used as a target, a weapon, and an accessory (Rouse, n.d.). In line with Wall's (2007) definitions, an example of *crime in the device* could be accessing child pornography on a mobile device. It is unlawful for anybody to collect and share sexually explicit photos of children. A *crime using the device* could be a fraudster using a voice-changing app to change his voice, allowing him to impersonate another individual (e.g., one with a Chinese accent). He could then use a voice over IP (VoIP) application to disguise a fraudulent phone number, making it look like he is calling from a phone number known to the victim, all in an attempt to trick the potential victim (identity spoofing) into providing confidential information to steal his identity. As for the third category, a *crime against the device* often seeks to compromise one or more of the CIA triad of cybersecurity fundamentals: confidentiality, integrity, and availability (Nurse, 2018). An example of this type of crime could be using a denial-of-service attack – an attempt to flood web services and to make them unavailable – against the server of an online banking service or using a brute-force attack to break weak passwords relied upon by online banking customers. These crimes often utilize dictionary or credential stuffing attacks, using a password dictionary containing millions (e.g., random passwords) of words that people regularly use in their passwords while credential stuffing uses exposed data (e.g., data breach) reducing the number of possible correct answers (Cloudfare, 2021).

If we are to understand cybercrime better, a possible avenue is to understand better how different humans interact. It is complicated to analyze cybercrime types when considering the myriad of actors within the cybercrime ecosystem. For this reason, it is imperative to understand the relationships between four of these key actors. As is the case with most social ills, cybercrime is a human problem.

FOUR KEY ACTORS WITHIN THE CYBERCRIME ECOSYSTEM

Biologists define an ecosystem as the interaction of a biotic community and its environment (Maimon & Louderback., 2019). Importing this concept to human societies, social scientists have proposed that human populations employ social organization and technology in their efforts to adapt to the environment (either natural or built) and evolve (Georgia State University, 2021). Drawing on these claims, the interactions among cybercrime *offenders*, *enablers* (i.e., individuals who support the online criminal operations), *targets* (i.e., individual victims or organizations), and *guardians* (i.e., official law enforcement agencies, private cybersecurity teams, and system administrators) form a unique ecosystem in which the activities of each actor influence the behaviors of other actors (Maimon & Louderback., 2019).

The offenders

Cybercriminals or *offenders* are individuals who use computers to attack other people's computer systems, networks, IoT devices, and data (e.g., personally identifiable data, health data, or research data). Similar to criminals in the physical world, cybercriminals' motivations to engage in online crimes may include prestige, recreation, ideology, revenge, and profit (Georgia State University, 2021; Maimon & Louderback, 2019; Seebruck, 2015). Their skill levels vary from very low to very high. Although several studies have shown that most cybercriminals have relatively low technical skills (Bossler, 2020; Holt et al., 2012; Leukfeldt, 2016; Maimon & Louderback, 2019; Musotto & Wall, 2020; Ribaux & Souvignet, 2020), other studies demonstrate that some online offenders' technical skills are proliferating (Nikkel, 2020; Wilson, 2014) and that they are engaging in sophisticated attacks (Holt & Bossler, 2014).

Dupont (2020) claimed that the industrialization of crime led to the search for rare *technical, entrepreneurial,* and *social* skills among criminals. Technical skills are often associated with using malware programming to access confidential data (Dupont, 2020). Some hackers also employ more complex attacks, using malware such as Emotet, Trickbot, and Cerberus to steal information (Interpol, 2020). As for social skills, cybercriminals often communicate through legitimate means, though usually via dark web channels, to meticulously plan and execute their unlawful online activities.

Entrepreneurial skills work the same way for online criminals as for legitimate businesspeople, as they can both turn personal data and intellectual property into profits (Dupont, 2020). Cybercriminals can also generate illegitimate profits by perpetuating crimes for other criminals. Both Lusthaus (2018) and Musotto and Wall (2020) argued that cybercriminals tend to work harder than people might believe, since they must combine their skills and employ various business strategies to attract (and profit from) other cybercriminals wanting their 'services.' Like on legitimate e-commerce websites, products, prices, and customers are differentiated on crime forums, and criminals have to fight to attract clients and increase their business (Musotto & Wall, 2020). In other words, the tactics they rely on are much closer to *The Wolf of Wall Street* than *The Godfather* (Musotto & Wall, 2020).

Cybercriminals communicate using different online mechanisms and use multiple techniques to get their attacks onto victims' computers and networks (Georgia State University, 2021). Among many subterfuges and fraudulent techniques, social engineering tactics (e.g., malicious emails, phishing, spear-phishing, romance scams, pretexting, and whaling attacks) are common forms of psychological manipulation used by cybercriminals to breach organization security measures through personal interactions (Jaf et al., 2018; Jakobsson, 2020; Nurse, 2018; Paganini, 2020; Pomerleau, 2019). Linton (2020) mentioned that given the right angle and the right pitch while communicating with potential victims, cybercriminals can make them do almost anything: social engineering, like martial arts, is all about using your opponents' force against them.

The enablers

Cybercrimes' *enablers* are individuals and criminal organizations that provide or facilitate services to those who wish to carry out cybercrimes (Georgia State University, 2021). These enablers may include coders or programmers of malicious software, distributors, and vendors who trade or sell hacking tools and stolen data (i.e., personal information from a data breach that could be used to commit fraud), teachers or *cyber-mentors* who exchange information regarding cybercrime techniques (i.e., modus operandi; procedures) and tools, and moderators and administrators of online marketplaces who maintain the criminal infrastructure, vouch for the goods, and enforce social norms in marketplaces (Georgia State University, 2021). Online offenders and enablers of cybercrimes can meet in offline social contacts or online environments (Leukfeldt, 2017). For example, a criminal organization might want to launder money from illicit activity. Thus, an enabler will provide the criminal organization access to money mules in many countries to disperse the funds globally. These money mules will have access to bank accounts to receive a portion of the overall ill-gotten gains to be distributed. Their job will be to redirect this sum to another bank account, to scramble the payment's initial money trail and avoid detection by financial institutions.

The victims

Victims of cybercrimes are individuals and companies who experience attacks on their computers, networks, mobile, and IoT devices. Unfortunately, victims' unawareness of their victimization, along with their unwillingness to report cybercrimes to law enforcement agencies, complicates the task of estimating the scope of cybercrime (Georgia State University, 2021). Even though online crime prevalence has considerably increased over the last two decades (Leukfeldt, 2017), only 10% of businesses impacted by a cybersecurity incident report it to law enforcement (Pomerleau, 2019). This low reporting rate not only applies to organizational victims of cybercrime but also to individuals (Leukfeldt, 2017). An example of victimization that is not systematically reported to law enforcement would be individuals becoming victims of identity theft after their personal information was made available on the dark web, typically following a data breach at an organization they have dealt with in the past. In such a case, cybercriminals might use these individuals' information to commit fraud (e.g., identity theft, fraudulent account opening, auto loan, credit card, line of credit applications). On the other hand, the fiduciary organization impacted by the data breach, either from being hacked or having inadequate security measures in place, is also victimized because the customer information they were responsible for protecting was stolen (Bentley et al., 2017).

The guardians

The list of relevant *guardians* in the context of cybercrimes includes law enforcement agencies (e.g., the FBI and local police agencies), governmental non-police organizations (e.g., the National Security Agency), private security and investigation teams, system administrators at various Internet Service Providers (ISPs), corporate and industrial asset protection teams (Georgia State University, 2021), as well as the general public (Nhan, 2010).

Law enforcement organizations serve as gatekeepers within the criminal justice system. They possess the legal power to investigate, collect evidence, and arrest suspects (Nhan, 2010). On the other hand, civilians in the private sector were at the forefront of policing cyberspace before law enforcement, and they still play a significant role in preventing, detecting, and responding to cybercrime investigations (Nhan, 2010). Computer security, cybersecurity, and anti-fraud professionals from various private sector organizations have been the front-line defense for their companies' infrastructure for many years.

However, as Pomerleau (2019) stipulated, the private sector does not have the necessary intelligence collection, legal authority, and enforcement capabilities to fully protect its network and infrastructure. While the government does possess the necessary authority and abilities, it does not have cybersecurity-specific expertise in the cyber-threats affecting the private sector (Pomerleau, 2019). The general public also plays an essential role in the detection of cybercrimes. As anyone can become a potential victim of cyber-crime, people must report cybercrime attempts to law enforcement. Their role is vital because if individuals do not report crimes, law enforcement cannot know the impact of these crimes on society. This situation leads to less invest-ment in cybercrime (e.g., developing expertise, human resources, investiga-tions) than in other crimes categorized as major crimes causing physical harm.

Many people believe that employee training is critical to notice and avoid cyber-threats. For many years, though, organizations and security teams have invested considerably in training employees to avoid clicking on unknown links, be suspicious of poorly written emails, and avoid opening potentially malicious attachments (Jakobsson, 2020). For Jakobsson (2020), such a training should not be the primary tool to prevent cybercrime; it should be the last resort. Chief Information Security Officers (CISOs) and their teams have created excellent awareness training by purchasing solu-tions – e.g., content libraries, administrative features, and assessment mea-suring – designed to educate employees about cyberattacks. Unfortunately, awareness is not enough to change behaviors and instill a security culture (Budge, 2021). Honest people can still send poorly written emails. Well-trained employees can also make mistakes and open an infected file, even though they have followed all their phishing and fraud detection training modules. If computer users could always detect cybercrime schemes, they would be far less likely to become victims. Unfortunately, this utopian situ-ation will probably never happen.

Jakobsson (2020) argued that it is a mistake to believe the end user (human) will always follow instructions. Solely focusing on security and privacy with-out considering the end user and user interfaces is a losing strategy for orga-nizations (Jakobsson, 2020). Indeed, we have to better understand what motivates users and how they interpret information. Whether it is a new mobile phone, a piece of software, an IoT device, or a computer, most users do not read the instructions. They do not want to know what can go wrong with their new device given various security configurations; they just want to use it (Jakobsson, 2020). Instead of increasing the training and awareness budget to solve user-related problems, which treat all employees as having the same motivations and psychological weaknesses, training should be tailored to specific issues and individuals. But above all, organizations should invest in user-related problems algorithmically (Briggs et al., 2017; Jakobsson, 2020).

HUMAN BEHAVIORS AS A CENTRAL ELEMENT OF CYBERCRIME

Human behaviors and actions lie at the center of every cybercrime. Organizations rely heavily on technology to manage the risk associated with cyber-threats. Unfortunately, many cybersecurity managers and law enforce-ment professionals still believe that technology is *the only way* to protect the organization. In fact, studies demonstrate that new technologies bring unintended consequences and that technological induced errors are often human-enabled (Nobles, 2018). Even with the implementation of the latest cybersecurity tools, systems, and technologies, we've still seen an increase in cyberattacks, and malicious actors can still access governments' and businesses' critical networks, systems, and data (Nobles, 2018).

Private and public organizations invest significant financial and human resources in cybersecurity systems and technology, ostensibly to reduce their risk of being the victim of cyberattacks. In 2020, the global cybersecurity market was worth US$173 billion, and it is expected to continue its stratospheric growth, with cybersecurity spending reaching US$270 billion by 2026 (Colombus, 2020). While small, medium, and large organizations' cybersecurity budgets differ in size, many organizations plan their annual cybersecurity investments based on a percentage of the IT budget or a set amount per employee. For example, according to a Deloitte & Touche survey of financial services organizations, organizations spend between 6% and 14% (10%, on average) of their IT budget on cybersecurity each year or between US$1,300 and US$3,000 per full-time employee (Comtois, 2019). A large financial institution such as J.P. Morgan Chase & Co. (NYSE: JPM) likely spends approximately US$600 million each year on cybersecurity, based on a 2018 estimate and assuming that their investment increases each year (Morgan, 2019).

Despite these investments in cybersecurity, the annual number of cyberattacks on companies has not decreased, and larger investments in cybersecurity do not necessarily translate into a higher cybersecurity maturity level (Comtois, 2019). Thus, investing in technology is not enough, since the human factor is still the weakest link in cybercrime management (Alavi et al., 2016; Dykstra, 2015; Edgar & Manz, 2017; Leukfeldt, 2017; Nobles, 2018; Proctor & Chen, 2015; Rubinoff, 2020). Consequently, humans need to be part of the solution and each organization's security strategy (Rubinoff, 2020).

Whether it is the company's system administrator who left generic passwords on the organization's critical applications, the cybersecurity employee who did not set up the security applications correctly, the IT employee who did not apply the necessary patches, or the business line employee who clicked on a fraudulent phishing link that gave hackers access to his organization's data and systems, humans always have a share of responsibility in the commission of a cybercrime. It could also be an employee of a third-party company, acting in good faith but inadvertently allowing a security breach by his actions within the system (Steinmetz et al., 2020). In other instances, customers may allow the crime, such as by becoming the victim of an online fraud scheme or love scam, entering a parent's credit card number into an unsecured video game website, or trying to pay a bill online but unwittingly using a fake website to enter payment information. Finally, of course, humans can be the offenders in these cybercrimes, whether by hacking or masterminding the crime. Thus, for each cybercrime committed, the human is involved at different levels in the commission of the crime, either as the cause of or solution to the security problem (Rubinoff, 2020).

THE HUMAN FACTOR IN THE LITERATURE ON CYBERCRIME

Recognizing the importance of the human aspect in cybercrime, some authors have already studied the interactions between humans, the tools and techniques used by hackers and fraudsters, and their motivations to influence victims successfully. Unfortunately, the importance of human factors in cybersecurity remains underappreciated (Nobles, 2018). Cybercrime was considered a computer science problem for a long time, so most social scientists do not see cybercrime prevention as their responsibility (Weulen Kranenbarg, 2020). Criminologists have also not devoted enough effort to understanding cybercrime prevention and the use of IT systems by cybercriminals (Weulen Kranenbarg, 2020). Some criminologists do provide empirical insight about traditional criminological explanations to explain cyber-offending (Holt & Bossler, 2014; Leukefeldt, De Poot, Verhoeven, Kleemans, & Lavorgna, 2017; Weulen Kranenbarg et al., 2017). However, more research on active defense methods, such as the study conducted by Siadi et al. (2020) on common types of online crime orchestrated by online scammers, is needed to potentially reduce the impact of cyber-offending on victims and organizations. Future similar studies would provide actionable intelligence to assist law enforcement with their investigations. As an example, after Siadi et al. (2020) shared their research with law enforcement, the Federal Bureau of Investigation (FBI) arrested 42 individuals in the US, 29 in Nigeria, and three others for alleged business email compromise attacks (The United States Department of Justice, 2018).

According to Soltanmohammadi et al. (2013), it is common knowledge that human errors enable approximately 80% of all cyberattacks. Nobles (2018) stressed that 95% of all cyber-incidents are human-enabled, while Van Zadelhoff (2016) claimed that human error is the most critical area of organizational vulnerability. Despite this evidence, security plans almost never consider human behaviors in terms of risk management. Part of the problem is that the risks associated with humans exceed cybersecurity professionals' expertise. The industry does not engage with human factor specialists such as cognitive and behavioral specialists to elaborate new and efficient strategies to tackle the human-enabled information security problems they face (Nobles, 2018). The analysis of employee behaviors by such professionals could provide practical insight into automation, information overload, technological determinist thinking, and procedures alignment, all helping to clarify operational effectiveness and impacts of technology on the workforce (Nobles, 2015). Businesses still pursue technical solutions to resolve behavioral-based risks instead of focusing on human decision-making and end-users' interactions with systems (Metalidou et al., 2014). But the human factor is *an end-user problem* (Jakobsson, 2020), and society needs to better understand the interaction between humans and technological devices such as computers and mobile devices. Until we do, cybercrime will remain a significant societal problem.

Humans build security to guard against bad actors (other humans) who are trying to take advantage of individuals' vulnerabilities, including those related to individuals' behavior while using a computer or a mobile device, their lack of technical knowledge regarding cyber-threats, or their lack of attention to best practices to avoid falling into cyber-threat traps. All cyberattacks involve human victims and attackers, but in some cases, a person could also be on both sides of the attack (e.g., a victim but also participating in the crime without necessarily realizing it) or in the middle of the attack (between the victim and the attacker, as a guardian).

A LOOK INSIDE THE ORGANIZATION

To analyze humans' involvement in cybersecurity problems and their potential role in solutions, organizations should consider various security strategies and the roles humans play in each strategy. From a governance standpoint, organizations can promote a security/compliance culture and encourage proper cyber hygiene at every level of the corporation. If we take a private organization as an example, it begins at the board level. Board members have legal and compliance accountabilities toward shareholders and regulators. They do not need to be cybersecurity technical experts, but they do need a relatively good understanding of the organization's cyber-risks and a detailed knowledge of how the organization manages its risks at the strategic and operational levels, to ensure the organization remains compliant and secure. To fulfill these responsibilities, they need to be aware of cyber-risks to ensure the organization remains compliant and secure.

For example, board members need to know what a ransomware attack is, how it could impact the organization's operations, and what leaders within the executive teams are doing to improve employees' responses to a potential attack. The goal is not to prevent every cyberattack, which is impractical, but to ensure that the organization is so resilient that if it is victimized, it will have the necessary capabilities and operational processes in place to recover swiftly from the incident – swiftly enough to minimize the impacts on its customers and investors – in line with its risk tolerance. A great way for board members to learn whether the organization is sufficiently ready to face such an attack is to read the post-mortem analysis of tabletop exercises or cyber-attack simulations. These practical scenarios evaluate what employees did right during the practice and focus on where they need to improve going forward.

Promoting good cyber hygiene also needs to come from the Chief Executive Officer (CEO) and the executive team, as the tone at the top is vital to effective security. Strong leadership from management can empower employees to make the proper decisions regarding ongoing and future IT investments to enhance security, implement new procedures, decide what level of training is required, and provide it appropriately throughout the organization. When made with the human factor in mind, such decisions can unify teams around the same goal: to rely on all employees and their interactions to protect the organization.

According to Rubinoff (2020), there are four steps to achieving proper cyber hygiene: (1) continuous training for all employees regardless of their hierarchical level, (2) promoting a culture of awareness within the organization, (3) installing patches (security updates) regularly, and (4) implementing the zero-trust model of security. In the zero-trust model, organizations do not automatically trust anything inside or outside of its perimeter, thus forcing the organization to authenticate everything (e.g., employees, connections, accesses) that is trying to connect with its network, only granting access to confirmed and known entities (Rubinoff, 2020). Focusing on better cyber hygiene and human-focused cybersecurity protocols is even more critical during crisis scenarios like the COVID-19 pandemic when most employees work from home. Adapting to COVID-19 required many organizations to work through a virtual private network to maintain customer service, which sometimes meant initiating high-level transactions (e.g., international wire transfers) from home, leading to increased risk from cyber-threats. In these particular circumstances, utilizing proper cybersecurity hygiene and security protocols, both of which should consider human behavior, is paramount.

Failure to maintain software patches is another critical vulnerability: cyber-attacks were responsible for approximately 60% of the data breaches in the last two years, many caused by a missing operating system patch or application patch (Sheridan, 2020). Patching might be expensive in terms of investments and operational costs. Still, those costs are minimal compared to the damages of a cyberattack – including significant reputation damage, compliance fines, and loss of customers. For example, the Marriott International hotel chain breach (2014–2018) compromised 500 million guest records, including 20.3 million encrypted password numbers, 5.25 million unencrypted password numbers, and credit card numbers. Marriott was fined US120 million dollars (Fruhlinger, 2020; Gates, 2021).

In most of these cyber-incidents, if the victimized organizations and their employees had installed security patches in time, their systems would have been protected, and the incidents could have been prevented. However, these security decisions need to be made by humans, and only humans, not machines, have leadership capabilities. Moreover, employees can also become insider threats to organizations when they turn against the company. Some organizations like WorldCom and Enron had to declare bankruptcy due to insider threats, while others like French Bank Société Générale suffered billions in losses (Binns, 2019; Pomerleau & Auger-Perreault, 2020).

Similar to Nobles (2018), Lapointe (2018) argued that the vast majority of cyberattacks and privacy breaches – 99% of the cases – are caused by human error giving access to corporate systems' confidential information. In this context, a human error is a non-malicious accident that could lead to a cyberattack, fraud, or breach of confidentiality. Employees can make numerous errors within organizations, but here is a non-exhaustive list of actions that may lead to a cyberattack or a leak of confidential information: (1) sending sensitive information to the wrong recipient by email, (2) clicking on a phishing email, (3) copying sensitive data to an incorrect server, (4) leaving a default password on sensitive equipment in the organization (servers, workstations, routers, firewalls, etc.), (5) providing too much access to a new employee, (6) leaving a password in the application code, and (7) writing down confidential information such as personally identifiable information (PII) on a piece of paper and not destroying it securely. These errors can be dramatic for an organization. They could lead to a breach of confidentiality involving identity theft for customers, damage the company's reputation (e.g., sending an email with confidential information to the wrong person), or open the door to a much larger cyberattack if an employee or a third party clicks on a phishing link.

CONCLUSION

Cybersecurity is a relatively new science of computing and human interactions that demands a broad, multidisciplinary effort (Millett et al., 2017). A better understanding of humans, human organizations, and their relationship with the use of technology and the Internet is necessary to develop a robust security science and deploy systems most effectively (Millett et al., 2017). Doing so will help make sure systems are doing what they were designed to do, which is to be secured against human adversaries (Millett et al., 2017). Like criminologists do for criminals operating in our physical world, cybersecurity professionals and researchers also need to think about how cybercriminals become criminals, why they commit a crime, how they think, how they live, and how they interact within their criminal path.

REFERENCES

Alavi, R., Islam, S., & Mouratidis, H. (2016). An information security risk-driven investment model for analysing human factors. *Information & Computer Security*, 24(2), 205–227.

Bentley, M. J., Oostman, R. K., & Ali Shah, F. S. (2017). We're sorry but it's not our fault: Organizational apologies in ambiguous crisis situations. *Journal of Contingencies and Crisis Management*, 26, 138–149. https://doi.org/10.1111/1468-5973.12169

Binns, C. A. (2019). Investigations: Fraud. In L. Shapiro, & M. H. Maras (Eds.), *Encyclopedia of security and emergency management* (pp. 1–6). Springer.

Bossler, M. A. (2020). Contributions of criminological theory to the understanding of cybercrime offending and victimization. In E. Leukfeldt, & T. J. Holt (Eds.), *The human factor of cybercrime* (pp. 29–59). Routledge.

Briggs, P., Jeske, D., & Coventry, L. (2017). Behavior change interventions for cybersecurity. *Behavior Change Research and Theory, 2017*, 115–136. https://doi.org/10.1016/B978-0-12-802690-8.00004-9

Budge, J. (2021). *Awareness isn't enough—It's time to change behaviors.* https://go.forrester.com/blogs/awareness-isnt-enough-its-time-to-change-behaviors/

Cloudfare. (2021). *What is credential stuffing? Credential stuffing vs. brute force attacks.* https://www.cloudflare.com/learning/bots/what-is-credential-stuffing/

Colombus, L. (2020). *2020 roundup of cybersecurity forecasts and market estimates.* https://www.forbes.com/sites/louiscolumbus/2020/04/05/2020-roundup-of-cybersecurity-forecasts-and-market-estimates/?sh=af8bc1a381d7

Comtois, J. (2019). *Financial services firms spend 6% to 14% of IT budget on cybersecurity – survey.* https://www.pionline.com/article/20190501/ONLINE/190509988/financial-services-firms-spend-6-to-14-of-it-budget-on-cybersecurity-survey

Dupont, B. (2020). The ecology of cybercrime. In E. Leukfeldt, & T. J. Holt (Eds.), *The human factor of cybercrime* (pp. 389–407). Routledge.

Dykstra, J. (2015). *Essential cybersecurity science: Build, test, and evaluate secure systems.* O'Reilly.

Edgar, T. W., & Manz, D. O. (2017). *Research methods for cyber security.* Syngress.

Fruhlinger, J. (2020). *Marriott data breach FAQ: How did it happen and what was the impact?* https://www.csoonline.com/article/3441220/marriott-data-breach-faq-how-did-it-happen-and-what-was-the-impact.html

Furnell, S. (2017). The evolving landscape of technology-dependent crime. In M. R. McGuire, & T. Holt (Eds.), *The handbook of technology, crime and justice* (pp. 65–77). Routledge.

Gates, M. (2021). *The rise of cyber due diligence in deal-making.* https://www.asisonline.org/security-management-magazine/articles/2021/01/the-rise-of-cyber-due-diligence-in-deal-making/

Georgia State University. (2021). *The cyber crime ecosystem.* Evidence-Based Cybersecurity Group. https://ebcs.gsu.edu/about/cybercrime-ecosystem/

Holt, T. J., & Bossler, A. M. (2014). An assessment of the current state of cybercrime scholarship. *Deviant Behavior, 35*(1), 20–40.

Holt, T. J., Strumsky, D., Smirnova, O., & Kilger, M. (2012). Examining the social networks of malware writers and hackers. *International Journal of Cyber Criminology, 6*(1), 891–903.

Interpol. (2020). *Interpol report shows alarming rate of cyberattacks during COVID-19.* https://www.interpol.int/News-and-Events/News/2020/INTERPOL-report-shows-alarming-rate-of-cyberattacks-during-COVID-19

Jaf, S., Ghafir, I., Prenosil, V., Saleem, J., Hammoudeh, M., Faour, H., & Baker, T. (2018). Security threats to critical infrastructure: The human factor. *Journal of Supercomputing, 74*(10), 4986–5002. https://doi-org.proxy1.ncu.edu/10.1007/s11227-018-2337-2

Jakobsson, M. (2020). *Security, privacy and user interaction.* Springer.

Lapointe, L. (2018). *The human fix to human risk.* Terranova Security.

Leukfeldt, E. R. (2016). *Cybercriminal networks: Origin, growth and criminal capabilities.* Eleven International Publishing.

Leukfeldt, E. R., De Poot, C., Verhoeven, M., Kleemans, E., & Lavorgna, A. (2017). Cybercriminal networks. In E. Leukfeldt (Ed.), *Research agenda: The human factor in cybercrime and cybersecurity* (pp. 33–42). Eleven International Publishing. https://www.researchgate.net/publication/317191029_Research_agenda_The_human_factor_in_cybercrime_and_cybersecurity

Leukfeldt, E. R. (2017). *Research agenda the human factor in cybercrime and cybersecurity.* Eleven International Publishing.

Leukfeldt, E. R., & Holt, T. J. (2020). *The human factor of cybercrime.* Routledge.

Linton, J. (2020). Foreword. In M. Jakobsson (Ed.), *Security, privacy and user interaction* (pp. vii–viii). https://doi.org/10.1007/978-3-030-43754-1

Lusthaus, J. (2018). *Industry of anonymity.* Harvard University Press.

Maimon, D., & Louderback., R. E. (2019). Cyber-dependent crimes: An interdisciplinary review. *Annual Review of Criminology, 2,* 191–216.

Mcguire, M. (2020). It ain't what it is, it's the way that they do it? Why we still don't understand cybercrime. In E. Leukfeldt, & T. J. Holt (Eds.), *The human factor of cybercrime* (pp. 3–28). Routledge.

Metalidou, E., Marinagi, C., Trivellas, P., Eberhagen, N., Skourlas, C., & Giannakopoulos, G. (2014). The human factor of information security: Unintentional damage perspective. *Procedia - Social and Behavioral Sciences, 147,* 424–428. https://doi.org/10.1016/j.sbspro.2014.07.133

Millett, L. I., Fischhoff, B., & Weinberger, P. J. (2017). *Foundational cybersecurity research: Improving science, engineering, and institutions.* The National Academies Press.

Morgan, S. (2019). *Global cybersecurity spending predicted to exceed $1 trillion from 2017-2021.* https://cybersecurityventures.com/cybersecurity-market-report/

Musotto, R., & Wall, D. S. (2020). More Amazon than mafia: Analysing a DDoS stresser service as organised cybercrime. *Trends in Organized Crime.* https://doi.org/10.1007/s12117-020-09397-5

Nhan, J. (2010). *Policing cyberspace: A structural and cultural analysis.* LFB Scholarly Publishing LLC.

Nikkel, B. (2020). Fintech forensics: Criminal investigation and digital evidence in financial technologies. *Forensic Science International: Digital Investigation, 33,* 200908. https://doi.org/10.1016/j.fsidi.2020.200908

Nobles, C. (2015). *Exploring pilots' experiences of integrating technologically advanced aircraft within general aviation: A case study.* CreateSpace.

Nobles, C. (2018). Botching human factors in cybersecurity in business organizations. *Holistica, 9*(3), 71–88. https://doi.org/10.2478/hjbpa-2018-0024

Nurse, C. R. J. (2018). Cybercrime and you: How criminals attack and the human factors that they seek to exploit. In A. Attrill-Smith, C. Fullwood, M. Keep, & D. J. Kuss (Eds.), *The Oxford handbook of cyberpsychology* (pp. 663–690). https://doi.org/10.1093/oxfordhb/9780198812746.013.35

Paganini, P. (2020). *The most common social engineering attacks (updated 2020).* https://resources.infosecinstitute.com/topic/common-social-engineering-attacks/

Pomerleau, P. L. (2019). *Countering the cyber threats against financial institutions in Canada: A qualitative study of a private and public partnership approach to critical infrastructure protection.* ProQuest Dissertations & Theses Global (2320957957). https://about.proquest.com/products-services/pqdtglobal.html

Pomerleau, P. L., & Auger-Perreault, M. (2020). Fraud risk management: Using fraud analytics to combat external and insider threats. In L. Shapiro, & M. H. Maras (Eds.), *Encyclopedia of security and emergency management* (pp. 1–9). Springer.

Powell, A., Flynn, A., & Henry, N. (2020). Sexual violence in digital society. In E. Leukfeldt, & T. J. Holt (Eds.), *The human factor of cybercrime* (pp. 134–156). Routledge.

Proctor, R. W., & Chen, J. (2015). The role of human factors/ergonomics in the science of security: Decision making and action selection in cyberspace. *Human Factors*, 57(5), 721–727.

Ribaux, O., & Souvignet, T. R. (2020). "Hello are you available?" Dealing with online frauds and the role of forensic science. *Forensic Science International: Digital Investigation*, 33. https://doi.org/10.1016/j.fsidi.2020.300978

Rouse, M. (n.d.). *Cybercrime*. https://searchsecurity.techtarget.com/definition/cybercrime

Rubinoff, S. (2020). *Research agenda: The human factor in cybercrime and cybersecurity*. https://www.researchgate.net/publication/317191029_Research_agenda_The_human_factor_in_cybercrime_and_cybersecurity

Seebruck, R. (2015). A typology of hackers: Classifying cyber malfeasance using a weighted arc circumplex model. *Digital Investigation*, 14, 36–45. https://doi.org/10.1016/j.diin.2015.07.002

Sheridan, K. (2020). *Missing patches, misconfiguration top technical breach causes*. https://www.darkreading.com/vulnerabilities—threats/missing-patches-misconfiguration-top-technical-breach-causes/d/d-id/1337410

Siadi, H., Koven, J., Felix Da Silva, C., Jakobsson, M., Bertini, E., Maimon, D., & Memon, N. (2020). A framework for analysis of attackers' accounts. In M. Jakobsson (Ed.), *Security, privacy and user interaction* (pp. 63–89). https://doi.org/10.1007/978-3-030-43754-1

Soltanmohammadi, S., Asadi, S., & Ithnin, N. (2013). Main human factors affecting information system security. *Interdisciplinary Journal of Contemporary Research in Business*, 5(7), 329–354.

Steinmetz, K., Goe, R., & Pimentel, A. (2020). Social engineering. In E. Leukfeldt, & T. J. Holt (Eds.), *The human factor of cybercrime* (pp. 173–193). Routledge.

The United States Department of Justice. (2018). *74 arrested in coordinated international enforcement operation targeting hundreds of individuals in business email compromise schemes*. https://www.justice.gov/opa/pr/74-arrested-coordinated-international-enforcement-operation-targeting-hundreds-individuals

Van Zadelhoff, M. (2016). *The biggest cybersecurity threats are insider your company*. https://hbr.org/2016/09/the-biggest-cybersecurity-threats-are-inside-your-company

Wall, D. S. (2007). Policing cybercrimes: Situating the public police in networks of security within cyberspace. *Police Practice and Research*, 8(2), 183–206.

Weulen Kranenbarg, M. (2020). Contrasting cyber-dependent and traditional offenders: A comparison on criminological explanations and potential prevention methods. In E. Leukfeldt, & T. J. Holt (Eds.), *The human factor of cybercrime* (pp. 194–215). Routledge.

Weulen Kranenbarg, M., Van Der Laan, A. M., De Poot, C. J., Verhoeven, M. A., Van Der Wagen, W., & Weijters, G. (2017). Individual cybercrime offenders. In E. Leukfeldt (Ed.), *Research agenda: The human factor in cybercrime and cybersecurity* (pp. 23–32). Eleven International Publishing.

Wilson, C. (2014). Cyber threats to critical information infrastructure. In L. J. Thomas, & N. Chen (Eds.), *Cyberterrorism: Understanding, assessment, and response* (pp. 123–136). Springer-Swansea University.

Chapter 4

Criminological, sociological, psychological, ethical, and biological models relevant to cybercrime and cybercriminals

INTRODUCTION

This chapter analyzes theoretical frameworks from various disciplines to better understand how different social science fields examine human factors within the cybercrime ecosystem. We will discuss numerous crime theories from criminology, sociology, anthropology, biology, psychology, ethics, and philosophy fields. We begin by discussing theoretical frameworks that are regularly used in the literature to explain crime, then focus on specific frameworks that are less common. Regardless of their popularity, all these frameworks must still be considered to explain why people commit a crime, the criminal environment, and particular ways in which cybercrime should be analyzed and addressed in the future.

Criminological and sociological models relevant to cybercrime

As of today, criminological research focuses primarily on criminal activities, subcultures, and criminal behaviors formed in physical spaces (Holt, 2020). The Internet transformed interpersonal communications by allowing individuals worldwide to share their interests and ideas across physical borders and language barriers (Holt, 2020). Technology and the online environment enable criminal organizations to operate in ways that were impossible in the physical world. Online environments and social media promote information-sharing and allow criminals to easily reach other criminal subcultures to introduce potential offending methods, without necessarily needing to know precisely who they are dealing with (Holt, 2020). Some of these interactions would not be possible in an offline environment due to legal risks and social rejections; thus, the online environment's anonymity greatly enhances the criminal possibilities afforded to cybercriminals (Holt, 2020).

Maimon and Louderback (2019) noted that the most common criminological theories on the underlying causes of cyber-dependent crimes are the General Theory of Crime developed by Gottfredson and Hirschi (1990), the Social Learning Theory by Akers (1973), the Social Control Theory by

DOI: 10.1201/9781003201519-4

Hirschi (1969), and the techniques of neutralization and deterrence by Sykes and Matza (1957) or Gibbs (1975). The *General Theory of Crime* suggests that individuals with low self-control have a higher propensity to take advantage of criminal opportunities offered to them and engage in various illegal activities (Maimon & Louderback, 2019). But while the General Theory of Crime has been applied in the criminology literature to offline offenders, findings regarding its application to online crime are mixed. For this reason, Maimon and Louderback (2019) claimed that *Social Learning Theory*, which explains that criminal behavior is learned through a process of imitation and influenced by positive peer reinforcement toward criminal behavior, is more appropriate to explain cyber-dependent crimes. For example, a study conducted by Hutchings and Clayton (2016) demonstrated that cybercriminals operating *booter services* websites offering distributed denial-of-service (DDOS) attacks for a fee learned their skills through interactions with other online community members that also shared favorable offending beliefs. This is only one example of the cybercrimes that are on sale. Hyslip (2020) described this relatively new way of doing business as cybercrime-as-a-service operations, noting that they have changed the criminal marketplace from a direct sales model to a managed service model where some criminals engage others to do the crimes for them.

Other studies, such as the one conducted by Cheng et al. (2013), relied on the *Social Control Theory*, which focuses on why people obey rules instead of breaking them (Schmalleger & Volk, 2001) to explain hacking. Cheng et al. (2013) found that employees who have an attachment to their jobs and the organization's commitment and norms showed significantly lower motivations to infringe the company's security policies. Other researchers investigated cyber-dependent crimes by analyzing the relationships between individual uses of neutralization techniques (Maimon & Louderback, 2019). Morris's (2011) study demonstrated that cybercriminals involved in low hacking levels (e.g., password guessing) rely on victims' denial as a neutralization technique. Cybercriminals use various neutralization techniques to minimize their deviance and justify their criminal activities and the impact of their crimes on victims. Offenders learn these techniques to justify breaking laws by denying responsibility, injury, or victimization (Brooks, 2016). Some of their irrational justifications are that victims should have protected themselves better by using strong passwords online or that their financial institution would reimburse victims for the money they were defrauded through an online scam.

The routine activity approach and the problem analysis triangle

The cybersecurity ecosystem can also be analyzed through a criminological lens using the *Problem Analysis Triangle*. According to this theoretical framework, crime will occur when offenders and targets converge in places where all three controllers – guardians, handlers, and managers – are ineffective, absent, or negligent (Eck, 2010; Miró Llinares & Johnson, 2018). The model is depicted as the crime triangle and is often called the problem analysis triangle, as premised on the routine activity theory (RAT) in criminology (Cyber-Trust Consortium, n.d.). To apply this theory to cybersecurity, one could use the crime triangle to explain the relationship between a *place*, a *malicious actor*, a *victim*, and a *guardian*. For instance, when a malicious and motivated actor (hacker) targets a suitable victim (organization/user) within a specific place (a critical system within the victim's infrastructure) and the victim lacks a guardian (an automated process within the security department), there is a high possibility for this victim to be under attack (Cyber-Trust Consortium, n.d.). Thus, to reduce the probability of a bad actor taking advantage of a victim and/or a place (as described above), organizations should aim to harden their critical systems, cloud access, and any essential IT components within their infrastructure. Doing so would reduce the chances of a malicious and motivated actor taking advantage of any vulnerabilities and significantly impact the organization's operations.

Environmental criminology

Cybercrime and criminal activities conducted online have received limited attention from environmental criminologists, potentially because cybercrime is a relatively new type of crime. It continually evolves, many victims do not report crimes, and there is limited data available to study the phenomenon (Miró Llinares & Johnson, 2018). Theories of environmental criminology (EC) differ from other criminological theories. Compared to foundational theories such as the ones discussed above, EC does not solely focus on criminals or what motivates them to offend. It concentrates instead of preventing criminal events by understanding the characteristics of the environments in which crimes occur (Cullen & Kulig, 2018; Miró Llinares & Johnson, 2018). In other words, certain aspects of the environment in which crimes are perpetrated may positively influence the commission of a crime, or they may reduce or deter criminals from taking advantage of potential vulnerabilities within that setting. EC shifts the focus from trying to explain criminal behavior to how criminal activities are shaped through opportunities generated by people's routine activities (Brantingham, Brantingham, Song, & Spicer, 2018; Miró Llinares & Johnson, 2018; Summers & Guerette, 2018). Therefore, EC is more in line with the routine activity theory from Cohen and Felson (1979) (Cullen & Kulig, 2018; Miró Llinares & Johnson, 2018). Cyberspace, as a convergence setting, does become a new 'place' in which cybercriminals may interact with other criminals in an attempt to take advantage of vulnerabilities that are present online (e.g., computer malware), along other Internet users (i.e., potential targets) interacting within cyberspace (Miró Llinares & Johnson, 2018).

As Miró Llinares and Johnson (2018) argued, people's routine activities are also relevant to cybercrime since 'people do engage in particular activities at particular cyber "space" at particular times' (p. 14).

Moreover, cyberspace can be divided into smaller spaces, such as social media networks (e.g., Facebook, Twitter, LinkedIn, Skype, Google Hangouts) where individuals may access personal information on public posts or accounts. Contacts and interactions between people also occur through web-pages, chat rooms, various online games, cyber 'places' for leisure, and both legitimate and underground digital channels. When criminal activities are perpetrated on social media in a public mode, it is relatively easy for people to notice and report them to law enforcement. However, some crimes may occur in private groups, private encrypted channels, among many other spaces, most of which lack guardianship and natural surveillance as they are not open to the public. Dark web online spaces, which is a part of the deep web, are not indexed by standard search engines and are often devoted to specific criminal activities (Miró Llinares & Johnson, 2018). Multiple examples of what can be purchased on the dark web are described by Maimon et al. (2020). Notably, they include a supply of secure sockets layer (SSL)/transport layer security (TLS) certificates – certificates fulfilling critical security functions in authenticating and verifying the identity of the host, client, or application (Maimon et al., 2020).

The online space allows a cybercriminal to reach many potential victims easily (e.g., by sending 1 million phishing emails) and simultaneously, no matter where they are located in the world (Miró Llinares & Johnson, 2018). Consequently, the cybercriminals' victim pool is staggeringly large, especially compared to the number of potential victims in a physical setting. Cyberspace also reduces the cost of traveling to a location to perpetrate the crime and makes it possible for victimization to occur asynchronously (e.g., when the victim clicks on the malicious link within a phishing email). The anonymity of cyberspace – the fraudster hiding behind an IP address – is also a critical component affecting cybercriminals' motivation for preferring online crime to physical crimes (Miró Llinares & Johnson, 2018). Geography is also critical in terms of online crime. Cyberspace also allows fraudsters and hackers to orchestrate an email attack from one country while the victims are located in different jurisdictions, making it harder for law enforcement to enforce regulations across countries and collaborate promptly (Miró Llinares & Johnson, 2018; Nish & Naumann, 2019; Pomerleau, 2019; Pomerleau & Lowery, 2020). Moreover, in cyberspace, one victim of a cyber-incident (e.g., downloading a virus attached to a document) may become the vector to infect other victims (e.g., sending the infected attachment to others), multiplying the impacts of a single crime attempt (Miró Llinares & Johnson, 2018). Hence, the justification of criminals' efforts to commit crimes online is often easier to make as only one action, such as sending an email, may reach a larger number of victims, successfully generating fraudulent revenue with considerably fewer efforts and risks.

As noted above, many strengths flow from the paradigm shift offered by the EC approach (Cullen & Kulig, 2018; Miró Llinares & Johnson, 2018). However, Cullen and Kulig (2018) are more critical toward EC than Miró

Llinares and Johnson (2018). Cullen and Kulig (2018) claimed that EC has various theoretical weaknesses that will need to be addressed in the future. They highlight four theoretical imperfections: (1) EC neglected to study what motivates offenders to commit crimes, (2) EC did not develop a full understanding of the risk of victimization, (3) EC relies primarily on informal social control, which is often ill-defined with unspecified components, and (4) EC does not explain the role and importance of inequality in the broader social environment properly (Cullen & Kulig, 2018).

Situational crime prevention

Situational crime prevention (SCP) stipulates that crime can be deterred by making strategic changes to an environment (Brooks, 2020). This theoretical framework combines various theoretical perspectives, including the routine activity approach, the rational choices perspective initially developed by Clarke and Felson (1993), and the crime pattern theory (CPT) (Brewer et al., 2019; Shariati & Guerette, 2017). SCP's underlying premise is that criminals are rational human beings who weigh the costs and benefits of their behaviors (Clarke, 1995). To reduce potential criminal activity, SCP crime prevention efforts focus on designing and manipulating the environment to make offenders' decisions to get involved in crime less attractive (Brewer et al., 2019).

As Shariati and Guerette (2017) and Brooks (2020) pointed out, traditional criminology frameworks concentrated primarily on explaining offenders' criminal nature as a means for reducing crime, while SCP sought to modify and alter environments that are favorable to crime behaviors, to make them less suitable for offending. The SCP uniquely aims to predict criminal behavior by focusing on what causes crime in its environmental settings, rather than arresting and punishing offenders (Clarke, 1997; Shariati & Guerette, 2017). More specifically, SCP focuses on *how* crime happens rather than *why* – and, therefore, on *how* it can be prevented. SCP techniques focus on (1) increasing the effort for the criminals (e.g., hardening targets, increasing controls), (2) increasing the risks to be caught (e.g., guardianship, natural surveillance), (3) reducing the rewards (e.g., concealing targets, disrupting markets), (4) reducing provocations (e.g., neutralizing peer pressures, discouraging imitations), and finally (5) removing excuses (e.g., posting specific instructions, alerting the conscience, setting rules) (Shariati & Guerette, 2017).

Although criminological research has found that SCP techniques can be successfully applied in conventional settings, it is still unclear whether SCP interventions can effectively prevent cybercrime (Brewer et al., 2019). According to Maimon and Louderback (2019), the escalation of cyber-dependent crime incidents during the past 15 years has forced criminologists, computer scientists, and information scientists worldwide to review the applicability of the SCP perspective in the context of different types of online crimes. For instance, Coles-Kemp and Theoharidou (2010) studied insider threats to information security, Morris et al. (2004) focused on malicious software, and

Brookson et al. (2007) applied SCP in the context of hacking (Maimon & Louderback, 2019). However, Maimon and Louderback (2019) argued that despite the growing number of individuals and organizations (both public and private) implementing security tools, additional cyber-threat prevention, detection systems, and stronger security policies in their computing environments, too few empirical investigations assess the effectiveness of these strategies in preventing and mitigating malicious cyber-dependent operations (Denning & Baugh, 2000; Harknett et al., 2010).

As Shariati and Guerette (2017) explained, the SCP follows three main steps: identify risk factors, formulate and implement appropriate solutions, and evaluate the results. On that front, two recent studies (Lévesque et al., 2013; Lévesque et al., 2016) employed clinical trials to assess antivirus products' effectiveness in detecting and preventing malware infections among computer users. Antivirus software allows users to keep their computer devices clean from malicious software (malware) such as viruses, worms, and trojans. These antiviruses are installed on computers and smartphones as the last defense against cyber-dependent crimes (Al-Ghaith, 2016). In their study, Lévesque et al. (2013) recruited 50 participants from the Université de Montréal campus. They provided each participant with a new laptop, then monitored their computer usage using various diagnostic tools over four months. The authors reported insightful results that need to be taken into consideration in an SCP context. For example, they found that one out of two new laptops would have been infected with malware within four months if the computers had no antivirus software installed. These scholars also found that 20% of the study computers were infected by malicious software that was not detected by the antivirus software installed on the machine.

In another study, Lévesque et al. (2016) monitored close to 27 million Windows 10 systems for four months. This study was conducted to test the probability of these computers being infected with malware. Lévesque et al. (2016) separated systems protected by a third-party antivirus product (the treatment group) from systems secured by Microsoft Windows Defender, Microsoft's default antivirus software (the control group). The authors found that 1.22% of the computer systems in the experimental group were infected by malware during the experimental period, while 14.95% of the computer systems in the control group could have been infected by malware if no antivirus product were protecting the system (Lévesque et al., 2016).

Anthropological criminology and ethnographic studies

Anthropological criminology has received more attention among scholars due to the increased focus on transnational crime and illegalized globalization (Sausdal & Vigh, 2019). Anthropologists aim to 'follow and stay with the movement' of the people and phenomena they study (Marcus, 1995, p. 106). Computer technologies and digital devices have become omnipresent in every aspect of human existence, and such development influences anthropologists to explore the significance of these technologies in crime and the relationship between the human and the machine (Van der Wagen, 2019; Van der Wagen & Pieters, 2015). Aas (2011) argued that anthropology is the appropriate discipline to answer a largely ignored call for ethnographic criminology at the methodological and theoretical levels (Sausdal & Vigh, 2019).

While quantitative studies may indicate to some level the scale of the cross-border and transnational crime problem, in terms of the revenues organized crime generates as a percentage of the global domestic product or the growth of legal trade, the underlying sociocultural practices remain under-researched with almost no useful empirical overviews (Bruinsma, 2015; Sausdal & Vigh, 2019). This led several scholars to analyze global forms of crime ethnographically (Sausdal & Vigh, 2019). Ethnographies are works consisting of in-depth interviews and observations of how people live in different contexts (Treadwell, 2020). An ethnographic approach is uniquely suited to study cybercriminals, as only embedded and long-term fieldwork provides the opportunity to witness crime and criminalization through groups' social formation, learning how these networks of criminals become socially embedded and incorporated (Sausdal & Vigh, 2019). This type of research methodology also allows scholars to explore how cybercriminals perceive the world as something meaningful to them (Sausdal & Vigh, 2019). An excellent example of such a research is the study conducted by Lusthaus (2018), who conducted 238 interviews and seven years of fieldwork in 20 countries, from Eastern Europe to West Africa, to study cybercriminals' underground economy cybercrime hotspots.

A more recent example is provided by Follis and Fish (2020). These authors used various methodologies and disciplines, including ethnographic and digital archive methods, to propose a novel 'boundary work' theoretical framework to articulate the relational approach to understanding hacker interactions, and to survey the field of contemporary state hacking. They use the term 'boundary work' to illustrate the strategic remapping of boundaries and borders corresponding to state domains and dividing state and society. For example, they contrast the actual nation-state hacking level of uncertainty and show how water became an object of concern and governance for some states to be positioned as a 'boundary object' between government and science (Follis & Fish, 2020). To fix the water problem, states focused on new areas of governance networks of scientific experts, water infrastructures, and hydro technologies to create the unity required of a technoscientific state (Follis & Fish, 2020). As Follis and Fish (2020) suggest, hacking and hackers themselves can be perceived as boundary objects sitting at the edge of many shifting state-society domains. Hacking is now a new technological innovation for states, a highly sought-after skill to generate economic development, and a strategic resource for national security (Follis & Fish, 2020). At the same time, it also remains a challenge depending on the type of targets, such as critical infrastructure or voting systems (Follis & Fish, 2020). These scholars provide an in-depth analysis of 'boundary workers' like cyber mercenaries, hacking teams of security contractors that are now populating a thriving market for state hacking practices.

Biosocial criminology

Boutwell et al. (2015) argued that evolutionary biology has not gained enough traction in the literature to explain criminal behaviors' origins. For decades, criminologists relied upon theories that attempted to organize a significant quantity of knowledge on antisocial, delinquent, and illegal behaviors, but without having a single framework unifying all this knowledge (Boutwell et al., 2015). Biosocial criminology views crime and antisocial behaviors as biological and social phenomena, since biology affects behavior and the environment affects biology (Rocque & Posick, 2017; Walsh, 2009; Walsh, 2014). Over the years, many scholars have discussed the future of biosocial criminology and how genetics could also influence delinquent and criminal behavior (Beaver et al., 2009; Beaver et al., 2015; Burt & Simons, 2014; Carrier & Walby, 2014; Carrier & Walby, 2015a; Carrier & Walky, 2015b; Gajos et al., 2016; Heylen et al., 2015; Posick et al., 2015; Rafter, 1997; Rafter, 2004; Rafter, 2006; Rafter, 2008a; Rafter, 2008b; Rafter et al., 2016; Raine, 2002; Rocque et al., 2012; Rocque et al., 2014; Vaughn, 2016; Walsh, 2009; Walsh & Wright, 2015; Wright & Boisvert, 2009).

Social learning theory and low self-control theory are two of the most empirically supported criminological theories (Pratt & Cullen, 2000). Previous empirical tests that relied on these perspectives primarily focused on associating low levels of self-control with delinquent involvement and exploring the relationship between frequent contacts with delinquent peers and antisocial behaviors (Beaver et al., 2009). On the one hand, theories such as the self-control theory (Gottfredson & Hirschi, 1990) claimed that parenting practices account for children's self-control, based largely on the way parents socialize their children, but ignored the role of biology and the evidence that self-control is part of genetics (i.e., originating in the pre-frontal cortex). On the other hand, purely biological theories on self-control are not beneficial to explain this issue either (Rocque & Posick, 2017). However, from a biological standpoint, Beaver et al. (2009) offered important implications for a theory originally brought forward by Gottfredson and Hirschi (1990). Using data from the National Longitudinal Study of Adolescent Health (Add Health) (Cleveland et al., 2005), the results of their study paint a very different picture than the one offered by Gottfredson and Hirschi (1990): once genetic effects were removed from their statistical model, the shared environment did not have any effect on the development of self-control (Brewer et al., 2019).

Moreover, a meta-analysis of the heritability of human traits by Polderman et al. (2015), based on 50 years of twin studies published between 1958 and 2012 on a wide range of traits (more than 14 million twin pairs across 39 countries), provides valuable insights. These scholars retrieved published classical twin studies in which observed variations in human traits were partitioned into genetic and environmental influences. The relative effects of genes and environment are not randomly distributed across all traits, but according to the authors they do cluster in functional domains (Polderman et al., 2015). Human traits and behaviors such as temperament, antisocial behavior, anxiety, depression, and substance use are heritable since no one trait had a weighted heritability estimate of zero (Polderman et al., 2015).

Rocque and Posick (2017) argued that biological research into criminology is not a paradigm shift but should be recognized as a regular science, like sociological criminology. They further suggested that sociology and biosocial criminology research are complementary. Since it is now clear that both biology and the environment are related to criminal behaviors, this knowledge should influence both theory and policymaking to reduce illegal activity (Rocque & Posick, 2017). From a biosocial criminology perspective, more studies should be conducted on cybercrime.

Psychology and cyberpsychology in the management of cybercrime

As cybercriminals' sophistication has increased, so too must the approaches to prevent, detect, and deter their behaviors (Nurse, 2018). Psychology plays a critical role in cybercrime. Some of the scams utilized by fraudsters take advantage of various human actions and mental weaknesses. Cyberpsychology research has made a significant incursion into cybercrime analysis by studying criminal behavior and its psychological and social impact on victims (Nurse, 2018).

As mentioned previously, humans are often the weakest link exploited by attackers, specifically because of how they make decisions. From a psychological perspective, Kahneman (2013) argued that the brain functions with *multiple tracks* and two general strands (Ayan, 2018) that drive the way people make choices (i.e., think fast and think slow). One system is fast, intuitive, and emotional. The other system is slower, more deliberate, and logical. System 1 is the automatic brain mode or the unconscious mind (e.g., daily routine, reading emails, etc.). System 2 is the analytic mode or more flexible conscious part (e.g., asking for something unusual; analyzing a situation and asking oneself questions before acting) of the brain. People's minds operate both unconsciously and consciously (Ayan, 2018). However, most of the employee errors that may lead to a cyberattack or a fraud are associated with System 1, using fast, intuitive, and emotional responses. Thus, positively influencing individuals to rely more frequently upon the second (analytic) mode, e.g., waiting a little longer to analyze the situation before clicking on a link within an email or opening an attachment, could prevent several frauds and cyberattacks.

The Chief Executive Officer (CEO) fraud scam is an excellent example of how fraudsters exploit System 1 to take advantage of individuals' psychological vulnerabilities. Cybercriminals will usually send an email emphasizing the urgency of a requested transaction (e.g., the money needs to be transferred as soon as possible), the status of the individual requesting assistance (e.g., the CEO), and the importance of maintaining the confidentiality of the deal (e.g., the employee should not advise his or her supervisor). Unfortunately, the urge to reply to an email from someone important within the organization led many finance and accounting professionals to become CEO fraud scam victims.

If these individuals had taken a moment to think about the nature of the request they received by email, using the more analytic System 2, they would have realized what the CEO or their representative was asking for did not make sense. For instance, even if the CEO had sent an email requesting a wire transfer of US$3M to an offshore bank, the employee would ask more questions about the legitimacy of the transaction. Furthermore, the same employee would verify whether the CEO is traveling in another country. He or she would further analyze the email requesting the transfer to make sure it was not spoofed, i.e., sent using a forged email address.

Cyberpsychology

According to Aiken (2016), cyberpsychology studies the impact of emerging technology on human behavior. This author argued that the new norms created due to the rapid acceleration of digitalization and the use of technology in our lives have led to what she calls *cyber-socialization*. The process of cyber-socialization is a lot faster than the normal process of socialization in the physical realm. Online communities and networks of contacts, friends, co-workers, and collaborators can easily connect based on relationship types and specific interests (e.g., gardening, sexual preferences, cars, cooking). In social psychology, these groups would be referred to as the reference groups – individuals with the same values, beliefs, habits, or behavioral patterns – for the new user that joined the online community (Aiken, 2016).

Cyberspace is a medium allowing people to meet other people, and without the Internet, many of them would not have created these friendships due to the distance. However, cyberspace may also lead to debatable friendships and social connections with individuals who do not necessarily want to become *real* friends. Cyberspace creates an opportunity for what Aiken (2016) refers to as *online syndication*, which is the possibility of finding other people with the same interests online.

Human behaviors have also been amplified and accelerated online. Aiken (2016) provides three examples: (a) people tend to be more generous (e.g., altruism) online that they are in the physical world, as they perceive cyberspace as an environment somehow carrying fewer risks; (b) people tend to be more trusting of other individuals they meet online and they also disclose information to them more quickly (e.g., quicker intimacy), and (c) due to an online disinhibition effect (i.e., acting drunk and having impaired judgment, similar to the effect alcohol can provide), individuals tend to be more adventurous and less inhibited online than they would be with other people outside of cyberspace. Overall, people tend to perceive cyberspace as an environment lacking authority, with more anonymity, and with a sense of distance to others that they are not used to in the physical world (Aiken, 2016).

Whitty and Young (2017) argued that cyberspace also offers unique opportunities for expressing the self. The anonymous nature of the Internet provides opportunities for people to be 'disembodied,' meaning they create and experience an online identity that is no longer constrained to a physical appearance (Whitty & Young, 2017). An example of the cyber effects of syndication and disinhibition would be the significant increase in online dating and cyber-romance. For example, Aiken (2016) noted a 2016 UK National Crime Agency (NCA) report reporting a sixfold increase in online-dating rape offenses in five years. Unfortunately, cybercriminals take advantage of this absence of guardianship and the fact that people tend to be more inclined to let their guard down in cyberspace.

Psychology also plays a vital role in understanding cybercriminals' behaviors and motivations for hacking and taking advantage of online victims. In committing a successful attack, the attacker experiences psychological benefits since he has a challenge, he entertains himself, and he can seek money from victims (Huang et al., 2018). As Huang et al. (2018) explained, a successful attack generates a sense of accomplishment for the hacker and may boost his reputation within the hacker community. According to these authors, to study cybercrime, it is imperative to understand what cybercriminals can gain from orchestrating successful attacks (e.g., Ran$umBin, a dark web service to monetize ransomware attacks) as well as how these gains may generate further attacks (Huang et al., 2018). They provide a formula to evaluate the characteristics that make a target valuable for cybercriminals and how they decide if an attack is worth pursuing or not:

$$Pe \times (Bpm + Bpp) \times Er > Cps + (Pa \times Pc \times Cc) + (Cim + Com)$$

Specifically, tracking the ease of attack (Pe), the monetary benefit (Bpm), the psychological benefit (Bpp), the ease of realization (Er), the psychological costs (Cps), the arrest rate (Pa), the ease of the judicial process involved in the conviction (Pc), the monetary opportunity cost if the attacker is convicted (Cc), the investment cost (Cim), and the monetary opportunity cost of the investment (Com) allows us to understand better how cybercriminals analyze the potential benefits versus the cost of investments and punishment (Huang et al., 2018).

Within this formula, the variables associated with the psychological benefit (Bpp) and the psychological costs (Cps) are of particular interest. The potential benefit of an attack (Bp) includes both the monetary benefit (Bpm) and the psychological benefits (Bpp). Thus, the benefit of an attack (Bp) equals the monetary benefit (Bpm) plus the psychological benefits (Bpp): Bp = Bpm + Bpp. The psychological benefit (Bpp) encompasses both the benefits for cybercriminals in committing a successful attack, thus generating a monetary benefit, and the psychological benefit of being recognized as having conducted a successful attack. The psychological costs (Cps) represent the psychological and mental energy required in committing a cyberattack and the fear of being caught or punished for conducting a specific type of attack.

PHILOSOPHICAL AND ETHICAL MODELS

Hard determinism and crime

According to Gilbert (2009), determinism has evolved from physical theories to the biological sciences over the last century. Previous empirical studies of genetics and neurobiology, Gilbert (2009) claimed, demonstrated that biological mechanisms beyond human control influence human behavior. The basic argument of hard determinists is that individuals in our society do not have free will. They are not self-made, and they do not have free choices, which means they cannot be truly and ultimately held responsible for their actions (Gilbert, 2009).

The hard determinist ethical position toward crime is that the criminal justice system should refrain from relying on retributive punishment, instead of trying to protect society through 're-education and deterrence' (Gilbert, 2009, p. 41). As Gilbert (2009) explained, people tend to believe that moral and ethical judgments come from another source than the physical brain. However, neurobiological determinism shows that an individual with a physical disability such as brain tumors (i.e., frontal damage to the brain) (Gilbert & Vranič, 2015) who commits a crime as a result of this physical disability is not responsible for his actions. Thus, this individual cannot be declared immoral and sentenced based on an immorality determination (Sapolsky, 2004). From this philosophical perspective, considering that individuals do not have free will and responsibility for their actions, society should be focusing on the prevention of crimes and deterrence of criminal activities, instead of prioritizing retribution and vengeance (Gilbert, 2009; Pereboom, 2001). There is no responsibility in the hard determinist's view (Pereboom, 2009), so retribution and determinism are incompatible (Gilbert, 2009).

From this perspective, Kant (1986, p. 215) explained that a person who has 'done wrong with his free will must repay in kind' through punishment that is equivalent to the harm done to others (Gilbert, 2009; Pereboom, 2009). Gilbert (2009) argued that acknowledging the increasing neurobiological evidence in connection with determinism does not necessarily mean criminals can easily get away with their crimes. Instead, the hard determinist perspective should be relied upon for future neurological interventions and treatments for criminals (Gilbert, 2009). Analyzing crime through a hard determinism lens requires rethinking many ethical issues, especially when deciding what kind of treatments should be provided to criminals (Gilbert, 2009; Gilbert & Vranič, 2015).

Contrary to advocates such as Pereboom (2005), Smilanksy (2011) claimed that the hard determinism position does not make sense when tackling criminal activities in the real world. Hard determinists strongly believe that there is no free will and no moral responsibility; thus, the fact that criminals might have hurt others is not their fault as it is not within their control (Smilansky, 2011). In Smilanksy's (2011) perspective, even though hard determinists agree with some form of punishment when there is no other alternative, such as incarcerating wrongdoers from lawful society, this philosophical position does not adequately explain how punishment will allow deterrence of crimes within society. For Smilanksy (2011), the hard determinist's view of punishment turns out to be similar to what he refers to as *funishment* or a 'practical reductio of hard determinism' (p. 354). Hard determinists believe it is impossible to allow incarceration in institutions of punishment as we know it today. Although they agree wrongdoers should be punished for their actions, they believe criminals should still have every opportunity to enjoy life through various measures of freedom in their interactions. In their view, no one deserves to be separated from the regular society and that this hardship needs to be compensated for (Smilansky, 2011).

For hard determinists, most criminals are incarcerated for crimes that are not life-threatening for others, so they should be quarantined – similar to a medical quarantine – instead of being imprisoned (Smilansky, 2011). While Smilanksy (2011) agrees that society might over-criminalize and over-punish in some instances, he describes funishment as equivalent to a 'five-stars hotel' (p. 355). This type of punishment would have significant practical implications since criminals currently have to balance the temptations of crime versus the risks – probabilities – of punishment. Notwithstanding that society might find new pharmaceutical and therapeutic methods in the future (Smilansky, 2011), current medical practices and science methodologies have not yet demonstrated evidence linking biological determinism and the propensity to commit a crime (Sapolsky, 2004). Neither have we found any evidence that potential offenders and actual criminals could function in society while also making the community safer, in the event that they do not have to undergo long periods of incarcerations (Smilansky, 2011).

Compatibilism and crime

On the other hand, compatibilists believe that free will and responsibility are compatible with neurobiological determinism, so compatibilists believe in several common forms of punishments (Gilbert, 2009; Smilansky, 2011). Compatibilists differ from hard determinists in their interpretation of the needed form of free will and the justification of punishment (Smilansky, 2017). Various forms of compatibilist free will exist. They allow for a *community of responsibility* and moral, personal beliefs, as well as practices demonstrating the compatibilist distinction and the differences in the degree of freedom and responsibility of individuals (Smilansky, 2017).

One of the main differences between the two paradigms is related to deterrence. According to Smilansky (2017), modern societies already have difficulty deterring crimes with actual unpleasant prison sentences. The excellent living conditions offered under the funishment strategy endorsed by the hard determinists would lead to an increase in criminal activities as fewer criminals would be deterred. This situation would also increase the number of criminals within the incarceration system (undeterred and often having better conditions incarcerated than free), thus increasing the costs of keeping criminals within these conditions (Smilansky, 2017). Also, the public sentiment regarding this new form of funishment would decline, as taxes would have to significantly increase to cover such a regime's costs, thus reducing law-abiding citizens' quality of life (Smilansky, 2017). Smilansky (2017) argued that the limitations of the hard determinist position should lead to a reevaluation of compatibilism. From a practical and theoretical standpoint, the hard determinism model cannot work on punishment, so compatibilism offers the best answer (Smilansky, 2017). From a neurobiology standpoint, there is still a lack of scientific evidence on the pre-frontal cortex's impact on cognition, emotional regulation, control of impulsivity, antisocial behavior, and moral reasoning. Each crime needs to be assessed on a case-by-case basis due to its specificity (Focquaert, 2019; Sapolsky, 2004).

Although a neurobiological framework may reduce the blame due to a biological malformation, it does not reduce the need to intervene against antisocial and criminal behaviors (Sapolsky, 2004). As Sapolsky (2004) mentioned in an analogy, 'To understand is not to forgive or to do nothing; whereas you do not ponder whether to forgive a car that, because of problems with its brakes, has injured someone, you nevertheless protect society from it' (p. 1794).

Over the last few decades, neuroscientific research has led to a better understanding of human behavior (prosocial, deviant, and antisocial behaviors), allowing scholars to identify multiple biological risk factors associated with violent crimes. Some of these factors are structural and functional brain impairments, genetic variants, hormone and neurotransmitter levels, and physiological indicators (Focquaert, 2019). Unfortunately, practically no scientific studies have been conducted on offenders' biomedical treatments (Focquaert, 2019). For this reason, more resources should be invested into studying criminal behaviors from a combination of both neurobiological and societal causes (Focquaert, 2019). This statement also applies to the study of cybercrime. More research should be conducted to assess how these biological risk factors apply to cybercriminals.

As we have discussed in this chapter, cybercrime and the cybercriminal mindset rely on various theoretical frameworks to analyze crime from different perspectives. Thus, meeting the cybersecurity challenge also needs partnerships with other disciplines than criminology to draw on what we know and understand human nature, how humans interact and manage systems, and how they deal with each other.

REFERENCES

Aas, K. F. (2011). Visions of global control: Cosmopolitan aspirations in a world of friction. In M. Bosworth, & C. Hoyle (Eds.), *What is criminology?* (pp. 406–417). University of Oxford Press.

Aiken, M. (2016). *The cyber effect: A pioneering cyber-psychologist explains how human behavior changes online.* Spiegel & Grau.

Akers, R. L. (1973). *Deviant behavior: A social learning approach.* Wadsworth Pub. Co.

Al-Ghaith, W. (2016). Extending protection motivation theory to understand security determinants of anti-virus software usage on mobile devices. *International Journal of Computers, 10,* 125–138.

Ayan, S. (2018). *The brain's autopilot mechanism steers consciousness.* https://www.scientificamerican.com/article/the-brains-autopilot-mechanism-steers-consciousness/

Beaver, K. M., Nedelec, J. L., da Silva Costa, C., & Vidal, M. M. (2015). The future of biosocial criminology. *Criminal Justice Studies, 28*(1), 6–17. https://doi.org/10.1080/1478601X.2014.1000002

Beaver, K. M., Shutt, J. E., Boutwell, B. B., Ratchford, M., Barnes, J. C., & Roberts, K. (2009). Genetic and environmental influences on levels of self-control and delinquent peer affiliation: Results from a longitudinal sample of adolescent twins. *Criminal Justice and Behavior, 36*(1), 41–60.

Boutwell, B. B., Barnes, J. C., Beaver, K. M., Haynes, R. D., Nedelec, J. L., & Gibson, C. L. (2015). A unified crime theory: The evolutionary taxonomy. *Aggression and Violent Behavior, 25*(Part B), 343–353. https://doi.org/10.1016/j.avb.2015.09.003

Brantingham, P. L., Brantingham, P. J., Song, J., & Spicer, V. (2018). Advances in visualization for theory testing in environmental criminology. In G. Bruinsma, & D. Johnson (Eds.), *The Oxford handbook of environmental criminology.* (pp. 238–272). Oxford handbooks in criminology and criminal justice, Oxford University Press. https://www.worldcat.org/title/oxford-handbook-of-environmental-criminology/oclc/1026702477

Brewer, R., De Vel-Palumbo, M., Hutchings, A., Holt, T., Goldsmith, J., & Maimon, A. (2019). *Cybercrime prevention: Theory and applications.* Palgrave.

Brooks, G. (2016). *Criminology of corruption: Theoretical approaches.* Palgrave Macmillan.

Brooks, A. (2020). *What is situational crime prevention? Investigating this crime reduction strategy.* https://www.rasmussen.edu/degrees/justice-studies/blog/situational-crime-prevention/#:~:text=Situational%20crime%20prevention%20is%20based,how%20it%20can%20be%20prevented

Brookson, C., Farrell, G., Mailley, J., Whitehead, S., & Zumerle, D. (2007). ICT product proofing against crime. *ETSI White Paper, 5,* 1–33.

Bruinsma, G. (2015). *Histories of transnational crime.* Springer.

Burt, C. H., & Simons, R. L. (2014). Pulling back the curtain on heritability studies: Biosocial criminology in the postgenomic era. *Criminology, 52*(2), 223–262.

Carrier, N., & Walby, K. (2014). Ptolemizing Lombroso: The pseudo-revolution of biosocial criminology. *Journal of Theoretical and Philosophical Criminology*, 6(1), 1–45.

Carrier, N., & Walby, K. (2015a). For sociological reason: Crime, criminalization, and the poverty of biosocial criminology. *Journal of Theoretical and Philosophical Criminology*, 7(1), 73–82.

Carrier, N., & Walky, K. (2015b). Is biosocial criminology a predisposition not to learn from social sciences? *Journal of Theoretical and Philosophical Criminology*, 7(1), 96–108.

Cheng, L., Li, Y., Li, W., Holm, E., & Zhai, Q. (2013). Understanding the violation of IS security policy in organizations: An integrated model based on social control and deterrence theory. *Computers & Security*, 39(Part B), 447–459. https://doi.org/10.1016/j.cose.2013.09.009

Clarke, R. V. (1995). Situational crime prevention. *Crime and Justice*, 19, 91–150. http://www.jstor.org/stable/1147596

Clarke, R. V. (1997). *Situational crime prevention*. Criminal Justice Press.

Clarke, R. V., & Felson, M. (1993). *Routine activity and rational choice*. Transaction Publishers.

Cleveland, H. H., Wiebe, R. P., & Rowe, D. C. (2005). Sources of exposure to smoking and drinking friends among adolescents: A behavioral-genetic evaluation. *Journal of Genetic Psychology*, 166, 153–169.

Cohen, L. E., & Felson, M. (1979). Social change and crime trends: A routine activity approach. *American Sociological Review*, 44(4), 588–608.

Coles-Kemp, L., & Theoharidou, M. (2010). Insider threat and information security management. In C. Probst, J. Hunker, D. Gollmann, & M. Bishop (Eds.), *Insider threats in cyber security. Advances in information security* (Vol. 49, pp. 45–71). Springer. https://doi.org/10.1007/978-1-4419-7133-3_3

Cullen, T. F., & Kulig, C. T. (2018). Evaluating theories of environmental criminology: Strengths and weaknesses. In G. Bruinsma, & D. Johnson (Eds.), *The Oxford handbook of environmental criminology*. (pp. 160–176). Oxford handbooks in criminology and criminal justice, Oxford University Press. https://www.worldcat.org/title/oxford-handbook-of-environmental-criminology/oclc/1026702477

Cyber-Trust Consortium. (n.d.). *The ever-evolving IOT landscape: Blessing or curse?* https://cyber-trust.eu/2020/10/12/the-ever-evolving-iot-landscape-blessing-or-curse/

Denning, D. E., & Baugh, W. E. (2000). Hiding crimes in cyberspace. In D. Thomas, & B. D. Loader (Eds.), *Cybercrime: Law enforcement' security and surveillance in the information age* (pp. 105–131). Routledge.

Eck, J. (2010). Places and the crime triangle. In F. Cullen, & P. Wilcox (Eds.), *Encyclopedia of criminological theory* (pp. 281–285). SAGE. https://study.sagepub.com/system/files/Eck%2C_John_E._-_Places_and_the_Crime_Triangle.pdf

Focquaert, F. (2019). Neurobiology and crime: A neuro-ethical perspective. *Journal of Criminal Justice*, 65, 101533. https://doi.org/10.1016/j.jcrimjus.2018.01.001

Follis, L., & Fish, A. (2020). *Hacker states*. The MIT Press.

Gajos, J., Fagan, M., & Beaver, A. (2016). Use of genetically informed evidence-based prevention science to understand and prevent crime and related behavioral disorders. *Criminology and Public Policy*, 15(3), 683–701.

Gibbs, J. (1975). *Crime, punishment, and deterrence*. Elsevier.

Gilbert, F. (2009). Does neurobiological determinism entail the end of criminal responsibility? In Center for Applied Ethics and Philosophy (Eds.), *Applied ethics: Life, environment and society* (pp. 37–45). Hokkaido University. https://www.academia.edu/14012139/Does_neurobiological_determinism_entail_the_end_of_criminal_responsibility

Gilbert, F., & Vranič, A. (2015). Paedophilia, invasive brain surgery, and punishment. *Journal of Bioethical Inquiry, 12*(3), 521–526. https://doi.org/10.1007/s11673-015-9647-3

Gottfredson, M. R., & Hirschi, T. (1990). *A general theory of crime*. Stanford University Press.

Harknett, R. J., Callaghan, J. P., & Kauffman, R. (2010). Leaving deterrence behind: War-fighting and national cybersecurity. *Journal of Homeland Security & Emergency Management, 7*(1), 1–24. https://doi.org/10.2202/1547-7355.1636

Heylen, B., Pauwels, L. J. R., Beaver, K. M., & Ruffinengo, M. (2015). Defending biosocial criminology: On the discursive style of our critics, the separation of ideology and science, and a biologically informed defense of fundamental values. *Journal of Theoretical & Philosophical Criminology, 7*(1), 83–95.

Hirschi, T. (1969). *Causes of delinquency*. University of California Press.

Holt, T. J. (2020). Cybercrime subcultures: Contextualizing offenders and the nature of the offence. In E. Leukfeldt, & J. Holt (Eds.), *The human factor of cybercrime* (pp. 159–172). Routledge.

Huang, K., Siegel, M., & Madnick, S. (2018). Systematically understanding the cyber attack business: A survey. *ACM Computing Survey, 51*(4), 1–36. https://doi.org/10.1145/3199674

Hutchings, A., & Clayton, R. (2016). Exploring the provision of online booter services. *Deviant Behavior, 37*(10), 1163–1178. https://doi.org/10.1080/01639625.2016.1169829

Hyslip, T. S. (2020) Cybercrime-as-a-service operations. In T. Holt, & A. Bossler (Eds.), *The Palgrave handbook of international cybercrime and cyberdeviance* (pp. 815–846). Palgrave Macmillan. https://doi.org/10.1007/978-3-319-78440-3_36

Kahneman, D. (2013). *Thinking, fast and slow*. Penguin Random House.

Kant, E. (1986). *Métaphysique des Mœurs. Première Partie, Doctrine du Droit*. Vrin.

Lévesque, F. L., Fernandez, J. M., Batchelder, D., & Young, G. (2016). Are they real? Real-life comparative tests of antivirus products. *Virus Bulletin Conference, 2016*, 1–11.

Lévesque, F. L., Nsiempba, J., Fernandez, J. M., Chiasson, S., & Somayaji, A. (2013). A clinical study of risk factors related to malware infections. In *Proceedings of the 2013 ACM SIGSAC Conference on Computer & Communications Security* (pp. 97–108). Association for Computing Machinery.

Lusthaus, J. (2018). *Industry of anonymity*. Harvard University Press.

Maimon, D., & Louderback., R. E. (2019). Cyber-dependent crimes: An interdisciplinary review. *Annual Review of Criminology, 2*, 191–216.

Maimon, D., Wu, Y., Stubler, N., & Sinigirikonda, P. (2020). Extended validation in the dark web: Evidence from investigation of the certification services and products sold on darknet markets. *EBCS Reports. 2*. https://scholarworks.gsu.edu/ebcs_reports/2

Marcus, G. (1995). Ethnography in/of the world system: The emergence of multi-sited ethnography. *Annual Review of Anthropology, 24*, 95–117.

Miró Llinares, F., & Johnson, S. D. (2018). Cybercrime and place: Applying environmental criminology to crimes in cyberspace. In G. Bruinsma, & S. D. Johnson (Eds.), *The Oxford handbook of environmental criminology.* (pp. 883–906). Oxford handbooks in criminology and criminal justice, Oxford University Press. https://www.worldcat.org/title/oxford-handbook-of-environmental-criminology/oclc/1026702477

Morris, R. G. (2011). Computer hacking and the techniques of neutralization: An empirical assessment. In T. J. Holt, & B. H. Schell (Eds.), *Corporate hacking and technology-driven crime: Social dynamics and implications* (pp. 1–17). IGI-Global.

Morris, M. R., Ryall, K., Shen, C., Forlines, C., & Vernier, F. (2004). Beyond social protocols: multi-user coordination policies for co-located groupware. In *Proceedings of the 2004 ACM Conference on Computer Supported Cooperative Work* (pp. 262–265). Association for Computing Machinery.

Nish, A., & Naumann, S. (2019). *The cyber threat landscape: Confronting challenges to the financial system.* https://carnegieendowment.org/2019/03/25/cyber-threat-landscape-confronting-challenges-to-financial-system-pub-78506

Nurse, C. R. J. (2018). Cybercrime and you: How criminals attack and the human factors that they seek to exploit. In A. Attrill-Smith, C. Fullwood, M. Keep, & D. J. Kuss (Eds.), *The Oxford handbook of cyberpsychology* (pp. 663–690). https://doi.org/10.1093/oxfordhb/9780198812746.013.35

Pereboom, D. (2001). *Living without free will.* Cambridge University Press.

Pereboom, D. (2005). Free will, evil, and divine providence. In A. Chignell, & A. Dole (Eds.), *God and the ethics of belief: New essays in philosophy of religion* (pp. 77–98). Cambridge University Press.

Pereboom, D. (2009). Defending hard incompatibilism again. In N. Trakakis, & D. Cohen (Eds.), *Essays on free will and moral responsibility* (pp. 1–33). Cambridge Scholars Press.

Polderman, T. J. C., Benyamin, B., de Leeuw, C. A., Sullivan, P. F., van Bochoven, A., Visscher, P. M., & Posthuma, D. (2015). Meta-analysis of the heritability of human traits based on fifty years of twin studies. *Nature Genetics, 47*(7), 702–709. https://doi.org/10.1038/ng.3285

Pomerleau, P. L. (2019). *Countering the cyber threats against financial institutions in Canada: A qualitative study of a private and public partnership approach to critical infrastructure protection.* ProQuest Dissertations & Theses Global (2320957957). https://about.proquest.com/products-services/pqdtglobal.html

Pomerleau, P. L., & Lowery, D. (2020). *Countering the cyber-threats to financial institutions.* Springer.

Posick, C., Rocque, M., & Delisi, M. (2015). Empathy, crime, and justice. In M. Delisi, & M. G. Vaughn (Eds.), *Handbook of biosocial criminology* (pp. 571–584). Routledge.

Pratt, T. C., & Cullen, F. T. (2000). The empirical status of Gottfredson and Hirschi's general theory of crime: A meta-analysis. *Criminology, 38*, 931–964.

Rafter, N. H. (1997). *Creating born criminals.* University of Illinois Press.

Rafter, N. H. (2004). Earnest A. Hooton and the biological tradition in American criminology. *Criminology, 42*(3), 735–772.

Rafter, N. H. (2006). H. J. Eysenck in Fagin's kitchen: The return to biological theory in 20th-century criminology. *History of the Human Sciences, 19*(4), 37–56.

Rafter, N. H. (2008a). *The criminal brain: Understanding biological theories of crime.* NYU Press.

Rafter, N. H. (2008b). Criminology's darkest hour: Biocriminology in Nazi Germany. *Australian and New Zealand Journal of Criminology, 41*(2), 287–306.

Rafter, N. H., Posick, C., & Rocque, M. (2016). *The criminal brain: Understanding biological theories of crime.* NYU Press.

Raine, A. (2002). The biological basis of crime. In J. Q. Wilson, & J. Petersilia (Eds.), *Crime: Public policies for crime control* (pp. 43–74). ICS Press.

Rocque, M., & Posick, C. (2017). Paradigm shift or normal science? The future of (biosocial) criminology. *Theoretical Criminology, 21*(3), 288–303.

Rocque, M., Welsh, B. C., & Raine, A. (2012). Biosocial criminology and modern crime prevention. *Journal of Criminal Justice, 40*(4), 306–312.

Rocque, M., Welsh, B. C., & Raine, A. (2014). Policy implications of biosocial criminology: Crime prevention, treatment, and offender rehabilitation. In B. B. Boutwell, K. Beaver, & J. C. Barnes (Eds.), *The nurture versus biosocial debate in criminology* (pp. 431–446). SAGE.

Sapolsky, R. M. (2004). The frontal cortex and the criminal justice system. *Philosophical Transactions: Biological Sciences, 359*(1451), 1787–1796.

Sausdal, D., & Vigh, H. (2019). Anthropological criminology 2.0: Ethnographies of global crime and criminalization. *Focaal, 85*, 1–14. https://doi.org/10.3167/fcl.2019.850101

Schmalleger, F., & Volk, R. (2001). *Canadian criminology today: Theories and applications.* Pearson.

Shariati, A., & Guerette, R. T. (2017). Situational crime prevention. In B. Teasdale, & M. Bradley (Eds.), *Preventing crime and violence. Advances in prevention science* (pp. 261–268). Springer. https://doi.org/10.1007/978-3-319-44124-5_22

Smilansky, S. (2011). Hard determinism and punishment: A practical "reductio." *Law and Philosophy, 30*(3), 353–367.

Smilansky, S. (2017). Pereboom on punishment: Funishment, innocence, motivation, and other difficulties. *Criminal Law & Philosophy, 11*(3), 591–603. https://doi.org/10.1007/s11572-016-9396-3

Summers, L., & Guerette, R. T. (2018). The individual perspective. In G. Bruinsma, & D. Johnson (Eds.), *The Oxford handbook of environmental criminology.* (pp. 84–104). Oxford handbooks in criminology and criminal justice, Oxford University Press. https://www.worldcat.org/title/oxford-handbook-of-environmental-criminology/oclc/1026702477

Sykes, G. M., & Matza, D. (1957). Techniques of neutralization: A theory of delinquency. *American Sociological Review, 22*(6), 664–670.

Treadwell, J. (2020). *Criminological ethnography: An introduction.* SAGE Publications Limited.

Van der Wagen, W. (2019). The significance of 'things' in cybercrime: How to apply actor-network theory in (cyber) criminological research and why it matters. *Journal of Extreme Anthropology, 3*(1), 152–168. https://doi.org/10.5617/jea.6895

Van der Wagen, W., & Pieters, W. (2015). From cybercrime to cyborg crime: Botnets as hybrid criminal actor-networks. *British Journal of Criminology, 55*(3), 578–595.

Vaughn, M. G. (2016). Policy implications of biosocial criminology. *Criminology and Public Policy, 15*(3), 703–710.

Walsh, A. (2009). *Biology and criminology: The biosocial synthesis.* Routledge.

Walsh, A. (2014). *Biosociology: Bridging the biology–sociology divide.* Transaction Publishers.

Walsh, A., & Wright, J. P. (2015). Rage against reason: Addressing critical critics of biosocial research. *Journal of Theoretical and Philosophical Criminology*, 7(1), 61–72.

Whitty, M. T., & Young, G. (2017). *Cyberpsychology: The study of individuals, society and digital technologies*. The British Psychological Society. Wiley.

Wright, J. P., & Boisvert, D. (2009). What biosocial criminology offers criminology. *Criminal Justice and Behavior*, 36(11), 1228–1240.

Chapter 5

Science and cybersecurity

INTRODUCTION

The early-2000s' sharp rise in global cybercrime incidents, followed by a steep increase in the volume of industry-based reports (e.g., those produced by consulting firms and think tanks), has highlighted the prevalence of cybercrime and its high costs to victims. Numerous studies report enthusiasm for discovering the new 'best solution' for a wide range of internet security issues, both individual and corporate. Unfortunately, few public and private organizations are systematically evaluating the efficiency of the security systems they are using before investing significant financial resources in additional tools. In 2021, the cybersecurity market is expected to reach US$60.2 billion, a 7% increase from the previous year (Help Net Security, 2021).

The cybersecurity discipline is populated with scholars trained to build security tools. In contrast, non-academic articles evaluating the effectiveness of security tools and policies leave something to be desired. The typical evaluations conducted by commercial and scholarly research laboratories are based on a variety of surveys and in-depth scans of collected or synthesized malicious traffic samples (Algaith et al., 2016; AV Comparatives, 2013; Garg et al., 2006; Gashi et al., 2009; Noureldien & Osman, 2000; Seeberg & Petrovic, 2007; Surisetty & Kumar, 2010). While this approach may test the tools' accuracy, it fails to consider how computer users (both legitimate and illegitimate) actually behave with their computers and the computer network. It also does not assess the effectiveness of security tools in preventing the development of cyber-dependent crimes. These reports and their conclusions should be taken with caution, since they lack rigorous scientific scrutiny and fail to adopt scientific research designs.

Maxion et al. (2010) argued that current cybersecurity research standards are too low. Cybersecurity research can be divided into two categories: *theoretical cyber* research uses pure mathematics or logic and deduction to demonstrate relationships, as is the case in other mathematical research areas, while *experimental cyber* research uses scientific methods to show a causal relationship, presume the relationship is valid, and use it to enhance the body of knowledge. But failing to ask whether theoretical results apply in real-life

DOI: 10.1201/9781003201519-5

situations may lead to the wrong conclusions in cybersecurity, since knowledge creation cannot solely be a collection of new tools (Maxion et al., 2010). For this to change, cybersecurity professionals and scholars should partner with researchers from a wide range of academic disciplines (e.g., criminology, sociology, psychology, computer science, computer information systems, and engineering) to find answers that may improve security professionals' operations in cyberspace (Maimon, 2020).

In this chapter, our objective is to explain various types of research applicable to cybersecurity, define scientific research, and emphasize the need to adopt rigorous scientific research designs in the cybersecurity discipline. Finally, we will discuss common methods to evaluate cybersecurity operations, then review the importance of field experiments, longitudinal surveys, and observations for improving cybersecurity.

THE IMPORTANCE OF QUANTITATIVE, QUALITATIVE, AND MIXED RESEARCH

From a social and economic perspective, both quantitative and qualitative research designs are potential tools for evaluating organizations' security posture, measuring the efficacy and the return on investment (ROI) of (a) deploying new security systems, (b) establishing new procedures, and (c) implementing and measuring the impact of new policies. Similarly, relevant quantitative, qualitative, and mixed research designs should prevail within the scientific field of cybersecurity, to demonstrate evidence of system efficacy, strategic value, and tools deployed in an organization's security architecture. However, most cybersecurity practitioners are not well versed in the art of scientific research. Likewise, cybersecurity researchers know how to conduct research and publish in scientific journals, but very few of them have *field experience* within companies' or governments' cybersecurity operations. There is a significant difference between generating potentially applicable research results and operationalizing them in a cybersecurity department.

Despite gaps in their research skills, practitioners do have acute expertise in relevant cybersecurity skills – including cybersecurity operations, encryption, security tools, automation, malware analysis, incidence response, and governance. For this reason, cybersecurity professionals should learn how to conduct research in cybersecurity or work with cybersecurity researchers to measure what works and what doesn't. This would allow academic researchers to broaden their depth of knowledge and work on more practical real-world projects, while also creating value for organizations by increasing operational efficiency and reducing the costs of deploying ineffective security systems. Many security tools generate a very high false-positive ratio, they do not detect the threats they were built for, or their implementation is too expensive to mitigate risks in a cost-effective way.

Quantitative, qualitative, or mixed methods?

In the cybersecurity literature, quantitative research is often seen as better than qualitative research, but several authors have suggested that both types of measurement are applicable (Cybenko & Landwehr, 2012; Herley & van Oorschot, 2018; Pfleeger, 2012; Pfleeger & Cunningham, 2010). Specifically, qualitative research consists of the collection and analysis of descriptive data. This type of research usually involves humans and often includes information about their emotional state, social characteristics, way of life, experiences, or perceptions. More specifically, qualitative data can be categorized and ordered, but it cannot be mathematically quantified. On the other hand, quantitative research involves collecting and analyzing numerical data, enabling the quantification or statistical exploration and explanation of data (Edgar & Manz, 2017).

When both quantitative and qualitative research methods are used in the same study, this is referred to as a mixed-method approach. For example, a mixed-method approach could qualitatively assess the content of human reactions to phishing attempts by email while also quantitatively measuring those responses by counting how many participants reported the phishing to the security operations center (Mäses et al., 2019). Mixed-methods approaches (e.g., sequential exploratory design, sequential explanatory design, convergent design) can help us better understand the complexity of individual end-user behaviors (both malicious and non-malicious), show how they differ under various work conditions (e.g., how they use a system), and try to predict the outcome (Dalal et al., 2021; Nicolau et al., 2017). All three methodologies (i.e., qualitative, quantitative, mixed) can produce reliable data for cybersecurity operations. If we want cybersecurity to grow and evolve, we must follow the example of several other fields (e.g., healthcare, climate change, policing, physics) and focus our research on rigorous scientific methods. The next two sections briefly introduce those methods and identify their benefits for cybersecurity research and practice.

SCIENCE, THEORIES, AND FACTS

Science is a powerful tool with which humans have made extraordinary societal and technological advancements. Science is based on what we can see, hear, and touch rather than on personal opinions and speculations (Chalmers, 2013). It is a method of inquiry, a process of asking multiple questions and rigorously testing hypotheses (Zakaria, 2020). Different branches of science – including physical science, life science, social science, mathematical science, and data sciences – have enabled us to understand where we stand in the universe, prevent and treat diseases, and even create the Internet (Edgar & Manz, 2017). According to Edgar and Manz (2017), science includes three components: (1) a philosophy, (2) a body of knowledge, and (3) a method or process to discover knowledge. As these authors explain, a philosophy of science defines what it means to be an observer of the universe from within it. The body of scientific knowledge encapsulates what we have learned about the universe. The scientific method is a rigorous process to generate evidence and assimilate knowledge based on observing the world (Edgar & Manz, 2017).

Specifically, the scientific method contains five steps: (1) formulating a question based on previous observations, measurements, or experiments; (2) formulating hypotheses; (3) making predictions from these hypotheses; (4) conducting experimental testing of the predictions; and (5) analyzing the results, modifying the hypotheses if needed, and repeating all five steps to generate new knowledge (Dykstra, 2015; Peisert & Bishop, 2007). Likewise, there are five essential principles governing scientific research. First, experiments should be *objective* and free of bias, considering all the data and not only the data validating the hypothesis. Second, the hypotheses themselves should be *falsifiable*, meaning that testing could legitimately show them to be false. Experiments should also be *reproducible*, meaning other researchers may reproduce the results, and their results should be *predictable*, allowing other scientists to predict future results. Finally, scientific data must be *verifiable*, meaning no conclusions are made until the results are verified through proper observations and experiments (Dykstra, 2015; Peisert & Bishop, 2007). For example, cybersecurity researchers could evaluate (test) whether an intrusion detection system (IDS) can identify a specific type of attack (Peisert & Bishop, 2007). As Peisert and Bishop (2007) explained, to eliminate any unconscious bias that the researchers could accidentally introduce, such an experiment should be *blind*, meaning in this case that the researchers do not know whether the data sent into the system contains the attack.

Science has evolved over the years, instilling confidence in what can be learned from observation. There are four essential characteristics of modern scientific research methods: (1) a rigorous and methodical approach to ensure the execution of research is adequately conceived and disciplined, (2) a process to research ground theories empirically and form conceptual models, (3) evidence driven by logical and reasoned thinking, and (4) a research culture characterized by a high level of skepticism, which is necessary to challenge older approaches and results and ultimately generate confidence in accepted knowledge (Edgar & Manz, 2017).

As Dykstra (2015) pointed out, there are numerous reasons why it is crucial to consider science. First of all, scientific research is respected as most of the population sees the value in scientific inquiry and scientific results. Indeed, science is becoming a *thing of admiration* as a more significant portion of the population now wants to identify with science. Science also provokes curiosity as it is a vehicle for both gaining information and generating more questions, in order to understand a given research domain more deeply. Furthermore, science can be relied upon to improve commercial efficiency and create potentially revolutionary innovations and applications.

Finally, science advances knowledge by allowing humans to create new knowledge about the world. This means that scientific researchers have the opportunity to contribute something new to the body of knowledge and advance the state of the art (Dykstra, 2015). Along similar lines, engineering uses scientific principles to apply the empirical knowledge generated through science to the design and construction of the machines, structures, and applications necessary to address societal problems and make processes more efficient (Edgar & Manz, 2017). Through research, science strives to explain different phenomena and identify which processes affect behavior in systems, allowing them to predict future events based on the current state and possible stimuli (Edgar & Manz, 2017).

There is an important difference between scientific fact and scientific theories. Briefly, facts can be observed and measured, while theories represent scientists' explanations and interpretations of those facts (Bradford, 2017). As Chalmers (2013) explained, facts are revealed to careful observers through the senses, they are independent of theories, and they constitute *a firm and reliable foundation* for scientific knowledge. Facts must be established before scientists can derive knowledge or build theories to explain or interpret the facts (Chalmers, 2013).

Edgar and Manz (2017) described a theory as a *proposed model or inner working*, allowing researchers to answer why a system behaves in a specific manner. In science, a theory is a foundational piece of knowledge around which research and even whole research fields are built. A scientific approach follows the life cycle of the scientific process, starting as a belief based on observations (Edgar & Manz, 2017). A good theory should encourage both testing and the expansion and evaluation of related hypotheses, since each theory should be testable and potentially falsifiable through observations, experiments, and logical reasoning (Edgar & Manz, 2017).

There are many benefits of using science in cybersecurity. However, it is also essential to understand what science is not. Science does not generate miracles or easy solutions, as it is a learning and discovery process with many failures and disappointments (Zakaria, 2020). Over time, the scientific community uses peer review to evaluate and eventually accept certain results and concepts as settled science. Disagreements within the scientific community do not mean that science is not working, since these debates and controversies are essential to settle or reject hypotheses. Even so, new evidence may disrupt settled science, as results will not necessarily hold forever (Denning & Johnson, 2021).

A great example of this is the COVID-19 pandemic. To effectively protect ourselves from the virus, the best option was to rely on scientific evidence. Of course, medical doctors and scientists had to change specific recommendations, conduct additional testing, and refine their strategies along the way based on the best evidence, including new and better data. As Gupta (2021) argued, a common problem with science, in general, is incomplete evidence due to the absence of long-term data. For good or bad, people tend to rely on theories, opinions, and perspectives not based on factual information. Thus, cybersecurity research should include long-term studies to establish more reliable evidence and form better theories.

SCIENCE IN CYBERSECURITY

Since science has been so fundamental in our lives, why do we not apply more science practices to cybersecurity research? Cyberspace is a combination of *hardware, data,* and *human interactions,* each playing a role in what characteristics are exhibited in cyberspace (Edgar & Manz, 2017). As a change in any one of these categories could alter specific components of the system's dynamics, the science of cybersecurity lies in understanding their interactions (Edgar & Manz, 2017). For example, humans may serve as developers and designers, users and consumers, practitioners, or active adversaries (Dykstra, 2015), but the human factor in cybersecurity is much less studied than its technological counterpart (Dalal et al., 2021). As in other fields, scientific exploration should pursue the knowledge needed to quantify security and predict what tools and practices will enable us to disrupt or hamper cyberattacks.

For Chief Security Information Officers (CISOs), information technology and security leaders, private and public sector executives, and cybersecurity practitioners, the use of scientific methods can make product and security system evaluations a strategic tool, enabling organizations to make better investment decisions and to deploy more efficient tools and policies. It can also avoid investing time, efforts, and resources in poor and unproductive places (Millett et al., 2017). More to the point, scientific cybersecurity can objectively demonstrate which practices and techniques work or do not work, to counter the all-too-common technique of trusting people's *opinions, wisdom, intuitive theories, ideologies, or beliefs* to make critical security decisions (Denning & Johnson, 2021; Dykstra, 2015; Millett et al., 2017).

Cybersecurity is an applied science that works best by focusing on observation and definition (Radley, 2018). It overlaps with other types of mathematical science (particularly mathematics and statistics), and it is strongly influenced by social sciences such as economics, sociology, psychology, and criminology. Cybersecurity is the application of security to cyberspace, after all, and applied research is a key step in the research life cycle. Scientific knowledge is used to solve a pressing problem (e.g., a compromised system, vulnerability, or threat) and generate a predictable outcome. This experimental method leverages controlled tests to capture *real-world behaviors* to determine how the system behaves, then conducts validation testing to see if the *right system* was built to fix it (Edgar & Manz, 2017). More precisely, *applied experimentation* clarifies the behavior of a system that exists while *applied research* seeks to understand an engineered system and how well it meets its security design requirements (Edgar & Manz, 2017).

As Edgar and Manz (2017) noted, essential aspects of cybersecurity cannot be formalized in mathematics given cyberspace's abstract nature – a large part of the difficulty in developing cybersecurity science. Every day, security practitioners have to deal with uncertainty and unknowns, make difficult choices, and manage crises that scientific methods could inform. These same practitioners have to face cyber-adversaries who are often challenging to comprehend (Dykstra, 2015). Thus, there is every reason to believe that traditional experimental and theoretical inquiry domains apply to cybersecurity studies. Our highest priority should be to establish research protocols to enable reproducible experiments (Dykstra, 2015; Jason, 2010).

To reach this goal, the data used in cybersecurity experiments needs to be published. In many studies conducted by think tanks and security solutions vendors, the data sets are not available for various reasons – often to maintain confidentiality or protect personally identifiable information (e.g., names, emails, IP addresses). In some cases, the data sets are also kept confidential by law (Peisert & Bishop, 2007). As Peisert and Bishop (2007) and Colfer (2011) articulated, sanitizing these data sets (i.e., destroying the data stored on a memory device) can alter properties affecting the analysis. This situation may lead to the creation of artificial data matching the relevant statistics of the real data sets. In these instances, should the final data sets be considered relevant statistics? For business purposes, that might be acceptable, but for research purposes, it is not in line with the best practices discussed earlier in this chapter.

There are multiple perspectives through which one can view scientific research in cybersecurity. The logical data and computer science informational aspects include the software, interfaces, and cyberspace artifacts (Edgar & Manz, 2017). It is also possible to study the physics that underlie cyberspace and study cybersecurity at the technical level of electrons, wires, computers, and other physical phenomenology (Edgar & Manz, 2017). Cybersecurity can also study the behavior of people in cyberspace. Individually, these are already challenging fields of study. Together, understanding them is even more difficult since each field calls for distinct expertise, e.g., researching cybersecurity through a technical computer science lens versus using a psychological and criminological perspective. Despite this challenge, cybersecurity needs more research to identify useful metrics for informing organizational practices, to understand what can be done in terms of corporate practices, and to discern to what extent these organizational practices enhance the organization's security posture (Dalal et al., 2021; Millett et al., 2017). We strongly believe that the human aspect of cybersecurity has not been sufficiently studied, especially in terms of how human interactions may impact a given organization's security posture. As discussed previously, humans are significant threats as they are intelligent and responsive. Their modus operandi, tactics, and defenses change over time.

Viruses and bacteria's can weaken our immune systems and blunt pharmaceuticals' effectiveness. A virus changes relatively slowly and is not intelligent, so it is possible to predict how it might change (Edgar & Manz, 2017). However, human threat actors communicate, share, sell exploits, and learn how cyber systems work very quickly (Colfer, 2011). This complexity makes cybersecurity research more demanding but also provides a lasting intellectual challenge for academics.

Consequently, as Edgar and Manz (2017) argued, there is a *coevolutionary process* that security practitioners and academics need to understand to help future-proof the knowledge gained from cybersecurity research. Cybercriminals change tactics and approaches very often, and organizations need to adapt continuously. For this reason, an organization should use security science to understand models, attacks, and defenses better; to clarify how systems are engineered, deployed, and maintained; and to know whether they should invest in new technology, develop and promulgate technologies, or establish new practices and policies to meet their security challenges (Millett et al., 2017). Using science in cybersecurity also means relying on predictive analytics and the data mining of active and passive observations, network probes, honeypots, and direct interactions with hackers, insiders, and cybercriminals (American Association for the Advancement of Science, 2014). These techniques help identify how best to respond to various types of attacks from a myriad of cyberattackers, but unfortunately, they are not regularly used by organizations. Much like medical science works to generate an immune response in the body, using science in cybersecurity allows experts to identify threats, adapt to those threats, and seek to eliminate them (American Association for the Advancement of Science, 2014).

Case reports

In any research field, a variety of methodological options exist for individuals interested in conducting research, each of which may be suitable depending on the purpose of the research, the type of research questions to be answered, and the availability of resources (Ponto, 2015). This section focuses on case reports, papers describing a new solution without providing context or assumptions (Edgar & Manz, 2017). These case reports are commonly used in the cybersecurity literature to describe a particular new technology. However, they are often relied upon without any associated performance or security experiments, or even a rigorous study of the technology's behavior and contexts (Edgar & Manz, 2017).

The cybersecurity community (e.g., vendors, consultants) often publishes white papers that are little more than glorified case reports. Any paper describing a technology, product, or algorithm without detailing the methodology of the study or the experiment conducted on the solution is essentially a case report – the lowest form of empirical research (Edgar & Manz, 2017). Case reports do not provide any information about the hypothetico-deductive experimental (a proposed description of the scientific method) setup (Edgar & Manz, 2017). Specifically, they do not describe the controls and assumptions for the particular study or the procedures used to analyze the data, the systems, and the policies. Thus, readers are left with the impression that the results were collected without evidence (Edgar & Manz, 2017).

From an academic perspective, while case reports in cybersecurity are frequent, their scientific contributions are too low to be useful. More rigorous research methods are needed to create new cybersecurity knowledge. New approaches based on science could help public and private organizations manage their cybersecurity operations from a practical perspective. These methods must be based on evidence instead of relying on vendors' opinions and professional experiences. Before looking at some of these methods, however, we need to explain the problems with surveys, benchmarks, and validation testing in cybersecurity.

THE PROBLEMS WITH SURVEYS, BENCHMARKS, AND VALIDATION TESTING IN CYBERSECURITY

Surveys

Check and Schutt (2012) defined survey research as 'collecting information from a sample of individuals through their responses to questions' (p.160). Survey research can use quantitative research strategies (e.g., questionnaires with numerically rated items), qualitative research strategies (e.g., open-ended questions), or both strategies (i.e., mixed-methods research) to describe and explore human behaviors (Ponto, 2015; Singleton, 2009). Researchers conduct these studies using scientifically tested strategies, valid and reliable instruments, and a rigorous approach (e.g., establishing representative samples and reducing nonresponse error), potentially generating significant and valuable results (Ponto, 2015). Nevertheless, survey research is prone to errors, particularly coverage errors (i.e., zero chance of individuals in the population to be included in the sample), sampling errors (i.e., individuals included in the sample do not represent the characteristics of the population), measurement errors (i.e., questions and instruments do not reflect the topic of interest or evoke truthful answers), and nonresponse errors (i.e., a lack of response from all individuals in the sample) (Check & Schutt, 2012; Dillman et al., 2014; Ponto, 2015; Singleton, 2009).

Thus, if individuals and organizations use surveys without a rigorous methodology, survey research can actually generate inaccurate results and invalid interpretations. Specifically, these results may not provide the truth about the efficiency and efficacy of certain cybersecurity tools or systems, despite their popularity in reports or white papers by vendors and consultants. In some of these reports, the methodology describing how the survey was conducted is not adequately explained, the participants were not objectively chosen, and the company did not use a representative enough sample to generalize the results they are explaining to readers and potential clients. In other words, sampling and measurement errors are often common in companies' surveys about their commercial benefits. The results of these surveys are often used for selling more costly cybersecurity products.

Benchmarks

When managing cybersecurity, it is normal for executives to ask if their security teams have the right number of employees, the appropriate skills and tools, and the latest systems in place to adequately protect the organization. A logical way to answer this question is to look at what others are doing, a process called benchmarking (Hewitt, 2018). Benchmarking is a tool or measurement process through which numerous artifacts (e.g., tools, procedures, performance measurements, detection ratios, and systems) can be compared. It is a standard tool used across industries to provide an approachable, inexpensive, and simple method for comparing solutions.

Even though benchmarks use real data, they do not attempt to replicate real conditions, as they only compare one result or situation to another one at a specific point in time. When these numbers are taken out of context, the resulting decisions may create security gaps within the organization instead of reducing them. For instance, benchmarks on the number of resources employed within a given cybersecurity department, the annual security budget, or the number and type of tools being deployed within the organization often contain misleading assumptions. Organizations differ in terms of their cybersecurity maturity level, the number of legacy systems, and the quality of data relied upon to create scenarios for detecting potential threats. Hence, benchmarks are not the best solution when security practitioners want to understand how a solution behaves under more realistic operational conditions (Edgar & Manz, 2017).

VALIDATION TESTING

Validation testing is a rigorous and controlled process allowing researchers to investigate and test the performance of an application to solve a problem (Edgar & Manz, 2017). Whereas benchmarks generate a series of *one-off tests*, validation testing uses a fully controlled environment that can study specific aspects of a problem and its potential solutions (Edgar & Manz, 2017). As Bucur and Babulak (2019) pointed out, new theoretical proposals need to be tested in a real environment, and validation testing can effectively test the applicability of cybersecurity tools and applications in real-life situations. For example, in the Security Content Automation Protocol Validation Program (SCAP), independent laboratories accredited by the National Institute of Standards and Technology (NIST) test security products and provide the results to NIST. The validations awarded to vendor products are publicly posted on the SCAP website, in a list of validated products and modules (National Institute of Standards and Technology, 2021). For example, researchers may want to validate if certain types of analytic tools (e.g., security information and event management systems, SIEMs) could impact the baseline ability of the system to detect attacks.

However, the primary challenge with validation testing is the difficulty of recreating realistically modeled environments and situations that organizations face, given the complexity of their environments, contexts, systems, vulnerabilities, data, employees, risks and threats, and individual third-party relationships. In other words, the theoretical side often dramatically differs from the practical side since organizations differ in how they manage cybersecurity within their operations. Validation testing is a great process for testing security products in a controlled environment, such as using a cloud infrastructure to test various threats and vulnerabilities scenarios. Still, the main challenge is to fully transfer these results to a real-life environment or to a specific organization, as the infrastructure used within the controlled environment is not identical to any real organization's infrastructure. Validating testing can demonstrate whether the security products do what they were intended to do in terms of performance, but it will not take into consideration behavior-based measures specific to the organization.

RESEARCH DESIGNS IN CYBERSECURITY

Numerous research designs may be used to improve the quality of the cybersecurity data available to decision-makers in public and private organizations. The following section provides a brief overview of several methods and techniques that should be more frequently relied upon in cybersecurity: fundamental observational and controlled research, case-control, simulations, longitudinal studies, the difference-in-differences (DID) research design, time-series design, and field experiments.

Fundamental observational and controlled research

Fundamental observational studies observe an entire system, without the presumption of any specific behavior, in *the wild* or its *natural habitat* (Edgar & Manz, 2017). In this type of study, the goal is to study the entire system without injecting or introducing a change or variable from the observer (Edgar & Manz, 2017). According to Peisert and Bishop (2007), 'if something cannot be observed (either directly or indirectly), it cannot be measured or studied' (p. 3). For example, it is possible to release a malware program and monitor it on an isolated network to analyze its propagation rate and validate specific controls. Observing this malware's behavior in the 'wild' will not determine the propagation rate as other factors may confound the analysis (Peisert & Bishop, 2007).

Another option is to use a controlled research environment. In a controlled environment, it is essential to know the nature of the hypothesis and the environment in which the experiment will be conducted. For instance, formulating a hypothesis about a potential relationship between a credential stuffing attack and the potential impact on the network, e.g., 'if we use a bot manager from company X, we will detect 40 percent more credential stuffing attacks than with company Y's bot manager,' then conducting a controlled experiment, could generate valid results (Peisert & Bishop, 2007). During the actual experiment, all variables are 'controlled' or kept constant, in order to isolate the specific effects of the variable under study – in this case, the use of a different bot manager. This improves the reliability and validity of the results (Peisert & Bishop, 2007). To establish a controlled environment in this example, we might ask questions like this: what is the attack and are both products looking for the same type of attack? Are both products testing against the same data set? Are both systems set up on a private access network? Are both systems reading data from the same locations on the network? Are the Internet protocol (IP) addresses of their hosts identical? And finally, are the operating systems and versions of the host identical? As Peisert and Bishop (2007) noted, if the answer to one of these questions is no, the experiment may have one or more uncontrolled variables, which means that the researchers will not be in a position to provide valid, reliable, and reproducible results.

Case-control

A case-control study is another category of observational research, using a comparison group in which existing records or information are used to identify subjects with (i.e., cases) and without (i.e., controls) the outcome of interest (Morrow, 2010). This research design is a common alternative to longitudinal (e.g., cohort study) research. While longitudinal studies look forward to understanding what will happen in the future, case-control studies look backward at something that already occurred (Edgar & Manz, 2017; Morrow, 2010). Case-controls are considered useful because (a) they allow researchers to gather important information in a short period, (b) they are relatively inexpensive to conduct, (c) they are helpful when the outcome is rare, (d) they can rely on only a few participants, and (e) they are practical for outcomes or conditions that may take a long time to manifest (Morrow, 2010).

In a cybersecurity context, an example of a case-control experiment could be to study a network compromised by malware and to compare it to a network without compromise – or to itself before the compromising event. Thus, the cases would be the infected machines. The controls would be a representative number of similar (e.g., with the same operating system, patches, and applications) but not currently infected devices (Edgar & Manz, 2017). The main disadvantages of case-controls are that they may be more susceptible to information bias (i.e., how the researchers will select the control group) and are not useful when the frequency of event occurrence is low (Morrow, 2010).

Simulations

Colfer (2011) argued that a significant gap in cybersecurity research is the lack of knowledge and understanding of the threat environment, due to the need to develop realistic security requirements. According to Colfer, one way to solve the security evaluation problem is by developing tools that could replicate realistic environments through testbeds (i.e., environments allowing researchers to verify a security technology and conduct experiments; Lee et al., 2018) and simulations (Colfer, 2011). Using computers to simulate complex models and cyberattacks in a simulated environment offers researchers the possibility to explore system interactions, component performance, and theoretical limits without compromising real systems that are in use within a given organization (Edgar & Manz, 2017).

For empirical research, a simulation is an essential tool for testing theories. In practice, it allows researchers to generate hypotheses (for later experimentation) on how cybercriminals could attack a system and take advantage of its known or unknown vulnerabilities. To make sure that the theoretical results may be replicated in the real world, the scenarios that are tested through testbeds and simulations need to be compared to real-world conditions, in order to gauge the effectiveness of the tools, controls, or systems under experimentation (Edgar & Manz, 2017).

Various attack scenarios can be simulated. One example could simulate a malicious bot attack through a 1-terabyte distributed denial of service (DDoS) attack, lasting for a few days, intended to take down the DNS service of the organization, then evaluate how security systems react to this attack. Researchers can also simulate cyberattacks through an intrusion detection honeypot (IDH). An IDH is a security tool that can be placed inside the network perimeter of an organization to generate alerts when an attack might be underway (Sanders, 2020). IDHs rely on deception through the use of systems, services, or tokens (e.g., honey systems, honey services, and honey tokens) to attract cyberattackers inside a system by convincing them to interact. The cybercriminals do not know the researchers are alerted to each of their moves, allowing them to study their behaviors (Sanders, 2020). They act like a virtual canary in a coal mine.

Simulations allow researchers to generate predictions about how a system might defend against a potential intrusion; they also provide a way to investigate the effectiveness of solutions, use possible controls, and examine multiple attack scenarios. Nonetheless, the results generated through simulations will only be as good as the models used in the simulations. The limits of these models need to be kept in mind when using these simulations to inform future strategic and operational security decisions (Edgar & Manz, 2017).

Longitudinal research

In medicine and health science, longitudinal studies are frequent. The primary objective of these studies is to collect sufficient information over time to ensure the entire life cycle (i.e., the full context) of the population under evaluation (e.g., participants, systems, processes) is considered (Edgar & Manz, 2017). Longitudinal studies provide the most in-depth understanding of a system as they capture data on how variables change over time, thus providing information on how participants evolve and the time sequences of events (Edgar & Manz, 2017). As Gupta (2021) noted, for instance, longitudinal studies on brain disease accumulated data over the past few decades on certain risk factors to the brain, showing that aside from age, most other risk factors for brain disease can be controlled. Along similar lines, the University of Exeter Medical School and King's College in London analyzed data from more than 19,000 people enrolled in the PROTECT study, which lasted 25 years (Gupta, 2021).

However, longitudinal studies about prevention and detection systems, the evolution of cyber-threats, or how human beings interact with computers and the cyberspace environment are not frequent, partly since they could span generations. For example, such a study could look at the evolution of virus prevention over time, but observing the same subjects (i.e., antivirus software) for the duration of the research (e.g., for ten years) could be a challenge (Edgar & Manz, 2017). Unfortunately, given the dynamics of cybersecurity research, human involvement as both cybercriminals and victims, and cyberspace's adversarial nature, conducting longitudinal studies in the wild would be very complicated and potentially costly. Reducing participant attrition and maintaining access to the same participants for an extended period would also be challenging, a situation that might impact the internal validity of the results (Edgar & Manz, 2017).

The difference-in-differences research method

As Wing et al. (2018) explained, the DID design is a quasi-experimental research design. DID is also known as a comparative interrupted time-series design or nonequivalent control group pre-test. It allows researchers to study causal relationships where randomized controlled trials (i.e., where participants are randomly assigned to an experimental group or a control group) are impossible, perhaps due to ethical factors. DID does not replace randomized experiments, but it provides a possible avenue to learn about causal relationships (Wing et al., 2018).

According to Dimick and Ryan (2014), this design can address a problem by examining a comparison group that is experiencing the same trends but is not exposed to a given policy change. The simplest form of this research design uses two groups (e.g., group A and group B) observed in two time periods (e.g., January and March of 2017) or two geographical areas (e.g., team A in Montreal, Quebec, and team B in Atlanta, Georgia) (Wing et al., 2018). More specifically, it compares the outcomes before and after a policy implementation in a study group without the exposure (group A) and one with the exposure (group B) (Dimick & Ryan, 2014). This procedure allows researchers to notice the changes in outcomes and to subtract one outcome from the other.

In these calculations, two differences in results are important: (1) the difference after versus before the policy change in the group exposed to the policy (B2 – B1), and the difference after versus before the policy change in the unexposed group (A2 –A1) (Dimick & Ryan, 2014). If there is no relationship between policy implementation and subsequent outcomes, the DID estimate equals 0. If the policy is associated with beneficial changes, then the outcomes following implementation will improve significantly in the exposed group (Dimick & Ryan, 2014). Assessments will be derived from regression models rather than a simple subtraction, allowing adjustments for other factors that may differ between the two groups under study. As Dimick and Ryan (2014) put it:

> Regression models also offer a way to estimate the statistical significance of the association between policy change and outcomes by including a variable that indicates if the observation is in the pre or post-period and another variable that divides the groups into those exposed and unexposed to the policy. (p. 2401)

Such an example could be applicable to two security operation center (SOC) teams or penetration testers, referred to in cybersecurity as red teams. For instance, we can assume the expertise, toolsets, techniques, and training of the members of each red team differ. This research method would enable researchers to evaluate the relative difference in response to *test cases*, to account for baseline differences, such as different reference points, different security experience, and different maturity levels (Edgar & Manz, 2017). Since it would not be possible here to measure the results of samples in a controlled experiment (i.e., measuring the difference in the resultant effect after treatment), the DID research method could be used to assess the capability of each red team in a pre-test mode and later in a post-test mode.

Both red teams would be attacking an environment with pre-built vulnerable web servers and databases. Later, the treatment would be exposing the red teams to copied environments with different defensive strategies and technologies (e.g., team A would be exposed to an environment following security best practices and team B would be exposed to an environment following best practices but also using network address randomization) deployed to protect the infrastructure of an organization (Edgar & Manz, 2017). By using a comparison group that is experiencing the same environment but is not exposed to the same defensive strategies, the pre-tests and post-tests for each team could be compared between the study group without the exposure (team A) and the study group with the exposure (team B). This research method demonstrates strong internal validity since the same factors affect all test subjects and it is possible to have confidence in the results, but the external validity of results (i.e., the results apply to similar groups in a different setting) from this method is not always applicable (Edgar & Manz, 2017).

Time-series design

Another reliable quasi-experimental method for cybersecurity research and practice is time-series design. This method takes multiple measurements over time to see how an intervention effect persists, and it is often used in medical treatment testing (Edgar & Manz, 2017). Since one desired outcome of science is the predictability of understanding, both in the present and (more importantly) in the future, time-series studies can enable better operational decisions (Edgar & Manz, 2017). In cybersecurity, these decisions might include how to best allocate funds to adequately mitigate cyber-risks, decide what controls to implement, and evaluate which systems work or do not work to detect trespassing by cyberattacks. As cybercriminals gain experience regarding the detection techniques used by organizations, they adapt their behaviors very rapidly to take advantage of vulnerabilities accessible to them. For this reason, this research design can be used to learn at the same time as the attackers, who attack critical organizational assets through several phases or stages.

A great example of research using this design is by Maimon et al. (2014), who used a time-series design in their criminological study of illegal online trespassers. In this research, they employed a large set of target computers built to be attacked (honeypots). To test their research hypotheses, Maimon et al. (2014) designed a randomized experiment: they used 80 public IP addresses provided by the information technology team of a large American university, and they deployed identical target computers on the university network. Within this infrastructure, they conducted two independent experiments to investigate the influence of a warning banner on the progression, frequency, and duration of system trespassing incidents at two different periods: (1) a two-month period from 1 April to 30 May 2011, and (2) a six-month period from 4 October 2011 to 3 April 2012. Once the honeypots were set up, the authors waited for system trespassers to use various software tools to bypass the security system in place and to infiltrate the infrastructure they were monitoring, to compare the activities on the system in line with the treatment and control conditions in place (Maimon et al., 2014).

To gain access to the target computers, system trespassers had to break into these systems successfully through frequently scanned and vulnerable entry points. After infiltrating the target computers, trespassers were assigned to either a treatment or a control target computer, and a system trespassing incident was initiated. The researchers monitored the different components of the system trespassing incident using specialized software, recording the system trespassing sessions for later analysis to allow the collection of meaningful data. In both experiments, the targeted computers (86 computers in the first experiment and 502 computers in the second) were set to either display or not display a warning banner once intruders had successfully infiltrated the systems. Results show that 1,058 trespassing incidents were observed in the first experiment and 3,768 incidents in the second. Also, their findings demonstrate that although a warning banner did not lead to immediate termination or a reduction in the frequency of trespassing incidents, it significantly reduced their duration, which is an evidence that these banners had a deterrent effect on system trespassers (Maimon et al., 2014).

Field research

According to the definition provided by Danelo (2017), field research is 'the collection of information outside a library, or workplace setting' (p. 1), and it is both a science and art. Field research generates new knowledge through practice, experiencing new situations, and appreciation. This research design may include cultural observations, expert interviews, and data collection, allowing a researcher to gather relevant information and determine common themes (Danelo, 2017). Since researchers are not working from their home office, they also need to be able to evaluate personal risks while conducting field research (Danelo, 2017). Barth et al. (2019) argued that field research lets researchers identify real-world problems. Like biologists observing animals interacting with their environment or sociologists interviewing people in their natural setting, cybersecurity researchers can use field research to research cybersecurity problems related to cyber-risks. Criminologists studying cybercrime also use field research to analyze crime to collect primary data in innovative ways (Bossler & Berenblum, 2019). The online fraud project conducted by the Evidence-Based Cybersecurity Group at Georgia State University, for instance, explores how online fraudsters use creative methods to deceive potential victims. This project focuses on online dating scams, online employment scams, business email compromise, and darknet auction scams (Georgia State University, 2021).

Another example of field research in cybersecurity is the study conducted by Nyre-Yu et al. (2019). In this research, a qualitative field study was conducted among three computer security incident response teams (CSIRTs) and included perspectives from government, academia, and private sector teams (Nyre-Yu et al., 2019). The methods used were observation – the researchers spent 3–5 business days with each team – and on-site interviews with analysts and managers, to capture insights with high ecological validity (i.e., the ability to generalize study findings to real-world settings). The resulting data and themes provided insights across multiple aspects of incident response, including information sharing, organization, learning, and automation of security tools (Nyre-Yu et al., 2019).

CONCLUSION

This chapter discussed the current state of research in cybersecurity to evaluate practices, systems, tools, and policies. Science is a rigorous process, and cybersecurity is more complex than just a technical problem. More emphasis should be given to studying the behaviors of people in cyberspace. Current research standards are too low, and the cybersecurity industry still heavily relies on the information provided by security vendors, who do not always explain in detail the methodology they use in evaluating their products. We strongly believe that a scientific approach should be used more often in cybersecurity to improve operational and strategic decisions and evaluate investments made in tools and systems. Because these financial investments are significant, they should be made on an evidence-based approach.

We also provided a brief overview of several research designs that could bring value in managing cybersecurity and various cyber-risks. Academics from different fields should partner with cybersecurity professionals to enhance cybersecurity research. Specifically, instead of focusing primarily on using surveys, case reports, and benchmarks, cybersecurity practitioners and academics should collaborate on research designs such as case-control, longitudinal study, time-series design, and field research to improve cybersecurity. In conclusion, we firmly believe that field research is the most exciting research design. This design should be used more frequently by researchers to create new knowledge, allowing practitioners to implement new strategies and security controls that will better protect their organizations.

REFERENCES

Algaith, A., Gashi, I., Sobesto, B., Cukier, M., Haxhijaha, S., & Bajrami, G. (2016). Comparing detection capabilities of antivirus products: An empirical study with different versions of products from the same vendors. In *2016 46th Annual IEEE/IFIP International Conference on Dependable Systems and Networks Workshop* (pp. 48–53). IEEE.

American Association for the Advancement of Science. (2014). *What is the science of cybersecurity?* https://www.aaas.org/news/what-science-cybersecurity

AV Comparatives. (2013). *File detection test of malicious software* (Technical Report, AV Comparatives). https://www.av-comparatives.org/wp-content/uploads/2017/03/avc_sum_201312_en.pdf

Barth, S., Hartel, P., Junger, M., & Montoya, L. (2019). Teaching empirical social-science research to cybersecurity students: The case of "thinking like a thief.". *IEEE Security & Privacy*, 17(3), 8–16. https://doi.org/10.1109/MSEC.2018.2888781

Bossler, A., & Berenblum, M. (2019). Introduction: New directions in cybercrime research. *Journal of Crime and Justice*, 42(5), 495–499. https://doi.org/10.1080/0735648X.2019.1692426

Bradford, A. (2017). *What is a scientific theory?* https://www.livescience.com/21491-what-is-a-scientific-theory-definition-of-theory.html

Bucur, C., & Babulak, E. (2019). Security validation testing environment in the cloud. In *IEEE International Conference on Big Data (Big Data)* (pp. 4240–4247). https://doi.org/10.1109/BigData47090.2019.9006202

Chalmers, A. F. (2013). *What is this thing called science?* University of Queensland Press.

Check, J., & Schutt, R. K. (2012). Survey research. In J. Check, & K. Schutt (Eds.), *Research methods in education* (pp. 159–185). SAGE Publications.

Colfer, B. J. (2011). *The science of cybersecurity and a roadmap to research.* Nova Science Publishers, Inc.

Cybenko, G., & Landwehr, C. E. (2012). Security analytics and measurements. *IEEE Security & Privacy, 10*(3), 5–8. https://doi.org/10.1109/MSP.2012.75

Dalal, R. S., Howard, D. J., Bennett, R. J., Posey, C., Zaccaro, S. J., & Brummel, B. J. (2021). Organizational science and cybersecurity: Abundant opportunities for research at the interface. *Journal of Business & Psychology*, 1–29. https://doi.org/10.1007/s10869-021-09732-9

Danelo, D. J. (2017). *The field researcher's handbook: A guide to the art and science of professional fieldwork.* Georgetown University Press.

Denning, P. J., & Johnson, J. (2021). The profession of IT: Science is not another opinion. *Communications of the ACM, 64*(3), 36–38. https://doi.org/10.1145/3447257

Dillman, D. A., Smyth, J. D., & Christian, L. M. (2014). *Internet, phone, mail, and mixed-mode surveys: The tailored design method.* Wiley.

Dimick, J. B., & Ryan, A. M. (2014). Methods for evaluating changes in health care policy: The difference-in-differences approach. *Journal of the American Medical Association, 312*(22), 2401–2402. https://doi.org/10.1001/jama.2014.16153

Dykstra, J. (2015). *Essential cybersecurity science: Build, test, and evaluate secure systems.* O'Reilly.

Edgar, T. W., & Manz, D. O. (2017). *Research methods for cyber security.* Syngress.

Garg, A., Vidyaraman, S., Upadhyaya, S., & Kwiat, K. (2006). Usim: A user behavior simulation framework for training and testing IDSes in GUI based systems. In *Proceedings of the 39th Annual Symposium on Simulation* (pp. 196–203). IEEE Computer Society.

Gashi, I., Stankovic, V., Leita, C., & Thonnard, O. (2009). An experimental study of diversity with off-the-shelf antivirus engines. In *Eighth IEEE International Symposium on Network Computing and Applications, 2009. NCA 2009* (pp. 4–11). IEEE.

Georgia State University. (2021). *Online fraud.* https://ebcs.gsu.edu/project/onlinefraud/

Gupta, S. (2021). *Keep sharp; Build a better brain at any age.* Headline Home.

Help Net Security. (2021). *Cybersecurity investments will increase up to 10% in 2021.* https://www.helpnetsecurity.com/2021/01/26/cybersecurity-investments-2021

Herley, C., & van Oorschot, P. C. (2018). Science of security: Combining theory and measurement to reflect the observable. *IEEE Security & Privacy, Privacy, 16*(1), 12–22. https://doi.org/10.1109/MSP.2018.1331028

Hewitt, C. (2018). *5 mistakes to avoid when staffing for security roles.* https://www.securityinfowatch.com/cybersecurity/information-security/computer-and-network-security-software/article/12430618/5-mistakes-to-avoid-when-staffing-for-security-roles

Jason. (2010). Science of cyber-security. The Mitre Corporation. Retrieved from https://irp.fas.org/agency/dod/jason/cyber.pdf

Lee, S., Lee, S., Yoo, H., Kwon, S., & Shon, T. (2018). Design and implementation of cybersecurity testbed for industrial IoT systems. *Journal of Supercomputing, 74*(9), 4506–4520. https://doi.org/10.1007/s11227-017-2219-z

Maimon, D. (2020). Relevance of evidence-based cybersecurity in guiding the financial sector's & efforts in fighting cybercrime. In P. L. Pomerleau, & D. L. Lowery (Eds.), *Countering cyber threats to financial institutions: A private and public partnership approach to critical infrastructure protection* (pp. 9–28). Palgrave Macmillan. https://doi.org/10.1007/978-3-030-54054-8_2

Maimon, D., Alper, M., Sobesto, B., & Cukier, M. (2014). Restrictive deterrent effects of a warning banner in an attacked computer system. *Criminology, 52*(1), 33–59. https://doi.org/10.1111/1745-9125.12028

Mäses, S., Kikerpill, K., Jüristo, K., & Maennel, O. (2019). Mixed methods research approach and experimental procedure for measuring human factors in cybersecurity using phishing simulations. In *Proceedings of the European Conference on Research Methods for Business & Management Studies.*

Maxion, R. A., Longstaff, T. A., & McHugh, J. (2010). *Why is there no science in cyber science? A panel discussion at NSPW.* https://dl.acm.org/doi/10.1145/1900546.1900548

Millett, L. I., Fischhoff, B., & Weinberger, P. J. (2017). *Foundational cybersecurity research: Improving science, engineering, and institutions.* The National Academies Press.

Morrow, B. (2010). An overview of case-control study designs and their advantages and disadvantages. *International Journal of Therapy & Rehabilitation, 17*(11), 570–574. https://doi.org/10.12968/ijtr.2010.17.11.79537

National Institute of Standards and Technology. (2021). *Security content automation protocol validation program.* https://csrc.nist.gov/Projects/scap-validation-program

Nicolau, B., Castonguay, G., Levine, A., Hong, Q. N., & Pluye, P. (2017). Applied mixed methods in oral health research: Importance and example of a training program. *JDR Clinical & Translational Research, 2*(3), 206–210.

Noureldien, N. A., & Osman, I. M. (2000). On firewalls evaluation criteria. In *TENCON 2000 Proceedings* (Vol. 3, pp. 104–110). IEEE.

Nyre-Yu, M., Gutzwiller, R. S., & Caldwell, R. S. (2019). Observing cyber security incident response: Qualitative themes from field research. *Proceedings of the Human Factors and Ergonomics Society Annual Meeting, 63*(1), 437–441. https://doi.org/10.1177/1071181319631016

Peisert, S., & Bishop, M. (2007). How to design computer security experiments. In L. Futcher, & R. Dodge (Eds.), *Fifth World Conference on Information Security Education. WISE 2007. IFIP Advances in Information and Communication Technology* (Vol. 237, pp. 141–148). Springer. https://doi.org/10.1007/978-0-387-73269-5_19

Pfleeger, S. L. (2012). Security measurement steps, missteps, and next steps. *IEEE Security & Privacy, 10*(4), 5–9. https://doi.org/10.1109/MSP.2012.106

Pfleeger, S., & Cunningham, R. (2010). Why measuring security is hard. *IEEE Security & Privacy, 8*(4), 46–54. https://doi.org/10.1109/MSP.2010.60

Ponto, J. (2015). Understanding and evaluating survey research. *Journal of the Advanced Practitioner in Oncology, 6*(2), 168–171.

Radley, A. (2018). *The science of cybersecurity: A treatise on communications security* (2nd ed.). CreateSpace.

Sanders, C. (2020). *Intrusion detection honeypots; Detection through deceptions.* Applied Network Defense.

Seeberg, V. E., & Petrovic, S. (2007). A new classification scheme for anonymization of real data used in IDS benchmarking. In *The Second International Conference on Availability, Reliability, and Security, 2007* (pp. 385–390). IEEE.

Singleton, R. A. (2009). *Approaches to social research.* Oxford University Press.

Surisetty, S., & Kumar, S. (2010). Is McAfee security center/firewall software providing complete security for your computer? In *Fourth International Conference on Digital Society, 2010* (pp. 178–181). IEEE.

Wing, C., Simon, K., & Bello-Gomez, R. A. (2018). Designing difference in difference studies: Best practices for public health policy research. *Annual Review of Public Health, 39,* 453–469. https://doi.org/10.1146/annurev-publhealth-040617-013507

Zakaria, F. (2020). *Ten lessons for a post-pandemic world.* W.W. Norton.

Chapter 6

Network security and intrusion detection systems

INTRODUCTION

Online offenders who engage in cyber-dependent crimes are eager to infiltrate and control targets' endpoint devices such as desktops, laptops, tablets, and mobile devices. To increase their probability of success, these offenders engage with online enablers who develop and sell the relevant sophisticated tools, thus supporting the offenders' illicit efforts. Similarly, they seek illegitimate access to computer networks to increase the number of potential endpoints and users they can target, all while disrupting the network owners' legitimate operations. In some cases, online offenders and enablers utilize a compromised network as a platform for engaging in subsequent online crimes. As such, network security aims to protect the network from illegal activity while allowing the network users to perform their critical functions within a secure online environment.

For their part, guardians (e.g., individual security professionals or cybersecurity teams) in charge of intrusion detection systems (IDSs) and the security of endpoint devices are constantly looking for efficient ways to prevent and detect cyber-dependent crimes and to respond to them accordingly. Endpoint protection platform (EPP) and endpoint detection and response (EDR) software products provide cybersecurity teams with a centralized platform to monitor endpoint devices continuously, unlike previous detection tools such as antivirus software. EPP and EDR products also promise to respond to suspicious user behaviors and potential security incidents via automation (Shread, 2020). This allows security professionals to stop threats and offers them new abilities to discover, investigate, and respond to these threats (Ozkaya & Aslaner, 2019).

To prevent threats from materializing, organizations utilize firewalls, intrusion prevention and detection systems, virtual private networks, network segmentation, data loss prevention (DLP) systems, security information and event management (SIEM) systems, honeypots, and security information management traffic systems to prevent, detect, and respond to various illicit attempts to access the network (Wheeler, 2011). However, current methodologies for evaluating different aspects of these security solutions rely primarily

DOI: 10.1201/9781003201519-6

on user surveys, third-party data, think tank analysts' reports, and vendors' analysis of their products.

Vendors make some information (i.e., datasets) publicly available to evaluate these tools, but it is not always usable for practitioners to improve the security posture of their organizations, due to data gaps and privacy concerns (Khraisat et al., 2019; Shiravi et al., 2012). Fortunately, some methods are documented in the literature to evaluate these tools' efficiency. However, they are either quantitative, based on risk management formulas and open-source databases that cannot easily demonstrate a true positive incidence for organizations' security postures, or they rest on a qualitative assessment based on reviewers' knowledge and opinions (Kiedrowicz & Stanik, 2018).

In this chapter, we will discuss some of the standard solutions that are used in cybersecurity to detect system intrusion and protect endpoint devices. Then, we will provide a critical assessment of some of the methodologies used to assess these solutions' effectiveness. In particular, we provide a list of challenges in assessing cybersecurity tools scientifically and outline various measures and research designs that can be utilized to improve cybersecurity. Finally, in the last section of this chapter, we offer a sample of recent scientific studies that may interest researchers and practitioners in cybersecurity.

NETWORK SECURITY AND INTRUSION DETECTION SYSTEMS IN CYBERSECURITY

Organizations face several cybersecurity threats that can affect the continuity of their operations, their reputation, and the creation of value for their shareholders. These threats can come from both outside the organization and within, forcing organizations to use an extensive set of security tools to protect their infrastructure, customer data, and a wide range of personal information and confidential proprietary information. In addition, some cybercriminals are becoming increasingly sophisticated and are highly motivated by profit. They have used sophisticated techniques to hide their identities and communications, distance their identities from illegal profits, and use infrastructures that are often difficult to compromise. Thus, it becomes increasingly important for computer systems to be protected using advanced IDSs capable of detecting modern cyberattacks, whatever their source (Khraisat et al., 2019).

Network security consists of policies, practices, and a set of rules designed to protect the integrity, confidentiality, and availability of an organization's computer networks and data. These elements are adopted by organizations to prevent, detect, and react to unauthorized access, misuse, modification, destruction, improper disclosure, or denial of a computer network and network-accessible resources (Fruhlinger, 2018; SANS, n.d.). The overall goal of network security is to create a connected network (e.g., computer networks and data using software and hardware technologies) that protects against illegal activity while allowing organizations to perform their critical functions within a secure environment (SANS, n.d.).

An intrusion can be defined as an attempt to destroy a computer or computer network's confidentiality, integrity, or availability (Cheng et al., 2020). Therefore, many practitioners and researchers have focused on detecting intrusions and determining how to best protect an organization against threats, particularly given the ever-increasing levels of intrusive activities and novel attacks (Gharib et al., 2016). More specifically, an IDS consists of network security equipment used to monitor a network transmission and send out alarms or take a responsive measure when suspicious activity is identified (Cheng et al., 2020).

Three common security strategies are known as the *prevention, detection*, and *response* triad. Prevention strategies make it possible to block all system access from intruders, in order to prevent derogatory actions. Detection is performed on those attacks that cannot be prevented, and the focus is on detecting – blocking – a subsequent transaction (i.e., attempt, connection, or compromise) from being committed. As for the response, this phase mainly consists of reacting to the effects of an attack, responding to the incident to stop the damage, and curing the affected nodes (Rathore et al., 2016).

IDSs can be categorized based on detection mechanisms and source(s) for which the detection is provided (Rathore et al., 2016). In terms of detection mechanisms, an IDS can be (a) *anomaly-based*, (b) *misuse-based*, or (c) *specification-based*, while it can also be *network-based, host-based*, or *hybrid* depending on the sources of the data and the systems being monitored (Rathore et al., 2016).

Intrusion detection system categories

As Rathore et al. (2016) explained, *anomaly-based detection* allows an IDS to detect the latest unknown attacks that may be encountered for the first time. It classifies behaviors in normal behaviors or attacks based on heuristics and signatures (Samrin & Vasumathi, 2017). Moreover, an anomaly-based IDS can perform what Thakkar and Lohiya (2020) referred to as *protocol analysis* to study the packet details. An important aspect to consider with anomaly-based detection capabilities is that for such detection techniques to work, the profile of the usual behavior – potential suspicious activities – must be updated periodically because of the changing behavior of the network with usage (Rathore et al., 2016). In other words, anomaly-based detection consists of creating a profile of statistically standard behavior of users and the network. This behavior is constantly monitored for a particular deviation, and when a variation occurs, it is treated as a potential intrusion (Rathore et al., 2016).

Misuse-based detection can be signature-based or rule-based. A signature-based detection will effectively detect attacks that have previously occurred, called *known attacks* (e.g., previous abnormalities in log files), but is not effective in detecting novel attacks (Samrin & Vasumathi, 2017; Scarfone & Mell, 2007). Signatures are patterns of previous attacks (e.g., more than five failed attempts to sign in) that are analyzed and then used for future detection, similar to how antivirus software is used to detect abnormal activities. Misuse-based detection compares signatures of well-known attacks to previously observed behaviors; thus, its drawback is that a new type of attack will not be recognized since there is no known signature (Samrin & Vasumathi, 2017).

In a *specification-based* IDS, some specifications and constraints for a standard application are defined. Then the application is monitored against those defined constraints, and if a deviation occurs, it will be detected as abnormal activity and a potential intrusion (Rathore et al., 2016). This type of IDS defines the desired behavior of a system in line with its functionalities and security policy. Any sequence of operations outside those specifications will be categorized as a security violation (Berthier & Sanders, 2011). This approach may be combined with an anomaly-based technique and an automated response to maintain high detection accuracy while reducing the costs associated with manually defining each specification (Berthier & Sanders, 2011). However, one of the limitations of this approach is the difficulty of verifying that the specifications are correct and adequately covering the organization's threat model (Berthier & Sanders, 2011).

A *network-based IDS* provides monitoring and analysis on each incoming packet of the network traffic and identifies intrusions on the network. It can be implemented on network devices like switch routers, servers, and gateways (Rathore et al., 2016). Similarly, a *host-based* IDS is concerned with the events that occur at each node. Therefore, it identifies any intrusion activity on a single node resulting from any event (e.g., changes in the critical system files on the host, repeated failed attempts to access the host, unusual process memory allocations, or unusual CPU activity) (Rathore et al., 2016). Finally, a *hybrid IDS* has both network-based and host-based features; thus, it performs intrusion detection on the host as well as on the whole network at the same time (Rathore et al., 2016).

Several systems can help mitigate the risks of various types of intrusions, insider threats, or data leakage within companies. In the following section, we discuss three of the leading security systems (tools) commonly used by organizations: (1) the endpoint detection system (EDS), (2) the SIEM system, and (3) the DLP system. The development of the cybersecurity toolset and its use depends on its missions, risk appetite, and overall information security program (Death, 2017).

Endpoint Detection Systems (EDSs)

EDR software products provide cybersecurity teams with a centralized platform to monitor endpoints. These endpoints are users' devices such as desktops, mobile devices, laptops, or Internet of Things (IoT) devices. Unfortunately, an endpoint may have been ill-configured or have security vulnerabilities (e.g., insufficient security updates), making them popular targets for various malware attacks to gain access to corporate networks (Sujeong et al., 2020). In this way, these endpoints can become the weakest security link (Deloitte, n.d.).

A Gartner analyst in 2013 coined the term 'endpoint threat detection and response system' (Osterman Research, 2019). The following year, Gartner defined an EDR as a tool focusing on detecting and investigating various activities (including potential threat activities) on hosts (i.e., endpoints) instead of at the network level (Osterman Research, 2019). To do that, an EDR records endpoint and network events, stores the detection activities, and investigates activities through behavioral analysis. These analytical capabilities allow for identifying tasks that improve the security state, blocking common attacks, and identifying early attacks (e.g., insider threat), all while responding to ongoing attacks (Osterman Research, 2019). According to Sujeong et al. (2020), recent endpoint detection technologies are limited to ensuring the visibility of anomalies within the corporate network, rather than using probability values to predict anomalies that may occur at the endpoints. However, ensuring visibility does position organizations better to respond to potential security incidents, primarily via automation (Shread, 2020).

Event log-based detection technology for endpoint security relies on rules and patterns, rendering it possible to respond to known attacks but making it more difficult to respond to unknown attacks (e.g., fileless malware attacks) or advanced persistent threats (APTs) (Sujeong et al., 2020). As a study conducted by Osterman Research (2019) shows, organizations primarily deploy EDR solutions in order to protect against fileless malware, improve post-breach remediation capabilities, and provide improved threat telemetry through automated communication processes from multiple data sources (Sumo Logic, 2019). In contrast to signature scanning or anomaly detection techniques, EDR tools search for threats by matching system events against a knowledge base of adversarial *tactics, techniques,* and *procedures* (TTP) (Hassan et al., 2020). As Hassan et al. (2020) explained, tactics describe 'why' an attacker performs a given action while techniques and procedures describe 'how' the action is performed.

Some of the companies offering EDR systems are Crowdstrike (Falcon), Check Point (Sandblast), Microsoft (MITRE ATT@CK), and Palo Alto (Cortex XDR), among many others (Shread, 2020).*

Security Information and Event Management (SIEM) systems

As Bucur and Babulak (2019) stipulated, one of the most critical cybersecurity management actions is log collection. Network components such as servers, firewalls, intrusion prevention systems (IPS), IDS, and applications can generate log files. These logs can confirm that suitable functionalities are being used and identify possible security issues (Bucur & Babulak, 2019), and they are available in different formats (e.g., Microsoft Windows OS uses event logs, Linux/Unix Syslog, or Rsyslog) (Bucur & Babulak, 2019). Often, cybersecurity professionals have to deal with applications where no standard log files have been defined. These log files may be formatted as text, XML, or many other formats, depending on the application type (Bucur & Babulak, 2019).

SIEM is prevalent in cybersecurity since it allows the collection and management of many types of information. SIEM can provide deep visibility into the network, systems, and applications. It ties other security tools (e.g., malware analysis, intrusion prevention tools) into a unified system that can trigger events and alerts (Death, 2017). A common challenge when using a SIEM system is deciding what logs to select and how to optimize the security log management (Raval & Verna, 2017). Organizations have limited resources, and with so many types of data sources and increasingly dynamic risks due to the leveraging of technology (e.g., IoT, device proliferation, bring your own device, cloud usage), security professionals need to make risk-based decisions about which logs will be integrated into the SIEM (Raval & Verna, 2017).

SIEM software uses analytics engines to match events against an organization's policies and to thwart attacks (Berman, 2018; Tehila, 2021). They also offer correlation tools, which means that two or more related events can trigger mitigation actions to detect attacks (Bucur & Babulak, 2019; Palomar et al., 2013), as well as the ability to retain data for some time (Berman, 2018). As Bucur and Babulak (2019) explained, SIEM manufacturers recently added artificial intelligence (AI) features to provide modeling and user behavior analysis. For instance, Microsoft Azure offers an extensive range of security options, including log file collection, stocking, and analysis tools including (a) activity logs, (b) activity log alerts, (c) metric alerts, (d) log profiles, and (e) event categories (Bucur & Babulak, 2019).

More specifically, when a SIEM identifies a potential threat through network security monitoring, it generates an alert and defines a threat level based on predetermined rules (Tehila, 2021). For example, suppose someone tries to log into an account ten times in 10 minutes. That frequency may be considered normal for the organization, but attempting to log in 100 times within 10 minutes would be flagged by the system as suspicious activity and a potential attack, requiring an investigation to corroborate the activity (Tehila, 2021). As Tehila (2021) argued, with endpoints dispersed outside the corporate network, cloud adoption on the rise, and the increased demand for remote workers to access new applications render the SIEM a critical tool. It provides security teams a centralized view of insights and activities within their IT environment, along with data analysis, event correlation, aggregation, reporting, and log management (Tehila, 2021).

Some companies offering SIEM are Splunk (Splunk Enterprise), Micro Focus (ArcSight Enterprise Security Manager), LogRhythm (LogRhythm NextGen SIEM Platform), IBM (QRadar SIEM), and LogPoint (LogPoint SIEM) (Gartner Peer Insights, 2021b).

Data Loss Prevention (DLP)

DLP is an enterprise program allowing organizations to stop various sensitive data from leaving the enterprise's infrastructure. DLP systems came into use in 2006 and gained some popularity in 2007 (AlKilani et al., 2019; Kanagasingham, 2008). Over the years, with recent high-profile data loss incidents coming to light, DLP technologies have solidified their role as important information security and privacy controls. A DLP system includes a set of rules and policies that classify data according to its type, to ensure that it is not maliciously or accidentally shared. More specifically, the system monitors end-user activities, data flow, and data sent over the network. If any suspicious activity is detected, a system alert is triggered so that a cybersecurity employee can investigate (AlKilani et al., 2019; De Groot, 2020).

Enterprise data exists in three central states, and DLP systems aim to protect the data at each stage: (1) data at rest, (2) data at the endpoint, and (3) data in motion (Hart et al., 2011; Liu & Kuhn, 2010). A DLP system identifies confidential data on network storage servers (e.g., credit card numbers or social security numbers), monitors network traffic (e.g., emails), and outputs channels to peripheral devices (e.g., USB ports). It either enforces data control policies or generates reports so that IT administrators or cybersecurity professionals can investigate potential breaches (Hart et al., 2011). For example, a DLP system may detect an employee using the corporate email network to send a file containing confidential information to his personal email address.

Some available Enterprise Data Prevention (DLP) tools are Symantec DLP by Symantec, Forcepoint DLP by Forcepoint, McAfee DLP by McAfee, Digital Guardian DLP by Digital Guardian, and Endpoint Protector by CoSoSys (Gartner Peer Insights, 2021c).

CHALLENGES IN EVALUATING SECURITY TOOLS

Within the literature on the effectiveness of cybersecurity tools, including those discussed above, there are three primary challenges related to accessing suitable datasets to produce scientific results applicable in the real world. First, a considerable number of researchers have attempted to evaluate what works and what does not (Gharib et al., 2016) when it comes to detecting abnormal behaviors and patterns that should be deemed high risks in terms of cybersecurity. However, many researchers (e.g., Alazab et al., 2014; Duque & Omar, 2015; Ji et al., 2016) use the same publicly available datasets to evaluate detection methods and do not focus on evaluating and assessing the datasets themselves (Gharib et al., 2016). As argued by Shiravi et al. (2012), 'running these systems over real labeled network traces with a comprehensive and extensive set of intrusions and abnormal behavior is the most idealistic methodology for testing and evaluation' (p. 358).

This public data allows researchers to conduct testing, but most of the datasets are relatively old and are not always applicable to the reality businesses face today. For example, the 1998 DARPA (Defense Advanced Research Project Agency) dataset was used to generate the Discovery and Data Mining (KDD) KDD Cup99 (41 features) dataset in 1999. However, as Khraisat et al. (2019) pointed out, most of these datasets are still being used today as a benchmark within the IDS research community. Thakkar and Lohiya (2020) argued that these publicly available datasets are statistically deficient and that the research community should consider this issue.

Some newer datasets – with real labeled network traces – are open to the research community: the Cooperative Association for Internet Data Analysis (CAIDA, n.d.), The Protected Repository for Defense of Infrastructure against Cyber Threats (PREDICT) (Scheper et al., 2011), The Internet Traffic Archive (LBNL/ICSI Enterprise Tracing Project) (Lawrence Berkeley National Laboratory, 2013), and DEFCON (Ring et al., 2019; Shiravi et al., 2012). However, most of these datasets are heavily anonymized with the payload entirely removed, resulting in decreased utility to researchers. In addition, the protocol information and destination are often removed, significantly affecting their effectiveness as benchmarking datasets (Shiravi et al., 2012). Overall, their low accuracy and unreliable ability to reflect real-world conditions are both problematic for research and a significant practical concern (Brown et al., 2009; Mchugh, 2000; Shiravi et al., 2012).

The second challenge is that it is complicated to access and collect data from real-world enterprise networks, due largely to business continuity, privacy, and integrity issues (Haider et al., 2017). Ahmed et al. (2016) clearly explained the research challenges of not having access to a proper dataset to improve the security posture of organizations, despite the many techniques available for anomaly detection: (1) a lack of universally applicable detection techniques, (2) data containing noise is difficult to segregate, (3) a lack of publicly available datasets, and (4) user behaviors evolve over time, so intrusion detection techniques need to be continuously adapted to meet intruders' novel attacks.

Another significant challenge is appropriately comparing two or more IDSs. The scarcity of a proper public dataset severely impairs the evaluation of IDSs, particularly affecting anomaly-based detectors. This issue has been pointed out by numerous scholars, such as Tavallaee et al. (2010). It has also been argued by Sommer and Paxson (2010) that 'the most significant challenge an evaluation faces is the lack of appropriate public datasets for assessing anomaly detection systems' (p. 5).

Surveys and think tanks reports

Many cybersecurity vendors use surveys to gather information from their users, to better understand the efficiency of the tools they offer. Most of these surveys are very interesting to read; they provide many statistics and helpful feedback from users on the benefits and challenges of using a specific tool. Gartner Peer Insights (2021a), for example, offers IDS surveys and customer reviews, a great source of information. Other than these surveys, security professionals often must rely on vendors' sale documentation to evaluate new solutions/tools and to make the best cybersecurity investment decisions for their organizations. However, several common problems plague these surveys: (a) security vendors are not conducting independent research, (b) the methodology to analyze the results is often not explained, (c) the readers cannot generalize from the findings, and (d) the answers to the survey questions do not always provide the information needed to address a given security issue.

Think tanks and research firms like Gartner and Forrester Research have security experts who review security solutions and tools and provide expert analysis. Some reports or survey data are free, but organizations must often purchase individual reports or yearly memberships for their practitioners to read these reports. For example, Gartner Magic Quadrant (i.e., challengers, leaders, niche players, and visionary security vendors) for intrusion detection and prevention systems (IDPS) (Lawson, Hils, & Neiva, 2017), which evaluates security and risk management for companies offering IDPS, can be purchased for US$1995. Forrester Research's The Top Trends Shaping Endpoint Security Suites in 2020 cost $US395 (Sherman et al., 2020). The New Tech's Zero Trust Network Access, Q2 2021 report, is available for $US2995 (Holmes et al., 2021), while their report analyzing 27 evaluation criteria of security analytics platform providers, titled The Forrester Wave: Security Analytics Platforms, Q4 2020, is available for individual purchase at US$2995 (Blankenship et al., 2020). The quality of these research firms' reports is undoubtedly much higher than the surveys conducted by security companies – which are selling their own products – since they often test the products of competing companies to be in a position to rank them.

However, think tank research significantly differs from academic research in evaluating these products. Even though some of their analysts have graduate degrees and academic training in a broad range of disciplines, their main research objectives differ (Christensen & Holst, 2020). As Christensen and Holst (2020) argued, think tank research rarely seeks to provide a complete picture of research on a specific issue. Instead, they usually take a certain angle on a larger debate. As a result, they do not always offer a representative picture of the state of the art, often focusing instead on politically relevant conclusions. In other instances, they will seek knowledge confirming their viewpoints while disregarding unpopular findings (Christensen & Holst, 2020). Accordingly, there is still a perception that think tank security research is not always as independent as it should be. As Chafuen (2016) mentioned, think tanks often do the opposite of what should be done in independent research: 'they start with a conclusion commissioned by private research funding or donors, then produce research accommodating a pre-determined narrative' (Chafuen, 2016). Thus, their studies raise specific methodological challenges, including their lack of independence (Christensen & Holst, 2020). Furthermore, unlike some academic research, their results are not free of charge or open to everyone seeking to improve the security ecosystem or the greater good.

Intrusion-detection assessment metrics

The efficacy of cybersecurity tools is often evaluated through user surveys, third-party data analysis, think tank analysts' reports, and vendors' information regarding their products. These sources of information offer insight about each tool, such as the key performance indicators (KPI) that most organizations use, how the tool allows better visibility of threats, frequent use cases deployed by organizations using the tool, its attack detection capabilities to detect possible security events or compromise, or its detection rates. Other reviews identify challenges companies using the products commonly have to overcome (e.g., lack of skilled security staff to operate the systems, time spent per alert, manual rule creation, system integration, or being overwhelmed by too many false positives) (Alien Vault, 2019).

When it comes to the work being done by the security operation center (SOC), events, alerts, and incidents can be integrated into SOC processes (Death, 2017). An *event* is a change to an expected behavior (e.g., by a process, system, workflow, or employee), an *alert* is provided by a security system or tool (e.g., SIEM) to identify an event or a combination of events, and an *incident* is a malicious event that may negatively impact the organization and must be remediated (Death, 2017). A common issue for organizations using these tools is that they regularly generate numerous events, which can significantly impact the productivity of security operations and reduce the tool's organizational value in terms of risk management. More specifically, analysts must work through more events to get to a potential cybersecurity incident, as there are too many false *events* or *alerts* consuming analysts' time. This high false-positive (FP) ratio often requires hiring more analysts, requiring more financial and HR investments to reduce the backlog of alerts.

Security professionals want security tools to collect, process, and contextualize a large quantity of data, then filter the noise out of events and alerts so analysts may focus on potential incidents. Intrusion-detection assessment metrics are derived based on four indicators: (1) a true positive state is when the IDS identifies an activity as an attack and the activity is actually an attack, (2) a true negative is successfully ignoring acceptable behavior, (3) a false positive state is when the IDS identifies an activity as an attack, but the activity is of acceptable behavior, and (4) a false negative state is the most serious dangerous state and it is when an IDS identifies an activity as acceptable while the activity is actually an attack (OWAPS, 2022).

As Dykstra (2015) noted, both FPs and FNs occur in imperfect systems. A *FP* occurs when the solution incorrectly identifies the presence of an event or phenomenon when it was absent, thus giving a false alarm. In contrast, a *FN* occurs when the solution incorrectly identifies the absence of an event or phenomenon when it was present (Dykstra, 2015). Death (2017) considered this the most dangerous condition. Unfortunately, evaluations of cybersecurity tools rarely consider the effectiveness of the tools in terms of FP or FN ratios, or the critical impact of those ratios on organizations' investment and risk management.

These alerts are also problematic for security operation centers (SOC) analysts, leading to *alert fatigue* (Goodchild, 2021; Halder & Ozdemir, 2018). Alert fatigue may occur when an overwhelming number of alerts are created, desensitizing security analysts to them due to the high FP ratio (i.e., false alerts) (Gillis, 2021). Security alerts have different levels of importance. Analysts may become complacent by assuming that what they are seeing is not significant enough to justify a response (e.g., Dave is once again logging into a production server as root, but we verified it with him last week, so it must be normal). Analysts might close the alert instead of escalating it to an incident severity level; thus, they are distracted from the real threats (Matteson, 2021). Similarly, if too many incidents are categorized as inconsequential, analysts may ignore some of the most critical incidents or flag the alerts as being false alarms (Gillis, 2021). Regardless of the statistics that cybersecurity vendors produce, optimal IDSs are those that achieve high detection rates while at the same time generating a small number of false alarms (Elhag et al., 2015).

THE WAY FORWARD IN PROTECTING THE NETWORK FROM INTRUSIONS

Data science: data analytics, machine learning, and artificial intelligence

To better understand and analyze these actual phenomena with data, various scientific methods, machine learning techniques, processes, and systems are used to manage security incidents (Sarker et al., 2020). This is commonly known as *data science*, a concept intended to make computing processes more actionable and intelligent compared to traditional methods (e.g., rule-based) widely used in cybersecurity operations (Sarker et al., 2020). As Sarker et al. (2020) pointed out, data science is a new strategy in cybersecurity compared to other traditional security solutions like firewalls, user authentication methods, access controls, and cryptography. Most of these traditional security solutions have their own merits but are no longer effective in dealing with current cybersecurity threats (e.g., unauthorized access, malware attacks, denial of service, phishing, social engineering, insider threat, and zero-day attacks). Traditional systems also used to be managed by security professionals, and data management was done in an ad hoc manner instead of being a priority (Sarker et al., 2020).

Unfortunately, with the increasing number of cyber incidents over the years, these conventional solutions have encountered numerous limitations in mitigating cyber-risks. Security is now all about data and behavioral analytics, so to manage cybersecurity adequately, security professionals should analyze raw data (e.g., files, logs, network packets, etc.) to transform it into effective decision-making (Sarker et al., 2020). Therefore, the cybersecurity community needs to develop more flexible and efficient security mechanisms to respond to novel threats, both intelligently and promptly (Sarker et al., 2020). This can only be done through better use of data. Effective tools must analyze a massive amount of relevant data generated from various network and system sources, as well as discovering insights or appropriate security policies with minimal human intervention in an automated manner (Sarker et al., 2020).

Many researchers use the term 'data science' to describe the interdisciplinary field of collecting and preprocessing data, then inferring or making decisions based on data analysis (Sarker et al., 2020). According to Sarker et al. (2020), understanding data involves studying, processing, and extracting valuable insights from a set of information. Thus, the development of data mining, knowledge discovery, and machine learning consists of creating algorithms and programs that learn on their own (Sarker et al., 2020). The original data analysis and descriptive analytics, from the statistical perspective, form the general concept of 'data analytics' (Cao, 2017; Sarker et al., 2020).

From a rule-based approach to data analytics

Data analytics has been used to prevent and detect fraud for decades, using methods that range from detection rules to artificial neural networks (Pomerleau & Auger-Perreault, 2020). Detection rules are based on expert knowledge and can be easily explained to client organizations, their management, or potential users. However, to keep up with the ever-changing tactics of cyberattackers, rules must continually be added to or adjusted to remain relevant, and monitoring their effectiveness is complicated. Most SOC cybersecurity tools rely on rules to create events, alerts, and potential cybersecurity incidents to be looked at by security analysts. They must also be maintained in an inventory and their performance tracked, leading to complex and time-consuming rules management systems. While a single rule is easily explainable, hundreds of rules may nullify that advantage (Ryman-Tubb et al., 2018).

Machine learning and artificial intelligence

Machine learning models – a core part of AI – have also been used to discover insights from data and to prevent and detect fraud, most notably in credit card fraud management (Pomerleau & Auger-Perreault, 2020; Sarker et al., 2020). While machine learning is not as often used in cybersecurity to reduce the FP ratios of events and alerts, organizations are deploying significant efforts to improve cybersecurity operations using machine learning and AI. Analyzing cybersecurity data and creating the right tools and processes to successfully protect against cybersecurity incidents requires more than a simple set of functional requirements and knowledge about risks, threats, or vulnerabilities. Extracting security incident patterns and insights from cybersecurity data is key to building a corresponding data-driven model and making a security system automated and intelligent (Sarker et al., 2020). Several machine learning models can be used to extract insights or patterns of security incidents effectively.

There are three categories of machine learning models: *supervised, unsupervised*, and *reinforcement* or semi-supervised learning (Edgar & Manz, 2017), with supervised and unsupervised learning being the most prevalent in fraud risk management (Pomerleau & Auger-Perreault, 2020). Supervised learning algorithms like decision trees, logistic regression, and support vector machines require labeled data, such as confirmed fraudulent transactions or security incidents. Unsupervised learning, such as clustering (e.g., K-means clustering, hierarchical clustering, or principal component analysis) (Edgar & Manz, 2017), does not use labeled data but helpfully facilitates the detection of anomalies (Pomerleau & Auger-Perreault, 2020). Semi-supervised learning (e.g., expectation-maximization, transductive support vector machine, or Markov decision processes) may be used when it is known that a small number of variables lead to a result, but the full extent of variables involved is unknown (Edgar & Manz, 2017).

As Sarker et al. (2020) explained, association rule learning is another example of how machine learning-based policy rules can prevent cyberattacks. In an expert system, the rules are usually manually defined by an engineer or computer scientist working in collaboration with a domain expert (i.e., cybersecurity professional), since both kinds of expertise are necessary (Khraisat et al., 2019; Kim et al., 2014; Sarker, 2019). On the contrary, association rule learning involves the discovery of rules or relationships among a set of available security features (e.g., malware analysis, spam analysis, and anomalies) or attributes (e.g., ID, key number, or letter in a customer database) in a given dataset (Agrawal et al., 1993; Sarker et al., 2020).

Using these techniques, computer scientists can manipulate and analyze security data more effectively and efficiently. This may generate valuable insights from data to improve the work of cybersecurity analysts working in a SOC, to make sure they spend most of their time working on potential security incidents instead of FP alerts. It also helps optimize cybersecurity solutions and build automated and intelligent security systems (Sarker et al., 2020). For instance, in terms of problem understanding, gathering security data from diverse sources and preparing the data to feed into various models (data-driven model building and updating) can improve the efficacy of cybersecurity teams. Overall, machine learning can significantly improve the cybersecurity landscape, and data science is rapidly advancing a new scientific paradigm (Cukier, 2010; Hey et al., 2009; Sarker et al., 2020).

For more information on the concept of cybersecurity data science, we strongly recommend reading the following publication:
Sarker, I. H., Kayes, A. S. M., Badsha, S., Alqahtani, H., Watters, P., & Ng, A. (2020). Cybersecurity data science: An overview from machine learning perspective. *Journal of Big Data*, 7(1), 1–29. https://doi.org/10.1186/s40537-020-00318-5

The use of honeypots in intrusion detection and network security

Since conventional systems, such as the ones discussed at the beginning of this chapter, may have enormous implementation costs and still create high FP ratios, they do not adequately mitigate an organization's risks. Another approach is to use a honeypot, a computer system serving as *bait* for cyberattackers. When cyberattackers infiltrate a honeypot system, security professionals or researchers may study the intruder's tactics, tools, and procedures (Malwarebytes Labs, 2021). A survey conducted by the Neustar International Security Council demonstrates that 72% of security professional respondents either already use or are willing to use honeypots or similar technologies (Turpitka, 2020).

As is the case with machine learning, the use of honeypots is not necessarily new in cybersecurity (e.g., Lance Spitzner published his book *Honeypots: Tracking Hackers* in 2003). However, as a cybersecurity strategy it has gotten considerable attention in the last few years. According to Sanders (2020), an intrusion detection honeypot is

a security resource placed inside your network perimeter that generates alerts when probed, attacked, or compromised. These systems, services, or tokens rely on deception to lure attackers in and convince them to interact. Unbeknownst to the attacker, you're alerted when an interaction occurs and can begin investigating the compromise. This approach lends itself to intrusion detection with a low false-positive rate and minimal maintenance overhead, lowering your cost to defend data. This method is also extensible, allowing you to configure increased interaction levels that help discern your attacker's tradecraft and goals. (p. 3)

In recent years, many researchers have studied different honeypot techniques, strategies, and infrastructure designs to develop real-time IDPS (Baykara & Das, 2018; Xiangfeng et al., 2014). Recent efforts include the design and implementation of a distributed IDS based on honeypots (Malaník & Kouril, 2013; Yang & Mi, 2010), using honeypots to detect man-in-the-middle attacks in cloud computing (Satyavathi et al., 2019), and capturing and analyzing malicious traffic in voice over IP (VoIP) environments using a low-interaction honeypot (Vargas & Kleinschmidt, 2015). Other scholars have focused on detecting malicious web URLs on client-side honeypot systems (Shukla & Singh, 2014), deploying honeypots for the analysis and visualization of malware activity and malicious connections (Koniaris et al., 2014), dynamic and hybrid honeypot models for scalable network monitoring (Chawda & Patel, 2014), honeypot applications in the security of employment networks (Guizhou & Liu, 2012), honeypots in high-interaction systems (Akiyama et al., 2012), the usage of autonomous hybrid honeypots for distributed heterogeneous computer systems in the education process (Fanfara et al., 2013), honeypot architecture for identifying malicious network activities (Sadasivam & Hota, 2015), aggressive web application honeypots for exposing attackers' identities (Djanali et al., 2014), and even characterizing unwanted traffic on IP networks via low-interaction honeypots (Puska et al., 2014).

The main reason why using honeypots is fascinating is that most experienced security practitioners know very well that even a *minimally* sophisticated attacker with enough tenacity, motivation, and resources will eventually penetrate the organization. Hence, it's important to consider that every company's security perimeter (if we can still call it a perimeter, since remote work and bring-your-own-device policies have decentralized most borders) will be compromised at one point or another. Thus, honeypots are extremely meaningful for detecting and tracking attackers after a system or the organization's security controls have been compromised. As Sanders (2020) wrote, an organization does not lose when attackers get in the system; it loses when the attacker exfiltrates intellectual property, customer data, credit card numbers, and other sensitive information that the organization should have appropriately protected.

Moreover, a research honeypot can also serve forensic purposes, quietly gathering data about the hackers who break in to better understand their modus operandi and improve future preventative and detective defense measures (Turpitka, 2020). It's also a low-cost and high-efficiency detection tool for an organization to implement (Sanders, 2020). As Turpitka (2020) noted, cybersecurity companies and antivirus providers are the most common users of honeypots, but the technology is also beneficial for both public and private organizations. For example, in retail, where credit card numbers are at high risk, a honeypot full of fake card numbers means successful attacks are inconsequential (Turpitka, 2020). Moreover, other industries that deal with sensitive data in high volumes (especially government, financial services, and healthcare) can benefit from hiding a decoy inside the data to detect potential insider threats, for example (Turpitka, 2020).

The value of using honeypots lies in their being probed and attacked, so studying an attack's phases should serve specific purposes within organizations in a broader context of security architecture (Sanders, 2020). A honeypot sits dormant; it is deceptive, discoverable, interactive, and monitored; and it does not trigger any alerts until someone communicates with it (Sanders, 2020). There are three primary types of honeypots: (1) a *honey system*, (2) a *honey service*, and (3) a *honey token*. As Sanders (2020) clearly explained, a honey system will mimic the interaction of an operating system (e.g., Windows 10) and the services it provides, a honey service (e.g., an FTP server with open guest access) mimics the interaction of a specific software or protocol function, and a honey token (e.g., an unused user account and password) mimics legitimate data.

It is important to incorporate various tools to assess the activities that the honeypot monitors (Turpitka, 2020). For example, if the honeypot is intended to run malware (by mimicking software applications and APIs to invite malware attacks), it is recommended to use various antiviruses and firewalls to detect malicious activities. Also, it is recognized as a best practice to use machine learning and next-generation approaches to analyze the monitored activities instead of creating heuristics and rules, which most often create a high number of alerts (Turpitka, 2020).

The literature often distinguishes low-level honeypots from high-interaction honeypots (Briffaut et al., 2013). Low-level honeypots emulate a limited part of the services, mainly the network protocols, and allow statistical results to be computed and attack activities to be modeled. By contrast, high-interaction honeypots deploy real operating systems that will enable complete information to be captured (Briffaut et al., 2013). Most security professionals know there are no simple algorithms to analyze data from multiple sources such as file activity, network interactions, process, thread creation events, etc. On the other hand, it is not recommended to create a high-interaction honeypot in which an attacker may execute an action on the operating system in production (Turpitka, 2020).

A honeypot must rely on a controllable environment to be safe; otherwise, the attacker may compromise the operating system, get access to the infrastructure, and even destroy it (Turpitka, 2020). In addition, cybersecurity practitioners using honeypots within their infrastructure should not expect speed and scalability from high-interaction honeypots: a reliable environment for multi-vector threats requires significant resources (Turpitka, 2020). Finally, simple rules should not be used to whitelist normal activities in the systems. Even though doing so may seem intuitive and straightforward, it may require many weeks of work to add several hundred new rules, and new potentially malicious activities will still show up (Turpitka, 2020).

An evidence-based approach

Taking an Evidence-Based Cybersecurity Approach to this common cybersecurity challenge, significant efforts should be made to better understand cyberattackers' online behaviors and responses to situational stimuli during system trespassing events initiated against different types of computing environments. To this end, organizations should learn from the unique experimental designs of Maimon et al. (2014, 2015, 2019) for the intentional deployment of target computing platforms and networks (i.e., network 'honeypots' or 'bait traps') to study the behaviors and techniques of cyberattackers as they attempt to further infiltrate and attack the 'baited' computing system. Findings from such studies will facilitate the design of computer systems that better predict attackers' decision-making processes during system trespassing events and, consequently, make their detection by IDSs and IT security teams easier to achieve.

> For more information about honeypots and how to implement them, we strongly suggest the book written by Sanders (2020):
> Sanders, C. (2020). *Intrusion detection honeypots: Detection through deception.* Applied Network Defense. https://www.amazon.com/dp/1735188301/ref=cm_sw_r_em_api_i_CJRyFbHD8YFWJ

CONCLUSION

Network security aims to protect the network from illegal activity while allowing network users to perform their critical functions within a secure online environment. Various IDSs and cybersecurity tools are available to manage cyber-risks. Current methodologies for evaluating these security solutions rely primarily on user surveys, third-party data, think tank analysts' reports, and vendors' analysis. Many tools and systems currently used by private and public organizations to manage cybersecurity generate too many false alarms and negatively influence security analysts, causing them to work on low-risk events instead of focusing on security incidents that can significantly impact organizations. Previous studies on network security and IDSs are quantitative, based on complicated risk formulas and open-source databases that are not easily applicable in the real world. Most of the existing machine learning techniques used in the literature were trained and evaluated on the knowledge provided by the old datasets, such as DARPA/KDD99, which do not include trending patterns of intrusions or account for evolving cyber-threats and insider threat activities.

This chapter demonstrated that managing network security risks requires a multi-pronged approach, combining the right cybersecurity tools with machine learning techniques and the deployment of honeypots. Research and best practices in network security and intrusion detection should be available for everyone to work together to improve organizations' security postures. Specifically, researchers and practitioners should partner together to evaluate network and IDSs while relying on an evidence-based approach to measure the efficacy of cybersecurity tools and strategies. Cyber operation strategies are frequently changing due to the evolving risks and may not remain effective over time. Thus, there is a need for newer and more comprehensive datasets that contain a broad spectrum of cyber-threats affecting organizations. This is why organizations need to work with researchers to constantly create new knowledge in cybersecurity. Cyber-threats are not static, so the tools and strategies used to counter them also need to be dynamic, flexible, and adaptable.

NOTE

* We identify certain companies' products in this chapter, but such identification does not imply a recommendation of these companies or tools by the authors.

REFERENCES

Agrawal, R., Imieliński, T., & Swami, A. (1993). Mining association rules between sets of items in large databases. In *Proceedings of the 1993 ACM SIGMOD International Conference on Management of Data* (pp. 207–216). Association for Computing Machinery. https://doi.org/10.1145/170035.170072

Ahmed, M., Mahmood, A., & Hu, N., J. (2016). A survey of network anomaly detection techniques. *Journal of Network and Computer Applications, 60*(2016), 19–31. https://doi.org/10.1016/j.jnca.2015.11.016

Akiyama, M., Kawakoya, Y., & Hariu, T. (2012). Scalable and performance-efficient client honeypot on high interaction system. In *2012 IEEE/IPSJ 12th International Symposium on Applications and the Internet* (pp. 40–50). https://doi.org/10.1109/SAINT.2012.15

Alazab, A., Hobbs, M., Abawajy, J., Khraisat, A., & Alazab, M. (2014). Using response action with intelligent intrusion detection and prevention system against web application malware. *Information Management & Computer Security, 22*(5), 431–449.

Alien Vault. (2019). *2019 SIEM survey report.* https://cybersecurity.att.com/resource-center/analyst-reports/siem-survey-report

AlKilani, H., Nasereddin, M., Hadi, A., & Tedmori, S. (2019). Data exfiltration techniques and data loss prevention system. In *2019 International Arab Conference on Information Technology (ACIT)* (pp. 124–127). https://doi.org/10.1109/ACIT47987.2019.8991131

Baykara, M., & Das, R. (2018). A novel honeypot based security approach for realtime intrusion detection and prevention systems. *Journal of Information Security and Applications, 41*, 103–116. https://doi.org/10.1016/j.jisa.2018.06.004

Berman, D. (2018). *What is a SIEM?* https://logz.io/blog/what-is-siem/

Berthier, R., & Sanders, W. H. (2011). Specification-based intrusion detection for advanced metering infrastructures. In *2011 IEEE 17th Pacific Rim International Symposium on Dependable Computing, Dependable Computing (PRDC)* (pp. 184–193). https://doi.org/10.1109/PRDC.2011.30

Blankenship, J., O'Malley, C., Balaouras, S., Bouffard, A., & Dostie, P. (2020). *The Forrester wave: Security analytics platforms, Q2 2020.* https://www.forrester.com/report/The+Forrester+Wave+Security+Analytics+Platforms+Q4+2020/-/E-RES157496?objectid=RES157496

Briffaut, J., Clemente, P., Lalande, J., & Rouzaud-Cornabas, J. (2013). *Honeypot forensics for system and network SIEM design.* https://www.researchgate.net/publication/236216116_Honeypot_forensics_for_system_and_network_SIEM_design

Brown, C., Cowperthwaite, A., Hijazi, A., & Somayaji, A. (2009). Analysis of the 1999 DARPA/Lincoln laboratory IDS evaluation data with netadhict. In *2009 IEEE Symposium on Computational Intelligence for Security and Defense Applications* (pp. 1–7). https://doi.org/10.1109/CISDA.2009.5356522

Bucur, C., & Babulak, E. (2019). Security validation testing environment in the cloud. In *2019 IEEE International Conference on Big Data* (pp. 4240–4247). https://doi.org/10.1109/BigData47090.2019.9006202

CAIDA. (n.d.). *The cooperative association for internet data analysis.* https://www.caida.org/catalog/papers/1996_caida/

Cao, L. (2017). Data science: Challenges and directions. *Communications of the ACM, 60*(8), 59–68. https://cacm.acm.org/magazines/2017/8/219605-data-science/fulltext

Chafuen, A. (2016). *Transparency and independence: Think tanks rather than lobbying tanks.* https://www.forbes.com/sites/alejandrochafuen/2016/05/02/transparency-and-independence-think-tanks-rather-than-lobbying-tanks/?sh=6e3f0fdb5ea9

Chawda, K., & Patel, A. D. (2014). Dynamic and hybrid honeypot model for scalable network monitoring. In *International Conference on Information Communication and Embedded Systems (ICICES2014)* (pp. 1–5). https://doi.org/10.1109/ICICES.2014.7033844

Cheng, J., Wang, L., Jia, G., & Liu, Q. (2020). Research on effectiveness evaluation model of intrusion detection system based on cost and performance. In *2020 IEEE 9th Joint International Information Technology and Artificial Intelligence Conference (ITAIC)* (pp. 1143–1147). https://doi.org/10.1109/ITAIC49862.2020.9338872

Christensen, J., & Holst, C. (2020). How do advocacy think tanks relate to academic knowledge? The case of Norway. *Scandinavian Political Studies, 43*(3), 223–239. https://doi.org/10.1111/1467-9477.12184

Cukier, K. (2010). *Data, data everywhere.* https://www.economist.com/special-report/2010/02/27/data-data-everywhere

Death, D. (2017). *Information security handbook.* https://www.packtpub.com/product/information-security-handbook/9781788478830

Deloitte. (n.d.). *Endpoint security risks are rising.* https://www2.deloitte.com/content/dam/Deloitte/lu/Documents/risk/lu-endpoint-security-risks-rising.pdf

De Groot, J. (2020). *What is data loss prevention (DLP)? A definition of data loss prevention.* https://digitalguardian.com/blog/what-data-loss-prevention-dlp-definition-data-loss-prevention

Djanali, S., Arunanto, F., Pratomo, B. A., Baihaqi, A., Studiawan, H., & Shiddiqi, A. M. (2014). Aggressive web application honeypot for exposing attacker's identity. In *The 1st International Conference on Information Technology, Computer, and Electrical Engineering* (pp. 212–216). https://doi.org/10.1109/ICITACEE.2014.7065744

Duque, S., & Omar, M. N. B. (2015). Using data mining algorithms for developing a model for intrusion detection system (IDS). *Procedia Computer Science, 61*, 46–51. https://doi.org/10.1016/j.procs.2015.09.145

Dykstra, J. (2015). *Essential cybersecurity science: Build, test, and evaluate secure systems*. O'Reilly.

Edgar, T. W., & Manz, D. O. (2017). *Research methods for cyber security*. Syngress.

Elhag, S., Fernández, A., Bawakid, A., Alshomrani, S., & Herrera, F. (2015). On the combination of genetic fuzzy systems and pairwise learning for improving detection rates on intrusion detection systems. *Expert System with Application, 42*(1), 193–202. https://doi.org/10.1016/j.eswa.2014.08.002

Fanfara, P., Dufala, M., & Chovancová, E. (2013). Usage of proposed autonomous hybrid honeypot for distributed heterogeneous computer systems in education process. In *IEEE 11th International Conference on Emerging eLearning Technologies and Applications (ICETA)* (pp. 83–88). https://doi.org/10.1109/ICETA.2013.6674409

Fruhlinger, J. (2018). *What is network security? Definitions, methods, jobs & salaries*. https://www.csoonline.com/article/3285651/what-is-network-security-definition-methods-jobs-and-salaries.html

Gartner Peer Insights. (2021a). *Intrusion detection and prevention systems reviews and ratings*. https://www.gartner.com/reviews/market/intrusion-prevention-systems

Gartner Peer Insights. (2021b). *Security information and event management (SIEM) reviews and ratings*. https://www.gartner.com/reviews/market/security-information-event-management

Gartner Peer Insights. (2021c). *Enterprise data loss prevention (DLP) reviews and ratings*. https://www.gartner.com/reviews/market/enterprise-data-loss-prevention

Gharib, A., Sharafaldin, I., Lashkari, A. H., & Ghorbani, A. A. (2016). An evaluation framework for intrusion detection dataset. *International Conference on Information Science and Security (ICISS)*, 2016, 1–6. https://doi.org/10.1109/ICISSEC.2016.7885840

Gillis, A. S. (2021). *Alert fatigue*. https://whatis.techtarget.com/definition/alert-fatigue

Goodchild, J. (2021). *SOC teams burdened by alert fatigue explore XDR*. https://www.darkreading.com/analytics/soc-teams-burdened-by-alert-fatigue-explore-xdr/d/d-id/1341017

Guizhou, J., & Liu, Z. (2012). New honeypot system and its application in security of employment network. In *2012 IEEE Symposium on Robotics and Applications (ISRA)* (pp. 627–629). https://doi.org/10.1109/ISRA.2012.6219267

Haider, W., Hu, J., Slay, J., Turnbull, B., & Xie, Y. (2017). Generating a realistic intrusion detection system dataset based on fuzzy qualitative modeling. *Journal of Network and Computer Applications, 87*(2017), 185–192. https://doi.org/10.1016/j.jnca.2017.03.018.

Halder, S., & Ozdemir, S. (2018). *Hands-on machine learning for cybersecurity: Safeguard your system by making your machines intelligent using the Python ecosystem*. Packt Publishing.

Hart, M., Manadhata, P., & Johnson, R. (2011). Text classification for data loss prevention. In S. Fischer-Hübner, & N. Hopper (Eds.), *Privacy enhancing technologies. Lecture notes in computer science* (Vol. 6794, pp. 18–37). Springer. https://doi.org/10.1007/978-3-642-22263-4_2

Hassan, W. U., Bates, A., & Marino, D. (2020). Tactical provenance analysis for endpoint detection and response systems. In *2020 IEEE Symposium on Security and Privacy (SP)* (pp. 1172–1189). https://doi.org/10.1109/SP40000.2020.00096

Hey, T., Tansley, S., & Tolle, K. (2009). *The fourth paradigm: Data-intensive scientific discovery.* https://www.microsoft.com/en-us/research/wp-content/uploads/2009/10/Fourth_Paradigm.pdf

Holmes, D., Blankenship, J., Bouffard, A., & Dostie, P. (2021). *New tech: Zero trust network access, Q2 2021.* https://www.forrester.com/report/New+Tech+Zero+Trust+Network+Access+Q2+2021/-/E-RES161768

Ji, S.-Y., Jeong, B.-K., Choi, S., & Jeong, D. H. (2016). A multi-level intrusion detection method for abnormal network behaviors. *Journal of Network and Computer Applications, 62,* 9–17. https://doi.org/10.1016/j.jnca.2015.12.004

Kanagasingham, P. (2008). *Data loss prevention.* SANS Institute. https://www.sans.org/reading-room/whitepapers/dlp/data-loss-prevention-32883

Khraisat, A., Gondal, I., Vamplew, P., & Kamruzzaman, J. (2019). Survey of intrusion detection systems: Techniques, datasets and challenges. *Cybersecurity, 2*(1), 1–22. https://doi.org/10.1186/s42400-019-0038-7

Kiedrowicz, M., & Stanik, J. (2018). Method for assessing efficiency of the information security management system. *MATEC Web of Conferences, 210,* 04011. https://doi.org/10.1051/matecconf/201821004011

Kim, G., Lee, S., & Kim, S. (2014). A novel hybrid intrusion detection method integrating anomaly detection with misuse detection. *Expert Systems with Applications, 41*(4), 1690–1700. https://doi.org/10.1016/j.eswa.2013.08.066

Koniaris, I., Papadimitriou, G., Nicopolitidis, P., & Obaidat, M. (2014). Honeypots deployment for the analysis and visualization of malware activity and malicious connections. In *2014 IEEE International Conference on Communications (ICC)* (pp. 1819–1824). https://doi.org/10.1109/ICC.2014.6883587

Lawson, C., Hils, A., & Neiva, C. (2017). Gartner magic quadrant for intrusion detection and prevention systems. Retrieved from https://www.gartner.com/en/documents/3571417/magic-quadrant-for-intrusion-detection-and-prevention-sy

Lawrence Berkeley National Laboratory. (2013). *LBNL/ICSI Enterprise Tracing Project.* http://www.icir.org/enterprise-tracing/Overview.html

Liu, S., & Kuhn, R. (2010). Data loss prevention. *IEEE Computer Society Digital Library, 12* (2010), 10–13. https://doi.org/10.1109/MITP.2010.52.

Maimon, D., Alper, M., Sobesto, B., & Cukier, M. (2014). Restrictive deterrent effects of a warning banner in an attacked computer system. *Criminology, 52*(1), 33–59. https://doi.org/10.1111/1745-9125.12028

Maimon, D., Testa, A., Sobesto, B., Cukier, M., & Wuling, R. (2019). Predictably deterrable? The case of system trespassers. In G. Wang, J. Feng, M. Bhuiyan, & R. Lu (Eds.), *Security, privacy, and anonymity in computation, communication, and storage* (pp. 317–330). Springer.

Maimon, D., Wilson, T., Ren, W., & Berenblum, T. (2015). On the relevance of spatial and temporal dimensions in assessing computer susceptibility to system trespassing incidents. *The British Journal of Criminology, 55*(3), 615–634. https://doi.org/10.1093/bjc/azu104

Malaník, D., & Kouril, L. (2013). Honeypot as the intruder detection system. In *WSEAS International Conference on Computers* (pp. 96–101). https://www.semanticscholar.org/paper/Honeypot-as-the-Intruder-Detection-System-Malan%C3%ADk-Kou%C5%99il/2f0a86543b9c0c18f08311539237f74fe3601dfa

Malwarebytes Labs. (2021). *What is a honeypot? How they are used in cyberse-curity.* https://blog.malwarebytes.com/101/2021/05/what-is-a-honeypot-how-they-are-used-in-cybersecurity/

Matteson, S. (2021). *Cybersecurity: There's no such thing as a false positive.* https://www.techrepublic.com/article/cybersecurity-theres-no-such-thing-as-a-false-positive/

Mchugh, J. (2000). Testing intrusion detection systems: A critique of the 1998 and 1999 DARPA intrusion detection system evaluations as performed by Lincoln laboratory. *ACM Transactions on Information System Security, 3*(24), 262–294.

Osterman Research. (2019). *The critical role of endpoint detection and response.* https://cdw-prod.adobecqms.net/content/dam/cdw/on-domain-cdw/brands/trend-mirco/the-critical-role-of-edr-osterman-whitepaper-april-2019.pdf

OWAPS. (2022). Intrusion detection. Retrieved from https://owasp.org/www-community/controls/Intrusion_Detection

Ozkaya, E., & Aslaner, M. (2019). *Hands-on cybersecurity for finance.* Packt Publishers.

Pomerleau, P. L., & Auger-Perreault, M. (2020). Fraud risk management: Using fraud analytics to combat external and insider threats. In L. Shapiro, & M. H. Maras (Eds.), *Encyclopedia of security and emergency management* (pp. 1–9). Springer. https://doi.org/10.1007/978-3-319-69891-5_296-1

Puska, A., Nogueira, M., & Santos, A. (2014). Unwanted traffic characterization on IP networks by low interactive honeypot. In *10th International Conference on Network and Service Management (CNSM) and Workshop* (pp. 284–287). https://doi.org/10.1109/CNSM.2014.7014175

Rathore, M., Ahmad, A., & Paul, A. (2016). Real time intrusion detection system for ultra-high-speed big data environments. *Journal of Supercomputing, 72*(9), 3489–3510. https://doi.org/10.1007/s11227-015-1615-5

Raval, V., & Verna, S. (2017). The practical aspect: Challenges of security log management. *ISACA Journal, 6*, 1–5.

Ring, M., Wunderlich, S., Scheuring, D., Landes, D., & Hotho, A. (2019). A survey of network-based intrusion detection data sets. *Computers & Security, 86*, 147–167. https://doi.org/10.1016/j.cose.2019.06.005

Ryman-Tubb, F. N., Krause, P., & Garn, W. (2018). How artificial intelligence and machine learning research impacts payment card fraud detection: A survey and industry benchmark. *Engineering Applications of Artificial Intelligence, 76*, 130–157. https://doi.org/10.1016/j.engappai.2018.07.008

Sadasivam, G., & Hota, K., C. (2015). Scalable honeypot architecture for identifying malicious network activities. In *2015 International Conference on Emerging Information Technology and Engineering Solutions* (pp. 27–31). https://doi.org/10.1109/EITES.2015.15

Samrin, R., & Vasumathi, D. (2017). Review on anomaly based network intrusion detection system. In *2017 International Conference on Electrical, Electronics, Communication, Computer, and Optimization Techniques (ICEECCOT)* (pp. 141–147). https://doi.org/10.1109/ICEECCOT.2017.8284655

Sanders, C. (2020). *Intrusion detection honeypots: Detection through deception.* Applied Network Defense. https://www.amazon.com/dp/1735188301/ref=cm_sw_r_em_api_i_CJRyFbHD8YFWJ

SANS. (n.d.). *Network security resources.* https://www.sans.org/network-security

Sarker, I. H. (2019). Context-aware rule learning from smartphone data: Survey, challenges and future directions. *Journal of Big Data, 6*(1), 1–25. https://doi.org/10.1186/s40537-019-0258-4

Sarker, I. H., Kayes, A. S. M., Badsha, S., Alqahtani, H., Watters, P., & Ng, A. (2020). Cybersecurity data science: An overview from machine learning perspective. *Journal of Big Data, 7*(1), 1–29. https://doi.org/10.1186/s40537-020-00318-5

Satyavathi, P., Devarapalli, D., & Reddy, K. (2019). *IDS with honeypot to detect man in the middle attacks in cloud computing.* https://doi.org/10.23956/IJARCSSE.V9I8.1063. https://www.semanticscholar.org/paper/IDS-with-Honey-Pot-to-Detect-Man-in-Middle-Attacks-Satyavathi-Devarapalli/c1c0832351580a92f9f6dde24f26d10a20ac157d

Scarfone, K., & Mell, P. (2007). *Special publication 800-94: Guide to intrusion detection and prevention systems (IDPS).* National Institute of Standards and Technology (NIST). https://tsapps.nist.gov/publication/get_pdf.cfm?pub_id=901146

Scheper, C., Cantor, S., & Maughan, W. D. (2011). *PREDICT: A trusted framework for sharing data for cyber security research.* BADGERS '11. https://www.semanticscholar.org/paper/PREDICT%3A-a-trusted-framework-for-sharing-data-for-Scheper-Cantor/30db4b22b346fa9451f17d1d71e0f760da53dc4f

Sherman, C., Maxim, M., Corey, B., & Dostie, P. (2020). *The top trends shaping endpoint security suites in 2020.* https://www.forrester.com/report/The+Top+Trends+Shaping+Endpoint+Security+Suites+In+2020/-/E-RES159055

Shiravi, A., Shiravi, H., Tavallaee, M., & Ghorbani, A. A. (2012). Toward developing a systematic approach to generate benchmark datasets for intrusion detection. *Computers & Security, 31*(3), 357–374. https://doi.org/10.1016/j.cose.2011.12.012

Shread, P. (2020). *Top endpoint detection and response (EDR) solutions.* https://www.esecurityplanet.com/products/top-endpoint-detection-response-solutions.html#methodology

Shukla, R., & Singh, M. (2014). PythonHoneyMonkey: Detecting malicious web URLs on client-side honeypot systems. In *INFOCOM Technologies and Optimization Proceedings of 3rd International Conference on Reliability* (pp. 1–5). https://ieeexplore.ieee.org/stamp/stamp.jsp?tp=&arnumber=7014753

Sommer, R., & Paxson, V. (2010). Outside the closed world: On using machine learning for network intrusion detection. *2010 IEEE Symposium on Security and Privacy, Security and Privacy (SP)* (pp. 305–316). https://doi.org/10.1109/SP.2010.25

Sujeong, K., Chanwoong, H., & Taejin, L. (2020). Anomaly based unknown intrusion detection in endpoint environments. *Electronics, 9*(6), 1022–1041. https://doi.org/10.3390/electronics9061022

Sumo Logic. (2019). *What is telemetry? The guide to application monitoring.* https://www.sumologic.com/insight/what-is-telemetry/

Tavallaee, M., Stakhanova, N., & Ghorbani, A. A. (2010). Toward credible evaluation of anomaly-based intrusion-detection methods. *IEEE Transactions on Systems, Man, and Cybernetics, Part C (Applications and Reviews), 40*(5), 516–524. https://doi.org/10.1109/TSMCC.2010.2048428

Tehila, S. (2021). *Building SIEM for today's threat landscape.* https://threatpost.com/building-siem-threat-landscape/166390/

Thakkar, A., & Lohiya, R. (2020). A review of the advancement in intrusion detection datasets. *Procedia Computer Science, 167,* 636–645. https://doi.org/10.1016/j.procs.2020.03.330

Turpitka, D. (2020). *When you can't stop every cyberattack, try honeypots.* https://www.forbes.com/sites/forbestechcouncil/2020/01/28/when-you-cant-stop-every-cyberattack-try-honeypots/?sh=76b624006cf2

Vargas, I., & Kleinschmidt, J. H. (2015). Capture and analysis of malicious traffic in VoIP environments using a low interaction honeypot. *IEEE Latin America Transactions, 13,* 777–783. https://doi.org/10.1109/TLA.2015.7069104

Wheeler, E. (2011). *Security risk management: Building an information security risk management program from the ground up.* Syngress.

Xiangfeng, S., Xue, H., & Yunhui, G. (2014). Research on the application of honeypot technology in intrusion detection system. In *2014 IEEE Workshop on Advanced Research and Technology in Industry Applications (WARTIA)* (pp. 1030–1032). https://doi.org/10.1109/WARTIA.2014.6976452

Yang, Y., & Mi, J. (2010). Design and implementation of distributed intrusion detection system based on honeypot. In *2010 2nd International Conference on Computer Engineering and Technology* (pp. V6-260–V6-263). https://doi.org/10.1109/ICCET.2010.5486267

Chapter 7

The Internet of Things (IoT), data security, and website security

INTRODUCTION

The Internet of Things (IoT) denotes the billions of physical devices around the world that connect to the Internet and use it to send and receive data, without requiring human-to-computer or human-to-human coordination. Since any physical object can be transformed into an IoT device if it connects to the Internet to be controlled or to share information, IoT devices are prevalent in all industries. They include cameras, smart kitchen appliances, smart locks, lightbulbs, thermostats, and more. However, since many of these devices are inadequately protected, they are subject to online attacks such as ransomware attacks. IoT security involves a multilayer approach, including tools and strategies designed to safeguard smart devices from unwanted access or manipulation.

This chapter will define the IoT, then review, and assess IoT risks and security tools. We begin the first half of the chapter with an overview of these risks, present some of the existing tools and best practices to protect IoT devices, and highlight the common matrices employed to assess IoT security risks. Next, we review the existing evidence on these technologies' success in accomplishing their security goals. Finally, we propose an operationalization of additional measures to deploy scientific research designs, allowing researchers and practitioners to increase the effectiveness of these tools in preventing IoT cyberattacks.

In the second portion of this chapter, we elaborate on personally identifiable information (PII) – such as social security numbers, dates of birth, and sensitive data such as credit card information – and why business data are among the most popular and sought-after commodities by cybercriminals. We also cover some of the most common tools and strategies employed to ensure data security, a key strategy to protect sensitive data and ensure employees' and customers' privacy rights. The third section of this chapter will review and assess some of the existing technologies organizations use to protect their data and websites. Many organizations use websites to share data with both clients and employees, for example, so they have deployed web vulnerability scanning tools and Transport Layer Security (TLS) certificates.

DOI: 10.1201/9781003201519-7

We will conclude the chapter by suggesting additional cybersecurity measures and recommending several rigorous investigation tools, best practices, and valuable methods for cybersecurity practitioners.

THE IoT

In recent years, objects connected to the Internet have often been the subject of critical articles on security and the protection of personal data. Consider these headlines: 'IoT is so bad, many companies can't tell when they're hacked' (Schwab, 2019); 'When coffee makers are demanding a ransom, you know IoT is screwed' (Goodin, 2020); 'Hackers could use IoT botnets to manipulate energy markets' (Newman, 2020); '50, 000 home cameras reportedly hacked, footage posted online' (Owaida, 2020); 'Medical devices on the IoT put lives at risks' (Raidman, 2020); and 'IoT security; IoT needn't be the Internet of threats' (Oueslati, 2021).

Let us begin by defining the IoT: the 'interconnection, via the Internet, of computing devices embedded in everyday objects, enabling them to send and receive data' (Chaabouni et al., 2019, p. 2671). As of 2021, there are 10.7 billion IoT devices connected, including more than 3 billion devices located in China (Holst, 2021). As Holst (2021) explained, the number of IoT devices worldwide is forecasted to reach 25.4 billion by 2030, tripling the 2020 level of 8.74 billion. IoT is the convergence of the Internet with RFID (radio frequency identification), sensor technology, and intelligent objects, in order to collect and process spatial and temporal information to enact specific events and solve various challenges (Chaabouni et al., 2019; Singh et al., 2014).

IoT devices collect data using sensors, offering numerous services to users based on the data analyses and according to user-defined parameters (Figliola, 2020). These devices are collecting and transmitting data from device to device, device to enterprise systems, and now even from devices to humans (Rizvi et al., 2018). For instance, an intelligent refrigerator uses sensors (e.g., cameras) to inventory its stored items. It can alert users when some items run low based on image recognition analyses (Figliola, 2020). Other sophisticated IoT devices, such as the Fitbit Sense smartwatch, can track physical changes during sleep to monitor short-term and long-term trends (Schlinger, 2020). It can also – among many other functionalities – recognize patterns, collect user preferences, and gather historical use data to recommend training/activities based on the wearer's individual stress level.

According to Figliola (2020), IoT devices may be used in many fields. In the *manufacturing industry*, the industrial Internet of things (IIoT) includes networked machines in a production facility communicating with each other to improve efficiency, productivity, and performance. In healthcare, devices in the Internet of medical things (IoMT) like heart monitors can collect patient health data and send it to healthcare providers. In *smart cities*, IoT devices and systems are used to plan transportation and in *smart grid*, it connects utilities (e.g., electricity, water, and gas), while residents of *smart homes* may rely upon IoT devices such as smart thermostats, light bulbs, doorbells, or home security systems.

Despite the unprecedented hype of the last few years, the IoT's expected growth and adoption rate is nowhere near earlier forecasts (Gilchrist, 2017). For example, based on Statista's 2016 forecasts (Statista Research Department, 2016), Alam (2018) predicted that 35.82 billion IoT devices would be connected by 2021. Intel Corporation (2015) was even more optimistic, forecasting 200 billion IoT devices by 2020. Instead, only about 10 billion devices are connected right now (Holst, 2021). Still, recent statistics provided by the Statista Research Department (2021) show that the total revenue generated by the global IoT market (enabled sensors) will exceed US$27 billion in 2022, which would represent an increase of approximately 365% since 2016.

WHAT RISKS ARE ASSOCIATED WITH THE IoT?

Current security issues, risks, and challenges may help explain why IoT's expected growth has not fully materialized. Despite the benefits, connecting people, computers, and data also comes with risks. Technological means have transformed the way we live: we communicate largely through automation and intelligent machines relieve us of many mundane tasks. Still, we must assess the security of any advancement: what are the risks associated with these new technologies, these new tools, and the manner in which consumers will be interacting with them?

We often hear IoT objects described as insecure devices that come off the shelf and are too frequently installed in weak or insecure networks. But why is this the case? As Gilchrist (2017) explained, from a manufacturer's perspective, these products' development life cycle often happens in agile start-up companies. The developers often design IoT devices as prototypes to show a software proof of concept, not necessarily as fully secured products ready to be sold to the general population (Gilchrist, 2017). However, business needs and financial constraints influence their companies to generate a positive return of investment (ROI) on the product, even if that means releasing it before the design team can redevelop, test, and verify the software, firmware, and hardware to eliminate potential security flaws and exploits (Gilchrist, 2017).

From a security perspective, in software development, one best practice is to take a proactive approach to threat modeling – also known as a defensive approach – during the initial design and specifications phase. This means predicting potential threats and designing specific defenses for them, or establishing creative and innovative ways to protect devices during the coding and crafting processes, instead of solely relying on future security updates and patches (Stewart et al., 2015). Adding additional security controls to the foundation of these devices does cost money, and these investments in security directly impact the product's ROI. However, integrated security solutions are cost-effective and more successful than implementing security controls later (Stewart et al., 2015).

Unfortunately, not all threats can be predicted in the design phase since *securing the unidentified* is still impossible. Thus, organizations also need to plan to use a reactive approach – a threat model known as the adversarial approach – in case some unplanned risks materialize and impact consumers' security and data (Stewart et al., 2015). Threat modeling is often associated with techniques such as ethical hacking, penetration testing, source code review, and fuzz testing, i.e., providing different types of input to software in an attempt to stress its limits and identify previously undetected flaws (Stewart et al., 2015).

Another risk that we need to consider with IoT devices is consumers' acceptance of risk and their nonchalance to vulnerabilities and threats (Gilchrist, 2017). From a business perspective, the customer experience is paramount. Security professionals often claim that what consumers want (e.g., easy installation and operation, plug-and-play devices, easy authentication) may trade security for convenience. A great example of a plug-and-play scenario is the Wi-Fi-enabled gateway routers that Internet Service Providers (ISPs) routinely offer to home customers. The installation process of this device is relevant to the IoT since the router is the customer's premises equipment gateway. For some ISPs, it is also the demarcation point of their responsibility for security (Gilchrist, 2017).

Customers want to plug in the Wi-Fi router and simply set their home devices (smartphone, laptops, and other Wi-Fi connected devices) to connect instantly, work seamlessly, and pair with any enabled devices – without having to follow instructions, study user manuals, or call Tech Support to ensure a proper installation (Gilchrist, 2017). Unfortunately, not all customers care about security, and they expect providers to ensure the services they are paying for are secure. In addition, most customers are not security experts, and they do not necessarily understand that if an intruder gets into their Wi-Fi network (e.g., via Dynamic Host Configuration Protocol (DHCP) or Universal Plug and Play (UPnP) protocol), he would not only gain unauthorized access to the Internet but also to all the home IP devices connected to the network (Gilchrist, 2017). To break into IoT software, firmware, and hardware, cybercriminals have many tools available, including wireless scanning and mapping attacks, protocol attacks, eavesdropping attacks, cryptographic algorithms, key management attacks, spoofing, application integrity attacks, denial of service or jamming attacks, and physical security attacks (e.g., tampering), and privilege escalation attacks (Russell & Duren, 2018).

In the following section, we will focus on four categories of threats: rogue firmware, backdoors, malicious certificates, and eavesdropping. First, firmware is a type of software engraved into a piece of hardware, so it should be free of vulnerabilities (Dow & Lea, 2019; Technopedia, 2021). Rogue firmware can be a significant IoT threat since hardware devices, toys, and home appliances may be vulnerable to innovative attack vectors if the firmware can be upgraded or downgraded – thereby exposing a vulnerable version of the firmware to the attackers (Gilchrist, 2017). Second, a backdoor is an illegitimate access path to a computer system, allowing intruders to bypass the system's customary security mechanisms to access the system remotely and without detection (Death, 2017; Posey, 2021).

Legitimate SSL (Secure Sockets Layer)/TLS certificates fulfill critical security functions in authenticating and verifying the identity of the host, client, and the applications. However, cybercriminals have also started to use these certificates maliciously to commit nefarious activities, so these certificates are not the safe option they once were (Gilchrist, 2017). Finally, eavesdropping on network traffic is when cybercriminals passively listen to network communications to access private information, such as node identification numbers, routing updates, or sensitive application data (Das et al., 2012).

Another critical risk to consider is the requirement for trust at the device level. Since IoT devices must be interconnected to communicate and share information, blindly trusting another device can have significant security consequences. The enterprise traffic runs *south-north* – traffic from users goes toward servers or the Internet at the top of the network architecture – while with IoT, much of the traffic flows laterally *east-west* between interconnected devices through gateways and controllers (Gilchrist, 2017). Even though the IoT could theoretically allow devices to communicate through a flat network, using the Internet democratically, in practice devices need to be authenticated to securely access networks. According to Gilchrist (2017), without global trust among the devices, we should be talking about an *intranet of things* instead of an IoT.

To avoid letting all devices connected to the Internet communicate, share information, and accumulate knowledge without traffic surveillance, we are now grouping devices and products into secure private intranets, even within the primary home networks (Gilchrist, 2017). Given the increasing volume of potential IoT devices, the only security alternative is to authenticate, encrypt data, and rely on virus scan and intrusion detection for every device sharing a private network. However, this is not always practical in a business environment. If only one trusted device is hacked, and the other devices on the network connect to it without any security or detection systems, all the devices could be compromised (e.g., by malware or ransomware) as well. Thus, any IoT device is a potential attack vector for the other interconnected devices. Indeed, both Locker ransomware and Crypto-ransomware attacks are popular (among cybercriminals) against IoT devices, as they can disrupt and paralyze an entire network to force individuals or organizations to meet their demands (Chakkaravarthy et al., 2020).

Furthermore, according to Anand et al. (2020), a significant number of IoT devices currently have no mechanisms for energy harvesting and security. These scholars claim that both factors should be prerequisites at the design phase and that all the aspects of the sensors' life cycle must be addressed from the deployment of IoT devices to their disposal. Also, since IoT devices are power-constrained, IoT end nodes are often the weakest point in an end-to-end system (Anand et al., 2020). More precisely, energy efficiency solutions in terms of power consumption and data transmission have become an urgent need for sustainable IoT.

Anand et al. (2020) argued that since IoT revolves around data, the fate of an IoT network depends on its security and privacy. Recent security breaches show that even resource-constrained IoT end nodes with limited functionality introduce substantial risk to the whole system. Most of the breaches were caused by the interconnected nature of IoT devices, which provides a large attack surface and numerous attack points for cybercriminals (Anand et al., 2020). While most security threats apply to IoT, they are not always specific to it. Still, the risks may be more prominent due to the number of devices available as potential targets. When we talk about billions of connected devices, the probability of the risk materializing at some point is substantial (Strous et al., 2021).

Online attacks against IoT

A recent collaborative investigation – conducted by Which (a UK consumer group), the NCC group (a global cyber and software resilience business operating across multiple sectors), and the Global Cyber Alliance (an international cross-sector effort dedicated to reducing cyber risk) – shows the vulnerabilities associated with IoT devices and how cybercriminals can easily target them. They conducted an experiment (i.e., a honeypot setup) in which they filled a house with numerous IoT devices, including consumer devices connected to the Internet (e.g., TVs, thermostats, and smart security systems), and then analyzed the number of attempted hacks that took place over several weeks (Coker, 2021; Laughlin, 2021). They identified 12,807 unique scans/hacks during a single week in June 2021 (Coker, 2021). That week, the most common method used by cybercriminals was attempting to log into the devices using weak default usernames and passwords (e.g., 'admin'). The researchers documented 2,435 specific attempts to maliciously log into devices using this method, also called *spray and pray attacks*, at one point reaching 14 attempts per hour (Coker, 2021; Laughlin, 2021).

The positive aspect of this study is that most of the devices withstood these attacks, except for a wireless camera from Amazon – the ieGeek security camera, which has since been removed from sale – which allowed a malicious actor to spy on the home (Coker, 2021). According to the researchers, an Epson printer was the most frequently targeted device in the house (Coker, 2021). However, the attacks failed as they had relatively strong default passwords in place. Unique default passwords also protected a Yale security system and a Samsung smart TV from attacks (Coker, 2021). These findings are in line with mounting concerns about the security of IoT devices as they become increasingly prevalent in homes throughout the world (Coker, 2021). A primary security measure is making sure to change the generic password on each IoT device, as a preventative control to block cyber-offenders from gaining control.

IoT architecture and protocol stack

IoT architecture consists of three main layers: (1) the perception/physical layer, (2) the network/transport layer, and (3) the application layer (Chaabouni et al., 2019; Krushang & Upadhyay, 2014; Noor & Hassan, 2019; Rizvi et al., 2018). Other scholars (Elrawy et al., 2018; Khan et al., 2012) add two additional layers: the middleware layer (responsible for service management over IoT devices providing the same services) between the network layer and the application layer and the business layer (responsible for the global management of IoT applications and service management over IoT devices) on top of the application layer.

The perception layer is the hardware layer, composed of different sensors and actuators that send and receive data using different communication standards (e.g., Bluetooth, RFID, 6LowPAN, Zigbee) (Chaabouni et al., 2019; Noor & Hassan, 2019; Rizvi et al., 2018). The network layer, which operates like the network layer in TCP/IP and has the same traditional security problems (see Chapter 2), ensures the effective routing/transmission of data/information, again using various communication protocols (e.g., Wi-Fi, 3G, GSM, IPv6) (Chaabouni et al., 2019; Rizvi et al., 2018). The application layer, also known as the software layer, is the top layer: it provides systems with business logic and offers user interfaces (UIs) to the end users (e.g., for traffic monitoring) (Chaabouni et al., 2019). This is the most complicated layer of the IoT architecture since there are numerous products, devices, and manufacturers, and there is no universal standard for the construction of the application layer (Rizvi et al., 2018).

As shown in Figure 7.1, each layer represents various vulnerabilities that cybercriminals can exploit. Since IoT devices are located at different physical locations, they can be vulnerable to environmental hazards (e.g., rain, snow, wind, malicious attacks, unintentional damage), and stored data may also be stolen via physical access (Chaabouni et al., 2019). Likewise, since their sensors are small, they can suffer from resource constraint issues (e.g., limited computational resources, memory, or energy). More specifically, as data and commands are exchanged (network layer), they can face (a) different network vulnerabilities such as data interchange vulnerabilities (i.e., data transfer issues due to network floods or malicious gateway access), (b) unauthorized access (e.g., impersonation attack, communication interception, password guessing attacks), or (c) numerous connectivity vulnerabilities (e.g., data integrity violation, low quality-of-service (QoS)) (Chaabouni et al., 2019). Also, the application layer can be exposed to software problems such as account enumeration, insecure account credentials, and lack of account suspension after a limited number of password guesses. Moreover, cloud applications (Mishra et al., 2017; Modi et al., 2013) can be attacked by

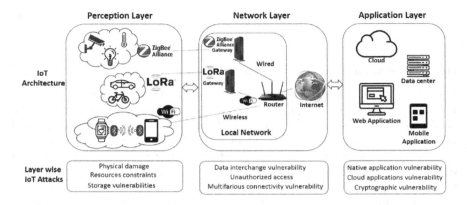

Figure 7.1 IoT architecture & layer wise attacks. (Chaabouni, N., Mosbah, M., Zemmari, A., Sauvignac, C., & Faruki, P. (2019). Network intrusion detection for IoT security based on learning techniques. *IEEE Communications Surveys & Tutorials, 21*(3), 2671–2701. https://doi.org/10.1109/COMST.2019.2896380)

viruses (e.g., trojan horses, worms) (Chaabouni et al., 2019). Since IoT is based on low computational capability devices, transport encryption is sometimes weak or neglected altogether. Therefore, communications are easily traceable and easily discovered (e.g., cipher text-only attack, man-in-the-middle attack) (Chaabouni et al., 2019).

IoT risk frameworks

As of today, there are no standard IoT risk frameworks available on the market. However, the National Institute of Standards and Technology (NIST) offers considerations for IoT, and existing risk assessment frameworks in information security can be slightly modified to handle IoT risks (Kandasamy et al., 2020). Moreover, the IoT Cybersecurity Improvement Act of 2020, was signed by then-US President Donald Trump on 4 December 2020, requiring Federal agencies to have cybersecurity requirements in order to protect controlled and owned IoT devices (Pingol, 2020).

Some popular IoT risk assessment frameworks are NIST IR 8228, OCTAVE for IoT, TARA for IoT, and ISO for IoT. The NIST (NISTIR 8228) has documented the potential challenges with IoT devices and risk considerations in achieving device and data security, both at rest and in transit (NIST, 2019). The purpose of this NIST publication was to enable both federal agencies and organizations to better understand and manage the cybersecurity and privacy risks associated with IoT devices throughout the devices' life cycles. Specifically, it encouraged readers to (1) understand risk considerations and mitigation challenges, (2) adjust organizational policies and processes, and (3) implement updated mitigation practices (Boeckl et al., 2019). OCTAVE (Operationally Critical Threat, Asset, and Vulnerability Evaluation) is a qualitative risk assessment framework with eight steps: (1) set up criteria for measuring risk, (2) develop asset profiles, (3) identify asset containers, (4) identify concerned areas, (5) identify threat schemes, (6) recognize risks, (7) examine risks, and (8) mitigate risk. It helps find various security vulnerabilities associated with IoT-based smart homes, identify the risks to people, and implement a four-phase approach to mitigate the identified risks: (1) establish drivers, (2) profile assets, (3) identify threats, and (4) mitigate risks (Kandasamy et al., 2020).

Threat Assessment & Remediation Analysis (TARA) is a predictive framework with three main advantages, according to Kandasamy et al. (2020): (a) it breaks down future attacks to a manageable list of potential attacks, (b) it improves the quality of risk and control evaluations, then communicates risks and recommendations to the organization, and (c) it can enhance outcomes, decrease the general effort of risk analysis, and facilitate better decisions. TARA was developed for a large and diverse environment within Intel, to assess the security risks of a very complicated and quickly evolving threat landscape (Kandasamy et al., 2020). The ISO/IEC 30141 provides the reference architecture needed to reduce the risks and maximize the benefits for IoT applications. Finally, ISO/IEC 27030 gives guidelines for security and privacy in IoT systems (Kandasamy et al., 2020). For more information about standards and information security frameworks, see Chapter 8.

IoT security tools and defense techniques for data security

The primary objectives of IoT security tools are to preserve privacy and confidentiality; ensure the security of IoT users, infrastructures, data, and devices; and guarantee the availability of the services offered by an IoT ecosystem (Noor & Hassan, 2019). As mentioned in Chapter 6 on cybersecurity tools, free datasets (e.g., KDDCUP99, NSL-KDD, and others) can be used to implement and validate network intrusion detection systems (NIDSs). However, these datasets have several data deficiencies, so they are not recommended to validate security tools' efficiency, nor are they recommended for IoT security network capabilities. More recent network datasets such as (a) the Sivanathan et al. (2017) IoT dataset (for smart cities and campuses), (b) CICIDS2017 (Sharafaldin et al., 2018; University of New Brunswick., n.d.-A; University of New Brunswick., n.d.-B), and (c) CSE-CICIDS2018 (University of New Brunswick., n.d.-C) can be used by both researchers and practitioners to evaluate tools. Chaabouni et al. (2019) claimed that the dataset of Sivanathan et al. (2017) is the only IoT network traffic dataset available in the literature. Nevertheless, it is designed for IoT device proliferation and not for intrusion detection. On the other hand, CICIDS2017 and CSE-CIC-IDS2018 have labeled records but do not target IoT system security, despite their up-to-date attack list (Chaabouni et al., 2019).

Free datasets can be used for NIDS implementation and validation, but since there are no datasets explicitly created for IoT networks, two strategies are possible: (1) download an available dataset targeting traditional systems, or (2) deploy open-source sniffing software on networks (Chaabouni et al., 2019). However, suppose companies are interested in investing additional financial resources in IoT security. In that case, big data and learning techniques (e.g., Apache Hadoop, Apache Spark, Apache Storm) (Amanullah et al., 2020) as well as deep learning (e.g., deep Eigenspace learning approach, Bi-Directional LSTM Recurrent Neural Network) are two other potential strategies to consider in securing IoT devices. Deep learning, a branch of machine learning, has shown promising results in previous studies for detecting security breaches (Amanullah et al., 2020). Furthermore, since IoT devices generate large volumes, variety, and veracity of data when big data technologies are incorporated, higher performance and better data handling can be achieved (Amanullah et al., 2020).

Jurcut et al. (2020) recommended other risk prevention methods for IoT such as honeypots (i.e., trapping adversaries), raising awareness through training, immediate responses to detected vulnerabilities, security on chips/ hardware (i.e., integrating security at the manufacturing stage), exhaustive security testing, and security on the software development life cycle (SDLC). They also noted that additional legislation such as the General Data Protection Regulation (GDPR) can improve awareness among the general public and influence companies to better secure devices and their clients' data. In addition, security solutions and techniques can be employed to improve the security of IoT systems. These techniques include security by design, using a security boot or root-of-trust mechanism (ENISA, 2019). A secure booting mechanism is a multilayered approach to IoT ecosystem starting from the initial secure boot, used to establish trust and integrity of the software on the IoT device. Elliptic curve digital signature algorithms (ECDSAs), secure hash algorithms (SHA), direct memory access (DMA), and physical unclonable functions (PUFs) are utilized to secure booting and remote attestation (Jurcut et al., 2020). Other technique options are access control, network access policy, device authentication, firewalls and IPS, updates and patches, and real-time operating systems (Jurcut et al., 2020).

As mentioned by ENISA (2019), best practices for IoT security include frequent vulnerability assessments, penetration tests, security maintenance, and threat intelligence tasks to prevent attacks and threats to the cloud, the network, and IoT end devices – as well as the applications developed for such devices. Moreover, low-powered IoT devices may not be able to create or store log files. Thus, service continuity, planning, and utilizing automatic backups or redundancy helps users prepare for malfunctions or service disruptions caused by security incidents (ENISA, 2019).

Besides, as Chaabouni et al. (2019) argued, traditional defense mechanisms such as filter packets, encryption, robust password authentication schemes, logging and auditing activities, IDSs, and IPS may be efficient to protect IoT devices in specific situations. For example, a popular strategy uses NIDS for connected smart things (Chaabouni et al., 2019). Still, they do not entirely make IoT devices secure.

Network Intrusion Detection Systems (NIDSs) in an IoT environment

NIDSs are tools that analyze network traffic to detect malicious behaviors. To build NIDS, Sharma and Dixit (2016) recommended collecting the traffic data from the network, analyzing the collected data, identifying relevant security events, and finally detecting and reporting malicious events. According to Chaabouni et al. (2019), researchers and professionals have two choices for performing these steps: use existing tools to facilitate their own NIDS implementation or develop an utterly new detection strategy. For existing tools, they can choose between using free datasets in an offline mode (since it is challenging to test proposals on real networks and those datasets are a good solution for benchmarking); free, open-source network sniffers (e.g., Tcpdump, Wireshark, Ettercap, Argus, EtherApe) to capture their own network traffic data; or a free, open-source NIDS that can be used and adapted depending on their objectives (Chaabouni et al., 2019).

An IDS deployed for an IoT system should analyze data packets and generate responses in real time (Elrawy et al., 2018). Also, it should be able to analyze data packets on different layers of the IoT network with different protocol stacks and adapt to other technologies in the IoT environment (Gendreau & Moorman, 2016). A system that monitors important operating system files is an example of a host-based IDS (HIDS), which is deployed on a particular endpoint and designed to protect it against internal and external threats. In contrast, a system that analyzes incoming network traffic is an example of a network-based IDS (NIDS), i.e., a solution designed to monitor an entire protected network. NIDS has visibility of all traffic flowing through the network and makes determinations based upon packet metadata and contents (Check Point, 2021). An NIDS sniffs network traffic packets to detect potential intrusions and malicious attacks, and it can be either software-based or hardware-based (Elrawy et al., 2018; Gautam & Om, 2016). For instance, Snort, Suricata, and Zeek are examples of NIDS; they can also be HIDS/ NIDS hybrids (Malhotra et al., 2021).

Basing IoT NIDS on machine learning techniques and deep packet inspection (DPI) are two strategies discussed in the literature to better protect IoT devices. Traditional NIDS suffer from a high false recognition rate, which can be reduced with machine learning techniques. Compared to a Signature/Non-Signature IDS, a machine learning-equipped IDS/NIDS differs as it employs statistical, genetic, and heuristics to disseminate complex attack patterns and improve the detection rate with reduced false negatives (Chaabouni et al., 2019). Various machine learning algorithms can be used to improve detection rates and quality, either individually or in combination: decision trees (DTs), support vector machines (SVMs), naive Bayes (NB), artificial neural networks

(ANN), k-means clustering, fuzzy logic, genetic algorithms, and stacked auto encoders (SAEs) (Chaabouni et al., 2019; Feng et al., 2014; Lin et al., 2015). Boukerche and Coutinho (2021) proposed categorizing current machine learning designs and solutions as device-oriented or network-oriented, and they investigated recent studies that designed machine-learning-based solutions to secure IoT applications. This proposed classification allows security practitioners to better identify and understand the challenges, requirements, and up-to-date common design principles for securing IoT devices and networks.

DPI is a function similar to a firewall, as it evaluates the contents of packets going through a checkpoint (Brooks, 2018). While conventional packet filtering only reads the header information of each packet – similar to reading the cover of a book – deep packet filtering is analogous to reading the book's content, which allows a better understanding of the traffic and the potential threats (Brooks, 2018). Scholars exhibit some divergence on DPI. Authors such as Trabelsi et al. (2016) and Jurcut et al. (2020) have contended that IoT devices require DPI capability to control the traffic. On the other hand, scholars like Elrawy et al. (2018) and Danda and Hota (2016) argued that using DPI technique for trusted operations within an IoT system is considered a violation of privacy.

Metrics to measure effectiveness

As Elrawy et al. (2018) explained, in a traditional communication network, IDS performance primarily uses the true positive rate (TPR) and the false positive rate (FPR) to evaluate the system's efficiency in identifying potential threats. However, in an IoT-based smart environment, the energy consumption, processing time, and performance overhead of an IDS are also critical to IoT devices' efficiency. Furthermore, due to IoT devices' power and memory limitations, these metrics are crucial for the IoT system's QoS. Therefore, they are considered essential performance metrics for an IDS designed for IoT-based smart environments. Elrawy et al. (2018) usefully compared IDSs designed for IoT systems, with a focus on their types, techniques, and features and a descriptive statistical analysis of the surveyed IDSs, in terms of the essential performance metrics affecting IDS suitability in IoT systems.

Recommended reference: Elrawy, M., Awad, A., & Hamed, H. Intrusion detection systems for IoT-based smart environments: A survey. *Journal of Cloud Computing*, 7(21), 1–20. https://doi.org/10.1186/s13677-018-0123-6

Examples of IoT security empirical research designs

In the IoT literature, scholars have discussed different IoT research designs to improve security in various fields of work. Chanson et al. (2019) proposed a design theory, including requirements, design principles, and features, for a blockchain-based sensor data protection system (SDPS). These scholars designed and developed an instantiation of an SDPS (a prototype CertifiCar) in three iterative cycles, intended to prevent the fraudulent manipulation of car mileage data (Chanson et al., 2019). The authors also applied the CertifiCar prototype to two additional use cases in pharmaceutical supply chains and energy microgrids. The results of their study suggest that the proposed design ensures the tamper-resistant gathering, processing, and exchange of IoT sensor data in a privacy-preserving, scalable, and efficient manner (Chanson et al., 2019).

Shukla et al. (2021) claimed that the traditional machine learning algorithms and healthcare IoT techniques lack real-world implementation for secure data transmission. Therefore, they introduced a novel research design in a healthcare blockchain for safe and reliable transactions in healthcare IoT. As stated by these authors, the use of fog computing (FC) extends the cloud services at the edge of networks. The integration of FC with blockchain helps overcome the issue of healthcare IoT device identification, authentication, and verification for scalable frequent data transmission in a decentralized environment (Shukla et al., 2021). In analyzing the results from the proposed novel Advanced Signature-Based Encryption (ASE) algorithm for throughput, packet error, reliability, and malicious node detection accuracy, the authors observed that the ASE algorithm in the FC environment outperformed the cloud and the other sophisticated techniques such as FogBus, Femto cloud, Blockchain Fog-based Architecture Network (BFAN), and BeeKeeper. Notably, they found that the malicious node detection accuracy of the ASE algorithm in the FC environment was 91%, compared to 83% in the cloud (Shukla et al., 2021).

Torabi et al. (2018) addressed the lack of IoT-specific empirical data by drawing upon more than 5 TB of passive measurements. To do so, the authors devised data-driven methodologies to infer compromised IoT devices and those targeted by denial-of-service attacks. Then, they performed a large-scale characterization analysis of their traffic, exploring a public threat repository and an in-house malware database (Torabi et al., 2018). Their study results exposed a significant 26,000 compromised IoT devices *in the wild*, with 40% being active in critical infrastructure (Torabi et al., 2018). Moreover, they uncovered new, unreported malware variants that specifically target IoT devices (Torabi et al., 2018). These empirical results show a first attempt to highlight the large-scale insecurity of the IoT paradigm and the alarming rise of new generations of IoT-centric, malware-orchestrated botnets.

WEBSITE SECURITY

As more people transact online through desktop computers or mobile devices, new threats target both IoT device vulnerabilities and online websites. Website security is vital as most of the worldwide population buys numerous goods and services through the Internet. According to Johnson (2021), as of January 2021, there were 4.66 billion active internet users worldwide (i.e., 59.5% of the global population); 92.6% of them (4.32 billion) accessed the Internet via their mobile devices (Johnson, 2021).

Data breaches regularly make headlines. Social engineering and phishing attacks often lead to exposure of information, even though organizations have protection mechanisms in place to prevent their customers from falling for these fraudulent online schemes (LeBlanc & Messerschmidt, 2016). Some of the data gathered by cybercriminals come from a lack of website security on transactional websites harnessing personal data, credit card data, and other data types that bad actors can use for nefarious means (e.g., identity theft, account takeovers, fraudulent documents). Individual personal identifiers (e.g., social security numbers, dates of birth), email dumps, and business data are among the most popular and sought-after commodities by cybercriminals (Sen, 2021). According to the latest estimates, cybercrime costs will grow by 15% per year over the next five years, reaching US\$10.5 trillion annually by 2025, up from US\$3 trillion in 2015 (Morgan, 2020). RiskBased Security (2021) noted that there were 1,923 breaches (49%) in 2020 that did not expose any actual records. However, the total number of records compromised in 2020 still exceeded 37 billion, representing a 141% increase compared to the previous year (Lohrmann, 2021).

Insecure web and cloud interfaces are vulnerabilities that may be an attack vector into an IoT system at the application layer. Also, cloud gateways must be equipped with security controls to restrict bad actors from modifying configurations (e.g., biometrics and multilevel authentication for access control) (Noor & Hassan, 2019). However, even with security controls in place, some vulnerabilities can be exploited by cybercriminals. The Open Web Application Security Project (OWASP), an international non-profit organization, published a list of the top ten web application security risks: (1) broken access control, (2) cryptographic failure, (3) injection, (4) insecure design, (5) security misconfigurations, (6) vulnerable and outdate components, (7) identification and authentication failure, (8) software and data integrity failures, (9) security logging and monitoring failures, and (10) server-side request forgery (OWASP, 2021).

Web defacement

As Davanzo et al. (2011) documented, web defacements are a common form of attack on websites. In these attacks, the legitimate site content is fully or partly replaced by the attackers. Generally, the attackers will show content that might be highly embarrassing to the site owner, such as disturbing images, music, political messages, or an association with a controversial social cause. Defacements are usually carried out by exploiting security vulnerabilities in the web hosting infrastructure. Still, there is increasing evidence of defacements obtained through fraudulent Domain Name System (DNS) redirects or hijackings (e.g., cache poisoning, NXDomain attack, phantom domain attack) (Davanzo et al., 2011; Ramdas & Muthukrishnan, 2019).

In recent years, criminologists and sociologists have conducted several studies to better understand why cybercriminals are attacking websites. Weijer et al. (2021) examined over 2 million web defacements performed by 66,553 hackers. These hackers targeted at least one website between January 2010 and March 2017. Six groups of defacers were distinguished based on the frequency and timing of their attacks (i.e., low and high sporadic defacers, low and high declining defacers, and low and high chronic defacers). The authors developed semi-parametric, group-based trajectory models through the use of zero-inflated, Poisson-based models to assess heterogeneity within this group of hackers, in an attempt to better understand the timing and frequency of performed defacements (Weijer et al., 2021). The study results demonstrated similarities to offline crime in that a small population of defacers accounted for most defacements against websites. Moreover, the authors concluded that defacers' motivations, methods, and targeting practices differed based on the frequency with which they performed defacements (Weijer et al., 2021).

Howell et al. (2019) used a sample of websites targeted by hackers in 2017 across the world. They examined the relationship between a country's structural characteristics and the frequency of website defacement reported for the country. Using Routine Activity Theory (RAT) to better understand website defacement, Howell et al. (2019) found that website defacements are less likely to occur in the presence of capable guardianship. Thus, they are more likely to occur when specific measures of target suitability (e.g., criminals' valuations of a product or target) are present. Also, using hackers' self-reported valuations of potential targets, they examined whether websites targeted for political reasons have different correlates than websites targeted for recreational reasons. Their findings show that recreational defacements are deterred by capable guardianship (e.g., computer emergency response teams (CERT) and a cyber defense military presence) and are influenced by specific measures of target suitability. In contrast, political defacements are not influenced by such measures (Howell et al., 2019).

Burruss et al. (2021) used a sample of 119 active website defacers (i.e., open-source data on the Zone-h website) who launched attacks against important websites. These scholars sought to determine whether different types of website defacers exist based on the volume of their attacks. The researchers used finite mixture modeling and multiple measures to model the changes in the counts of defacements, to determine whether different distributions exist based on the volume of defacements. After they categorized hackers by attack volume (i.e., low-volume defacers versus high-volume defacers), they used a negative binomial regression to validate whether the correlates of defacement vary across the distributions. Then, using data gathered on the clear web, the researchers included a series of binary measures indicative of hackers being active on Facebook, Twitter, Instagram, and Telegram (Burruss et al., 2021).

Burruss et al. (2021) identified two unique groups of website defacers: low-volume defacers (69%) and high-volume defacers (31%). Furthermore, they demonstrated that (a) social media presence, (b) the content of the defacement, and (c) the type of defacement predict group membership. For the low-volume defacers (about 69% of the sample), Facebook membership was the only social media variable that was predictive (b = −0.560), decreasing the defacement counts by about 43%. On the other hand, for the high-volume defacers, Twitter and YouTube were both significant predictors of an increase in defacement counts: Twitter increased counts by a factor of 2, while YouTube reduced counts by about 74%. Thus, social media may serve as a valuable platform to reach and possibly deter repeat offenders (Burruss et al., 2021).

An example of evidence-based research design

Bad actors are not only defacing websites. They can also create their own secure websites to lure potential victims. A great example of this is the study conducted by Maimon et al. (2020). In March 2019, the Evidence-Based Cybersecurity Research Group (EBCS) at Georgia State University, in collaboration with Venafi, released a detailed report demonstrating a steady supply of SSL/TLS certificates on several darknet markets. TLS is an updated and more secure version, and it is the successor protocol to SSL. It works the same way as SSL, using encryption to protect data transfers and information, to keep an internet connection secured.

These SSL/TLS certificates were offered for sale either as part of crimeware services and products (e.g., malicious websites) or as a standalone product. Prices ranged from US$260 to US$1600, depending on the type of certificate and scope of additional services offered. In the same advertisements, several vendors also offered Extended Validation (EV) certificates for sale. These certificates confirm the legal identity of the owner by a designated certificate authority (CA) and are normally designed to confer the highest level of trust (Maimon et al., 2020). As a research methodology, the researchers analyzed online markets and hacker forums that were active on the Tor network from October 2018 to April 2019, seeking 'for sale' listings of TLS certificates. In doing so, they discovered close to 70 relevant online market webpages on the Tor network.

Maimon et al. (2020) also did two case studies associated with UK website security. First, they approached a vendor on Telegram with a request to design a retail website with an EV certificate on it, with the goal of being contacted by future customers over Telegram, and second, they obtained EV certificates for UK-based organizations. In this second case study, the research team approached a vendor to purchase EV certificates and several authenticated documents: a certificate of incorporation for a UK-based retail website, registration of a UK-based retail company on the Dun and Bradstreet website, and a confirmation email from a CA for the approval of an EV certificate request (Maimon et al., 2020). To further test the possibility of creating a fake online bank in the United States, the researchers reached out to the vendor again and asked him to provide them with a quote for a US-based online loan and payday website. A few days after the group of researchers placed their order, they received official documents from the Division of Corporations in Delaware, indicating the formation of a new company that carried the entity name they provided to the vendor (Maimon et al., 2020). These documents included the new financial institution name and the name of the filing individual, as well as a physical address for the new company.

The findings reported in this study demonstrate that the process employed by some certificate authorities to validate the true identity of companies and organizations is highly problematic. Also, it shows that at least one organized crime group operating worldwide knew enough to issue EV certificates to nonexistent retail and financial organizations in both the UK and US (Maimon et al., 2020). These online vendors harnessed their knowledge of CA validation processes to sell fraudulent EV certificates to interested parties. The findings presented in this study add to the ongoing debate regarding the effectiveness and necessity of EV certificates in increasing trust among internet users (Maimon et al., 2020). More alarmingly, the findings demonstrate that cybercriminals can easily create fake online banking websites to launder illicit funds, commit fraud, and enable numerous criminal activities, all while using a *supposedly* secure and official website to lure potential victims or entice criminals into hiding or moving money worldwide.

THREAT HUNTING: A PROACTIVE APPROACH TO MITIGATING RISKS TO IoT, DATA SECURITY, AND WEBSITE SECURITY

Beyond incident response and threat intelligence operations, threat hunting can provide an extra layer of defense for public and private organizations' networks (Collins, 2018). As discussed previously, various technological tools and machine learning capabilities can be deployed to protect assets. However, we still lack efficient detection methods for advanced persistent threats – which are usually hidden or unknown, emerging in the form of zero-day attacks – and organizations often lack sufficiently trained experts to mitigate those threats (Bhardwaj & Goundar, 2019).

Collins (2018) defined threat hunting as 'an advanced security analysis process that leverages deep knowledge of a network or organization to catch subtler, more deeply embedded attackers than a Security Operations Center (SOC) finds' (p. 1). For Taschler (2021), threat hunting is the practice of proactively searching for cyber-threats that may have gone undetected in networks, devices, systems, or applications. Cyber-threats may be malicious actors, advanced persistent threats, technical vulnerabilities, or even insider threats. Having a proactive approach to searching for threats is vital. As Bhardwaj and Goundar (2019) pointed out, security teams need to work 24/7 to protect the organization, while cyberattackers only need to be successful once to penetrate organizations and cause significant damage.

In many organizations, analysts working in SOCs initiate threat hunting when they identify something suspicious, such as network conditions or activities that cannot be easily explained, to identify security incidents or catch potential attackers. Threat hunting can become a research process in three phases: trigger, hunt, and export (Collins, 2018). Rather than waiting for a specific trigger, however, the hunt should begin with a security analyst's intuition about what could potentially affect the network. During the hunt phase, the analyst finds something odd in the network, tests out hypotheses, and draws conclusions. The export phase is when an analyst communicates the results of his investigation to the security team, sometimes recommending new defense configurations or additional controls (Collins, 2018). Bhardwaj and Goundar (2019), however, suggested that the threat hunting process should be divided into five steps: (1) generate a hypothesis, (2) validate the hypothesis, (3) seek evidence, (4) discover patterns, and (5) enhance systems. In addition, threat hunters should verify endpoint detection logs, using behavioral analytics, network threat analytics, and application threat analytics (Bhardwaj & Goundar, 2019).

In our view, instead of initiating threat hunting when something unusual in the network is identified, security professionals should integrate threat hunting techniques and strategies on an ongoing basis. Threat hunting should become an additional full-time practice in cybersecurity operations, in order to prevent and detect potential vulnerabilities that could affect IoT devices, the security of data, and website operations. Also, the analysts hunting these threats should know what works and what does not work in mitigating threats. Finally, threat hunting processes and techniques (e.g., machine learning, AI-based techniques, intelligence gathering) should be automated (Karuna et al., 2021), so that cybersecurity analysts and professionals become more efficient and proactive in mitigating cyber-threats to IoT, data, and websites.

CONCLUSION

In this chapter, we identified various risks to IoT and data security, then summarized existing evidence about security technologies' success in accomplishing their goals. We also proposed ideas for additional measures to deploy scientific research designs, allowing both researchers and practitioners to increase their organizations' security posture and effectiveness in preventing IoT cyberattacks, securing data, and protecting websites. In the future, both cybersecurity researchers and practitioners will have to improve and test various tools, techniques, and strategies to protect critical assets. These security actors will have to continue innovating and searching for future threats if they want to secure IoT devices, data, and websites.

REFERENCES

Alam, T. (2018). A reliable communication framework and its use in Internet of things (IoT). *International Journal of Scientific Research in Computer Science, Engineering, and Information Technology, 3*(5), 450–456. https://www.researchgate.net/publication/325645304_A_Reliable_Communication_Framework_and_Its_Use_in_Internet_of_Things_IoT

Amanullah, M. A., Habeeb, R. A. A., Nasaruddin, F. H., Gani, A., Ahmed, E., Nainar, A. S. M., Akim, N. M., & Imran, M. (2020). Deep learning and big data technologies for IoT security. *Computer Communications, 151*, 495–517. https://doi.org/10.1016/j.comcom.2020.01.016

Anand, P., Singh, Y., Selwal, A., Alazab, M., Tanwar, S., & Kumar, N. (2020). IoT vulnerability assessment for sustainable computing: Threats, current solutions, and open challenges. *IEEE Access, 8*, 168825–168853. https://doi.org/10.1109/ACCESS.2020.3022842

Bhardwaj, A., & Goundar, S. (2019). A framework for effective threat hunting. *Network Security, 2019*(6), 15–19. https://doi.org/10.1016/S1353-4858(19)30074-1

Boeckl, K., Fagan, M., Fisher, W., Lefkovitz, N., Megas, K. N., Nadeau, E., & Piccarreta, B. (2019). *NISTIR 8228 considerations for managing Internet of Things (IoT) cybersecurity and privacy risks.* NIST. https://nvlpubs.nist.gov/nistpubs/ir/2019/NIST.IR.8228.pdf

Boukerche, A., & Coutinho, R. W. L. (2021). Design guidelines for machine learning-based cybersecurity in Internet of things. *IEEE Network, 35*(1), 393–399. https://doi.org/10.1109/MNET.011.2000396

Brooks, C. (2018). *What is deep packet inspection? How it works, use cases for DPI, and more.* https://digitalguardian.com/blog/what-deep-packet-inspection-how-it-works-use-cases-dpi-and-more

Burruss, G. W., Howell, C. J., Maimon, D., & Wang, F. (2021). Website defacer classification: A finite mixture model approach. *Social Science Computer Review, 1*, 1–13. https://doi.org/10.1177/0894439321994232

Chaabouni, N., Mosbah, M., Zemmari, A., Sauvignac, C., & Faruki, P. (2019). Network intrusion detection for IoT security based on learning techniques. *IEEE Communications Surveys & Tutorials, Communications Surveys & Tutorials, 21*(3), 2671–2701. https://doi.org/10.1109/COMST.2019.2896380

Chakkaravarthy, S. S., Sangeetha, D., Cruz, M. V., Vaidehi, V., & Raman, B. (2020). Design of intrusion detection honeypot using social leopard algorithm to detect IoT ransomware attacks. *IEEE Access, 8*, 169944–169956. https://doi.org/10.1109/ACCESS.2020.3023764

Chanson, M., Bogner, A., Bilgeri, D., Fleisch, E., & Wortmann, F. (2019). Blockchain for the IoT: Privacy-preserving protection of sensor data. *Journal of the Association for Information Systems, 20*(9), 1271–1307. https://doi.org/10.17705/1jais.00567

Check Point. (2021). *What is an intrusion detection system?* https://www.checkpoint.com/cyber-hub/network-security/what-is-an-intrusion-detection-system-ids/#

Coker, J. (2021). *Smart home experiences over 12,000 cyber-attacks in a week.* https://www.infosecurity-magazine.com/news/smart-home-experiences-cyber/

Collins, M. (2018). *Threat hunting: A guide to proactive network defense* (1st ed.). O'Reilly Media.

Danda, J. M. R., & Hota, C. (2016). Attack identification framework for IoT devices. In S. Satapathy, J. Mandal, S. Udgata, & V. Bhateja (Eds.), *Information systems design and intelligent applications. Advances in intelligent systems and computing* (Vol. 434). Springer. https://doi.org/10.1007/978-81-322-2752-6_49

Das, S. K., Kant, K., & Zhang, N. (2012). *Handbook on securing cyber-physical critical infrastructure.* Morgan Kaufmann.

Davanzo, G., Medvet, E., & Bartoli, A. (2011). Anomaly detection techniques for a web defacement monitoring service. *Expert Systems with Applications, 38*(10), 12521–12530. https://doi.org/10.1016/j.eswa.2011.04.038

Death, D. (2017). *Information security handbook.* Packt Publishing.

Dow, C., & Lea, P. (2019). *Mastering IoT: Build modern IoT solutions that secure and monitor your IoT infrastructure.* Packt Publishing.

Elrawy, M., Awad, A., & Hamed, H. (2018). Intrusion detection systems for IoT-based smart environments: A survey. *Journal of Cloud Computing, 7*(21), 1–20. https://doi.org/10.1186/s13677-018-0123-6

ENISA. (2019). *Good practices for security of IoT.* https://www.enisa.europa.eu/publications/good-practices-for-security-of-iot-1

Feng, W., Zhang, Q., Hu, G., & Huang, J. X. (2014). Mining network data for intrusion detection through combining SVMs with ant colony networks. *Future Generation Computer Systems, 37*, 127–140. https://doi.org/10.1016/j.future.2013.06.027

Figliola, P. M. (2020). *The Internet of things (IoT): An overview.* https://fas.org/sgp/crs/misc/IF11239.pdf

Gautam, K. S., & Om, H. (2016). Computational neural network regression model for host-based intrusion detection system. *Perspective in Science, 8*, 93–95. https://doi.org/10.1016/j.pisc.2016.04.005

Gendreau, A. A., & Moorman, M. (2016). Survey of intrusion detection systems towards an end-to-end secure Internet of things. In *2016 IEEE 4th International Conference on Future Internet of Things and Cloud (FiCloud), IEEE* (pp. 84–90). https://doi.org/10.1109/FiCloud.2016.20

Gilchrist, A. (2017). *IoT security issues* (1st ed.). DeG Press.

Goodin, D. (2020). *When coffee makers are demanding a ransom, you know IoT is screwed.* https://arstechnica.com/information-technology/2020/09/how-a-hacker-turned-a-250-coffee-maker-into-ransom-machine/

Holst, A. (2021). *Number of Internet of things (IoT) connected devices worldwide from 2019 to 2030 (in billions).* https://www.statista.com/statistics/1183457/iot-connected-devices-worldwide/

Howell, C. J., Burruss, G. W., Maimon, D., & Sahani, S. (2019). Website defacement and routine activities: Considering the importance of hackers' valuations of potential targets. *Journal of Crime & Justice, 42*(5), 536–550. https://doi.org/10.1080/0735648X.2019.1691859

Intel Corporation. (2015). *A guide to the Internet of things; How billions of online objects are making the web wiser.* https://www.intel.fr/content/www/fr/fr/internet-of-things/infographics/guide-to-iot-new.html

Johnson, J. (2021). *Global digital population as of January 2021.* https://www.statista.com/statistics/617136/digital-population-worldwide/

Jurcut, A., Niculcea, T., Ranaweera, P., & LeKhac, A. (2020). Security considerations for Internet of Things: A survey. *S.N. Computer Science, 1*(193), 1–19. https://doi.org/10.1007/s42979-020-00201-3

Kandasamy, K., Srinivas, S., Achuthan, K., & Rangan, V. P. (2020). IoT cyber risk: A holistic analysis of cyber risk assessment frameworks, risk vectors, and risk ranking process. *EURASIP Journal on Information Security, 2020*(1), 1–18. https://doi.org/10.1186/s13635-020-00111-0

Karuna, P., Hemberg, E., O'Reilly, U.-M., & Rutar, N. (2021). *Automating cyber threat hunting using NLP, automated query generation, and genetic perturbation.* Cornell University. https://arxiv.org/abs/2104.11576

Khan, R., Khan, S. U., Zaheer, R., & Khan, S. (2012). Future Internet: The Internet of things architecture, possible applications, and key challenges. In *2012 10th International Conference on Frontiers of Information Technology, IEEE* (pp. 257–260). https://doi.org/10.1109/FIT.2012.53.

Krushang, S., & Upadhyay, H. (2014). A survey: DDOS attack on Internet of things. *International Journal of Engineering Research and Development, 10*(11), 58–63. http://www.ijerd.com/paper/vol10-issue11/Version_3/I10115863.pdf

Laughlin, A. (2021). *How a smart home could be at risk from hackers.* https://www.which.co.uk/news/2021/07/how-the-smart-home-could-be-at-risk-from-hackers/

LeBlanc, J., & Messerschmidt, T. (2016). *Identity and data security for web development: Best practices* (1st ed.). O'Reilly.

Lin, W. C., Ke, S. W., & Tsai, C. F. (2015). CANN: An intrusion detection system based on combining cluster centers and nearest neighbors. *Knowledge-Based Systems, 78*, 13–21. https://doi.org/10.1016/j.knosys.2015.01.009

Lohrmann, D. (2021). *2020 data breaches point to cybersecurity trends for 2021.* https://www.govtech.com/blogs/lohrmann-on-cybersecurity/2020-data-breaches-point-to-cybersecurity-trends-for-2021.html

Maimon, D., Wu, Y., Stubler, N., & Sinigirikonda, P. (2020). *Extended validation in the dark web: Evidence from investigation of the certification services and products sold on darknet markets. EBCS Reports, 2.* https://scholarworks.gsu.edu/ebcs_reports/2

Malhotra, P., Singh, Y., Anand, P., Bangotra, D. K., Singh, P. K., Hong, W.-C., & Calafate, C. T. (2021). Internet of things: Evolution, concerns and security challenges. *Sensors, 21*(5), 1809–1842. https://doi.org/10.3390/s21051809

Mishra, P., Pilli, E. S., Varadharajan, V., & Tupakula, U. (2017). Intrusion detection techniques in cloud environment: A survey. *Journal of Network and Computer Applications, 77*, 18–47. https://doi.org/10.1016/j.jnca.2016.10.015

Modi, C., Patel, D., Borisaniya, B., Patel, H., Patel, A., & Rajarajan, M. (2013). A survey of intrusion detection techniques in cloud. *Journal of Network and Computer Applications, 36*(1), 42–57. https://doi.org/10.1016/j.jnca.2012.05.003

Morgan, S. (2020). *Cybercrime to cost the world $10.5 trillion annually by 2025.* https://cybersecurityventures.com/hackerpocalypse-cybercrime-report-2016/

Newman, L. H. (2020). *Hackers could use IoT botnets to manipulate energy markets.* https://www.wired.com/story/hackers-iot-botnets-manipulate-energy-markets/

NIST. (2019). *Considerations for managing Internet of things (IoT) cybersecurity and privacy risks: NISTIR 8228.* NIST. https://csrc.nist.gov/News/2019/nist-publishes-nistir-8228

Noor, M. B. N., & Hassan, W. H. (2019). Current research on Internet of things (IoT) security: A survey. *Computer Networks, 148*, 283–294. https://doi.org/10.1016/j.comnet.2018.11.025

Oueslati, H. (2021). *IoT security: IoT needn't be the Internet of threats.* https://www.cpomagazine.com/cyber-security/iot-security-iot-neednt-be-the-internet-of-threats/

Owaida, A. (2020). *50,000 home cameras reportedly hacked, footage posted online.* https://www.welivesecurity.com/2020/10/14/50000-home-cameras-reportedly-hacked-footage-posted-online/

OWASP. (2021). *OWASP top 10.* https://owasp.org/www-project-top-ten/

Pingol, E. (2020). *U.S. IoT improvement act becomes law.* https://www.trendmicro.com/us/iot-security/news/6613

Posey, B. (2021). *Backdoor (computing).* https://searchsecurity.techtarget.com/definition/back-door

Raidman, D. (2020). *Medical devices on the IoT put lives at risk.* https://www.darkreading.com/iot/medical-devices-on-the-iot-put-lives-at-risk/a/d-id/1337448

Ramdas, A., & Muthukrishnan, R. (2019). A survey on DNS security issues and mitigation techniques. *2019 International Conference on Intelligent Computing and Control Systems (ICCS),* 2019, 781–784. https://doi.org/10.1109/ICCS45141.2019.9065354.

RiskBased Security. (2021). *2020 year end report; Data breach quickview.* https://pages.riskbasedsecurity.com/en/en/2020-yearend-data-breach-quickview-report

Rizvi, S., Kurtz, A., Pfeffer, J., & Rizvi, M. (2018). Securing the Internet of Things (IoT): A security taxonomy for IoT. In *17th IEEE International Conference on Trust, Security and Privacy in Computing and Communications/12th IEEE International Conference on Big Data Science and Engineering (TrustCom/BigDataSE): Trust, Security and Privacy in Computing and Communications* (pp. 163–168). https://doi.org/10.1109/TrustCom/BigDataSE.2018.00034

Russell, B., & Duren, D. V. (2018). *Practical Internet of things security: Design a security framework for an Internet connected ecosystem.* Packt Publishing.

Sen, R. (2021). *Here's how much your personal information is worth to cybercriminals – and what they do with it.* https://theconversation.com/heres-how-much-your-personal-information-is-worth-to-cybercriminals-and-what-they-do-with-it-158934

Schlinger, A. (2020). *The 18 best fitness watches to track your workouts.* https://www.menshealth.com/fitness/a19543741/best-fitness-watches-track-workouts/

Schwab, K. (2019). *IoT security is so bad, many companies can't tell when they're hacked.* https://www.fastcompany.com/90292568/iot-security-is-so-bad-many-companies-cant-tell-when-theyre-hacked

Sharafaldin, I., Lashkari, A. H., & Ghorbani, A. A. (2018). Toward generating a new intrusion detection dataset and intrusion traffic characterization. *ICISSp,* 1, 108–116.

Sharma, S., & Dixit, M. (2016). A review on network intrusion detection system using open-source snort. *International Journal of Database Theory and Application,* 9(4), 61–70. http://article.nadiapub.com/IJDTA/vol9_no4/5.pdf

Shukla, S., Thakur, S., Hussain, S., Breslin, J. G., & Jameel, S. M. (2021). Identification and authentication in healthcare Internet-of-things using integrated fog computing based blockchain model. *Internet-of-Things,* 15, 100422. Science Direct. https://doi.org/10.1016/j.iot.2021.100422

Singh, D., Tripathi, G., & Jara, A. J. (2014). A survey of Internet-of-Things: Future vision, architecture, challenges, and services. In *2014 IEEE World Forum on Internet of Things (WF-IoT)* (pp. 287–292). https://doi.org/10.1109/WF-IoT.2014.6803174.

Sivanathan, A., Sherratt, D., Gharakheili, H. H., Radford, A., Wijenayake, C., Vishwanath, A., & Sivaraman, V. (2017). Characterizing and classifying IoT traffic in smart cities and campuses. In *IEEE Conference on Computer Communications Workshops (INFOCOM WKSHPS)* (pp. 559–564). https://doi.org/10.1109/INFCOMW.2017.8116438.

Statista Research Department. (2016). *Internet of Things (IoT) connected devices installed base worldwide from 2015 to 2025 (in billions).* https://www.statista.com/statistics/471264/iot-number-of-connected-devices-worldwide/

Statista Research Department. (2021). *Global Internet of Things enabled sensors market in 2016 and 2022.* https://www.statista.com/statistics/773994/global-internet-of-things-enabled-sensors-market-size/

Stewart, J. M., Chapple, M., & Gibson, D. (2015). *CISSP (ISC)2 certified information systems security professional official study guide.* Sybex.

Strous, L., von Solms, S., & Zúquete, A. (2021). Security and privacy of the Internet of things. *Computers & Security, 102,* 102148. https://doi.org/10.1016/j.cose.2020.102148

Taschler, S. (2021). *What is proactive threat hunting?* https://www.crowdstrike.com/cybersecurity-101/threat-hunting/

Technopedia. (2021). *Firmware.* https://www.techopedia.com/definition/2137/firmware

Torabi, S., Bou-Harb, E., Assi, C., Galluscio, M., Boukhtouta, A., & Debbabi, M. (2018). Inferring, characterizing, and investigating Internet-scale malicious IoT device activities: A network telescope perspective. In *2018 48th Annual IEEE/IFIP International Conference on Dependable Systems and Networks (DSN)* (pp. 562–573). https://doi.org/10.1109/DSN.2018.00064.

Trabelsi, Z., Zeidan, S., & Masud, M. M. (2016). Network packet filtering and deep packet inspection hybrid mechanism for IDS early packet matching. In *2016 IEEE 30th International Conference on Advanced Information Networking and Applications (AINA). IEEE* (pp. 808–815). https://doi.org/10.1109/AINA.2016.178

University of New Brunswick. (n.d.-A). *Intrusion detection evaluation dataset (CIC-IDS2017).* https://www.unb.ca/cic/datasets/ids-2017.html

University of New Brunswick. (n.d.-B). *Intrusion detection evaluation dataset (ISCXIDS2012).* https://www.unb.ca/cic/datasets/ids.html

University of New Brunswick. (n.d.-C). *CSE-CIC-IDS2018 on AWS; A collaborative project between the Communications Security Establishment (CSE) & the Canadian Institute of Cybersecurity (CIC).* https://www.unb.ca/cic/datasets/ids-2018.html

Weijer, S. G. A. V. D., Holt, T. J., & Leukfeldt, E. R. (2021). Heterogeneity in trajectories of cybercriminals: A longitudinal analyses of web defacements. *Computers in Human Behavior Reports, 4,* 100113. https://doi.org/10.1016/j.chbr.2021.100113

Chapter 8

Data privacy, training, and awareness and cybersecurity frameworks

INTRODUCTION

Leadership is paramount in cybersecurity management. An organization's culture depends on how its leaders define security and promote a culture of security among employees and stakeholders. As such, many leaders embrace compliance with various cybersecurity frameworks (e.g., National Institute of Standards and Technology (NIST) or ISO 27000) in their quest to develop cybersecurity policies. These policies should include compliance with data privacy rules (e.g., the General Data Protection Regulation (GDPR)), which have evolved considerably over the years. Another critical element involves implementing cybersecurity training and awareness sessions among computer and network users.

This chapter will first review data privacy policies, assessment tools, and existing cybersecurity training and awareness policies, along with programs developed to train computer network users in various organizations. We will then discuss the common matrices security teams use to assess tools' and policies' effectiveness in achieving a more secure cyber infrastructure, in light of the relevant academic research. Following a review of the scientific evidence, we will propose the operationalization of additional data privacy and cyber training-related measures, then offer relevant research designs to facilitate rigorous investigations of these policies' effectiveness in protecting data privacy and reducing the risk of cybercrime.

Data privacy

Data is now the most critical asset for organizations (Chavalit & Hohler, 2020), as personal data is the new oil of the Internet and the new currency of the digital environment (Gilchrist, 2017). As a result, the privacy and security concerns introduced by the Internet, new technologies, artificial intelligence, and big data are growing at an unprecedented rate (Lee Williams, 2016). As Lee et al. (2016) explained, data privacy is about how organizations access, collect, and utilize data, and about the data subject's legal rights. Since the use of data is growing exponentially every day, protecting information is now an extremely challenging task (Chavalit & Hohler, 2020). Failure to protect data adequately can significantly damage an organization's reputation, reduce customers' trust, and lead to substantial fines (Chavalit & Hohler, 2020).

According to Chavalit and Hohler (2020), data protection is the practice of preserving information from compromise, loss, and disruption. The scope of data protection includes the classification, categorization, and retention of all data in an organization. Specifically, companies need to ensure data is available at all times and understand the sensitivity and type of data they collect, process, and store within their infrastructure (Chavalit & Hohler, 2020). They also need to act as fiduciaries to ensure data is appropriately retained based on business needs and at the same time consider various regulations that may apply depending on where they do business.

Digital risks

To gain a competitive advantage, capitalize on digital information, and own personal data, businesses of all types must manage risks and protect data privacy through cybersecurity. As more knowledge and processes get digitized, more risks may occur – the Internet of Things (IoT), for example, exponentially increases the amount of user data via connected devices – and an organization's evolution is influenced by the way it manages risks of all kinds (e.g., reputational, ethics, conformity, regulation, market, strategic, and credit) (Carataș et al., 2019; Williams, 2016). Other risks in the digital transformation process may be associated with culture, talents, good judgment, risk appetite, risk management ability, and the use of the legacy systems (old technology). Digital risk refers to the entire range of digital behavior influencing the effectiveness and response to risk of 'all processes and decisions that include automation, for digital surveillance and warning actions' (Carataș et al., 2019, p. 243). Overall, given that there are numerous hostile actions carried out in cyberspace capable of affecting the confidentiality, integrity, and availability (CIA) of the information systems' functioning, the use of new technologies may generate risks that can seriously affect the individual or the organization (Carataș et al., 2019).

According to Carataș et al. (2019) organizations use data governance 'to manage, engage, and assure data' (e.g., an enterprise hard copy or digital assets) (p. 243). Hence, defining data becomes a key business process and is part of data governance best practices. However, it can be challenging to define what *data* means for the company, decide where to store or locate it (e.g., multiple systems, cloud providers, and other third parties), and understand how it can be used (Carataș et al., 2019). Moreover, to adequately protect data, security professionals need to understand why cybercriminals would be interested in accessing certain datasets (the value of the data), and how they can better secure that data based on the associated risks.

Data breaches

Unfortunately, data breaches continue to impact organizations worldwide, and not a day goes by without some data breach affecting personal information. Many data breaches result from human factors, whether accidental (e.g., an employee or a contractor), intentional (e.g., an insider threat), or malicious (e.g., a cybercriminal group). As argued by Williams (2016), there is often also little transparency about how much data organizations collect about users and how they use it, despite the enormous quantity of data collected about each of us (e.g., through IoT devices, geo-localization, transactional data) that has inherent monetary value for bad actors.

One recent data breach that compromised millions of potential victims' identities is the Equifax data breach in 2017, where data from more than 143 million people (more than 40% of the US population) were exposed, including names, addresses, date of birth, social security numbers, and driver's licenses (Fruhlinger, 2020). Ultimately, this led to a US$575 million settlement (Swinhoe, 2021). Moreover, there was an ethics violation and data leak at Cambridge Analytica, as well as a Facebook data breach that became public in 2018 – a political consulting company collected and used the personal data of 87 million Facebook users, using it to create personalized voting ads supporting Donald Trump (Carataş et al., 2019). The Marriott data breach is another significant case, as it was confirmed in 2018 that a Chinese spy agency hacked the data of 500 million guests of the Marriott hotel chain, starting in 2014, forcing the organization to pay a US$124 million fine (Gressin, 2018; Swinhoe, 2021).

Among many other potential examples (e.g., 3 billion Yahoo accounts in 2017, 700 million LinkedIn users in 2021, 533 million Facebook users in 2019, 330 million Twitter users in 2018, and 100 million T-Mobile customers) (Abrams, 2021; Tungall, 2021), Capital One bank suffered a breach in 2019, affecting 100 million customers in the US and 6 million in Canada, when a former employee of Amazon, Paige Thompson, illegally obtained personal information of Capital One Bank credit card customers by exploiting a configuration vulnerability in Capital One's web application firewall (Swinhoe, 2021). More recently, in 2021, SolarWinds, a major US information technology firm, was the victim of an unprecedented cyberattack via third-party application programming interface (API) keys that spread to its clients (e.g., large private organizations and government agencies) and went undetected for months, more evidence of third-party risks (Jibilian & Canales, 2021).

CYBERSECURITY GOVERNANCE

As Moschovitis (2018) suggested, an organization's cybersecurity governance is analogous to driving a car. If the vehicle's wheels are out of alignment, the driver must fight the steering wheel to keep the car straight on the road.

Similarly, an organization's business goals, information technology, and cybersecurity must be aligned to ensure smooth governance. Because governance is 'the collective set of principle-guided actions that when applied guide a company to fulfillment of its goals,' Moschovitis (2018, p. 47) argued, company leaders must think about, agree on, and consistently apply cybersecurity governance to generate results.

Misalignment in this context could include technology being out of sync with business needs or the cybersecurity team not protecting the right assets. In both examples, technology and cybersecurity are not working together to support the organization's business goals. The causes of misalignment are often very complex and intertwined, driven by hidden layers of confusion, lack of leadership, indifference, and office politics. To manage cybersecurity adequately in such a challenging business context, and to make sure cybersecurity management aligns with the organization's business goals, cybersecurity professionals and leaders must avoid poor governance and management at all costs (Moschovitis, 2018). In addition, executives in both public and private organizations must strengthen their internal cybersecurity programs and prepare for the fallout, as only one thing is sure: preventive measures will inevitably fail at some point (Garcia et al., 2017).

Thus, having a holistic strategy is vital. A holistic approach in managing cybersecurity risks consists of (a) identifying risks and the risk appetite of the organization, (b) analyzing and evaluating those risks, (c) treating the risks, and (d) monitoring them on an ongoing basis. As Boehm et al. (2018) argued, implementing a holistic approach to manage cyber-risk requires a top-management overview of the enterprise and its multilayered risks. Exhibit 1 in their paper illustrates the traditional cybersecurity focus versus a holistic approach to managing cybersecurity. Risks may come from within or outside the organization. Furthermore, security executives have to plan responses to potential attacks on external, unrelated entities that can have cascading effects on their organization, the economy, and society (Garcia et al., 2017). For example, given a series of successful cyberattacks against one or many financial institutions in a short period, citizens would have difficulty getting access to their accounts, withdrawing cash, or using their credit cards, while stock exchange trading floors may also be prohibited from conducting market transactions (Pomerleau, 2019).

As Garcia et al. (2017) noted, 'the core challenge for state cybersecurity professionals is not technical; the cutting edge cybersecurity is governance' (p. 253). All technology and security solutions must be configured and implemented by humans. They describe cybersecurity governance as 'the process through which humans understand organizational risk, prioritize resources, and establish procedures to erect technical defenses against computer-based attacks' (p. 254). When it comes to cybersecurity, organizations should seek to become as resilient as possible against internal and external threats that may significantly impact their functions and results. This resilient posture requires three core actions: (1) the deployment of technical and administrative controls to harden vulnerable information assets, (2) user awareness programs and training to maximize compliance with established controls, and (3) the collection and dissemination of information needed to adapt the current security posture to emerging threats (Garcia et al., 2017).

Information security control frameworks

A control framework can be defined as a set of measures put in place to protect an organization's information assets. There are several established control frameworks in the security industry, which individual organizations can customize based on their specific needs. However, the role of governance is generally limited to (a) selecting a control framework, (b) modulating the control framework based on the business context, compliance, and risks specific to the organization, (c) establishing current and target maturity levels, (d) establishing a security program to achieve the target maturity levels, and (e) measuring the effectiveness of controls and the security program. In short, governance asks, 'are we doing the right things?'

Information security governance (ISG) frameworks provide organizations with the means of comprehensively dealing with the security of their information assets. This process needs to involve every stakeholder through governance and management processes (Rebollo et al., 2014). Some organizations will fully implement a specific framework, while others will use sections and recommendations from many frameworks in implementing their ISG. The following section will review some of the most common information security frameworks, guidelines, standards, and recent regulations that have significantly impacted how organizations implement new policies, procedures, and controls to mitigate information security and cyber-risks.

ISO 27001 and 27002

International Organization for Standardization (ISO) 27001 is one of the most prevalent information security standards. Many organizations use it as a baseline for their ISG and operations. As a supplement to ISO 27001, ISO 27002 provides guidelines on implementing the information security controls in Annex A of ISO 27001 (IT Governance, 2021). Both standards are often used together, but only ISO 27001 is required for certifying an Information Security Management System (ISMS). Organizations that have adopted most or all of the requirements in ISO 27001 often need to measure the adequacy of their ISMS, in order to identify deficiencies and opportunities for improvement (Monev, 2020). As Monev (2020) explained, since the integral components of the standard target continuous improvement (like all ISO standards), security control effectiveness measurement, and compliance assessments, cybersecurity experts can significantly benefit from analyzing the results of an ISMS maturity assessment to better protect their organizations.

For instance, ISO/IEC 27002:2013 guides the application of information security by using commonly accepted security controls to enhance security governance and management within organizations (ISO, 2013). Forms of controls involve 14 security areas as defined in ISO/IEC 27001 (ISO, 2013).[i] ISO/IEC 27002:2013 establishes guidelines and general principles to initiate, implement, maintain, and improve information security management in a system. Likewise, ISO/IEC 27002:2013 contains best practices in security management and control in the field of information security management (Sihwi et al., 2016). Thus, ISO 27001 puts a governance framework around the ISO 27002 catalog of controls to extract a framework adapted to a given company in any industry.

National Institute of Standards and Technology (NIST)

The NIST is a US Department of Commerce physical sciences laboratory, chartered to promote technical innovation and industrial competitiveness (Pomerleau & Lowery, 2020). NIST's activities include a wide array of technology-related research endeavors, and it serves as a technical authority on the establishment and maintenance of technical standards in the fields of cybersecurity/information technology, engineering, and nano-scale technologies (National Institute of Standards & Technology (NIST), 2017). In addition, the NIST cybersecurity framework serves as a set of detailed guidelines and industry best practices, designed to assist governmental and private organizations alike with effectively reducing and mitigating potential cybersecurity risks (Pomerleau & Lowery, 2020).

Originally designed to be versatile, the framework was constructed around the fundamental premise that recommended guidelines, standards, policies, procedures, and protocols can only be effective if implemented across the organization as a whole – not just by the organization's internal IT department (National Institute of Standards & Technology (NIST), 2018). Thus, it can serve as a foundational baseline for an organization's cybersecurity policies or enhance existing policies and procedures (Pomerleau & Lowery, 2020). Central to this framework are five continuous core functions: *Identify, Protect, Detect, Respond,* and *Recover.* Collectively, these five distinct operational pillars form the essential components of a holistic cybersecurity program that revolves around the three basic types of cyber threats: *perimeter threats* (e.g., firewalls and antivirus protection), *intranet threats* (e.g., portable data devices and network protection), and *human security* (e.g., poor cyber hygiene practices and potential insider threats) (National Institute of Standards & Technology (NIST), 2017). Beyond the NIST Cybersecurity Framework, NIST also provides *NIST Special Publication 800-30*, an overarching cyber risk assessment framework for conducting risk assessments of individual organizational-level networks, based on federal information systems assessment standards (National Institute of Standards & Technology (NIST), 2012).

LAWS, REGULATIONS, AND INDUSTRY STANDARDS

The General Data Protection Regulation (GDPR)

Regulations in charge of personal data and cybersecurity are fundamental in data classification. Companies that manage to classify data can also safely protect it, using programs to evaluate and identify the content of their data assets. As an example, the European Union adopted in 2018 the GDPR, which applies to all organizations that use personal data of users from the EU, regardless of their location. Hence, it imposes internet privacy on a global level (Carataş et al., 2019). According to Wolford (2021), GDPR is currently the world's strictest privacy and security law. GDPR requirements apply to each member state of the European Union, aiming to create more consistent protection of consumer and personal data across EU nations. Some of its key privacy and data protection requirements include: (1) requiring the consent of subjects for data processing, (2) anonymizing collected data to protect privacy, (3) providing data breach notifications, (4) safely handling the transfer of data across borders, and (5) requiring certain companies to appoint a data protection officer to oversee GDPR compliance (De Groot, 2020a).

Payment Card Industry Data Security Standard (PCI DSS)

The PCI Security Standards Council (PCI SSC) was launched in 2006 to improve the security of payment accounts (PCI Security Standard Council, 2021a). This standard supported the evolution of the Payment Card Industry Data Security Standard. The PCI Security Standards Council (PCI SSC) is an independent organization created by the major payment card brands (Visa, MasterCard, American Express, Discover, and JCB) (Bonner et al., 2011). It applies to all entities that process payment cards or store, process, or transmit cardholder data, including merchants, issuer banks, acquirer banks, and card brands (Rahaman et al., 2020). Different levels of compliance apply depending on the volume of transactions.

Payment Card Industry Data Security Standard (PCI DSS) is technical, prescriptive, and detailed. Therefore, it could be used as a basis for a framework of security controls. In addition, it may extend the scope of credit card data protection to any other type of data necessary to conduct business. As explained by Crozier and Law (2019), under the PCI DSS, the 12 security requirements are categorized under six broader objectives: (1) to build and maintain secure networks and systems, (2) protect cardholder data, (3) maintain a vulnerability management program, (4) implement strong access control measures, (5) regularly monitor and test networks, and (6) maintain an information security policy (Crozier & Law, 2019; PCI Security Standards Council, 2021b). All entities in the PCI ecosystem need to comply with the standard. Each entity needs to obtain a compliance report from qualified security assessors and approved scanning vendors to maintain its membership status. For example, a merchant needs to send its compliance report to the acquirer bank, while a card issuer and acquirer banks need to send their compliance reports to the payment brands. This standard plays an essential role in evaluating industry participants' security and compliance status and in supervising the entities responsible for conducting compliance assessments (Rahaman et al., 2020).

Health Insurance Portability and Accountability Act (HIPAA) – health-related information

In the US, it is more common to see regulations that cover specific industries. One example in the health sector is the Health Insurance Portability and Accountability Act (HIPAA), originally introduced in 1996 (Arora et al., 2014). HIPAA enables the transfer of health insurance coverage for American workers and their families when they change employers. It was implemented primarily to reduce fraud and abuse cases in the field of healthcare (US Department of Health & Human Services, n.d.-a). More specifically, HIPAA dictates standards for the protection of healthcare information, electronic billing, the protection of data, and the confidential treatment of health information.

The HIPAA Privacy Rule specifically protects the privacy of individually identifiable health information, called protected health information (PHI) (US Department of Health & Human Services, n.d.-b). This privacy rule applies to health plans, healthcare clearinghouses, and any healthcare providers who transmit healthcare information (US Department of Health & Human Services, n.d.-c). There are three parts to the HIPAA Security Rule, all of which are necessary to comply with the HIPAA compliance checklist: (1) technical safeguards (e.g., implementing tools for encryption and decryption, implementing a means of access control), (2) physical safeguards (e.g., inventory of hardware, policies for the use and positioning of workstations), and (3) administrative safeguards (e.g., introducing a risk management policy, testing of contingency plans) (HIPAA Journal, 2021). The main security objective is always to protect patient identity and data in such a way that if unauthorized individuals (e.g., hackers) do gain access to the data, they would not be able to link it to a specific patient or health file being shared with other partners (Arora et al., 2014).

New York Department of Financial Services (NYDFS) cybersecurity regulations

New York Department of Financial Services (NYDFS) is a relatively new regulation, first released on 16 February 2017, promoting the protection of clients' personal information as well as the computer systems of all financial institutions and other lenders (e.g., mortgage companies and insurance companies) doing business in the state of New York (De Groot, 2020b). To comply with the NYDFS standards, organizations must adhere to several essential requirements. First, they must have a comprehensive cybersecurity policy in place, and this policy must address concerns in alignment with industry best practices and ISO 27001 standards. NYDFS also requires covered institutions to have reporting procedures, policies in place regarding third-party security, qualified cybersecurity personnel, limited access privileges, and to notify NYDFS of all cybersecurity events that could cause material harm (De Groot, 2020b).

Furthermore, the cybersecurity policy must be aligned with the NIST Cybersecurity Framework by identifying all cybersecurity threats (internal and external), employing a defense infrastructure to protect against threats, using a system to detect cybersecurity events, responding to all detected threat events, working to recover from each cyber incident, and fulfilling requirements for regulatory reporting (De Groot, 2020b). As an example, the NYDFS' breach prevention regulations require notice to the NYDFS superintendent within 72 hours if there is 'a reasonable likelihood of materially harming any material part of the normal operation(s) of the Covered Entity' (Casetext, 2021; Galli, 2018). In addition, covered entities not respecting NYDFS requirements may face financial penalties and their violations may become public (De Groot, 2020b).

CYBERSECURITY TRAINING AND AWARENESS

In May and June 2021, International Data Group (IDG), an American media and research company, conducted a 26-question survey (Global Intelligence Report on Cybersecurity) of 2,741 security, IT, and business professionals around the world, security professionals, and worldwide line-of-business employees across industries: the US and Canada (23%), EMEA (36%), APAC (27%), Latin America (7%), and Africa (7%) (CSO, 2021). The results show that organizations with mandatory security training in place are less likely (vs. organizations without mandatory security training) to expect incidents of industrial espionage (44% vs. 51%), data theft and sabotage (52% vs. 62%), and theft of digital identities or access to the data (57% vs. 64%) (CSO, 2021). Only 49% of respondents reported having a mandatory IT security training and awareness program in place for some time, while 20% responded that they had just implemented one. In contrast, 29% had yet to roll out or had no plans to introduce such training for all employees. Participants with most of their data in the cloud were more likely to have mandatory training (70% vs. 49%) than other respondent segments, and those with a zero-trust approach in place were more likely to have mandatory training in place (54% vs. 40%) than participants that did not have such a security strategy within their organization (CSO, 2021).

Shaw et al. (2009) defined cybersecurity awareness as 'the degree of understanding of users about the importance of information security and their responsibilities and act to exercise sufficient levels of information control to protect the organization's data and networks' (p. 92). The primary purpose of cybersecurity educational tools is to increase cyber literacy relating to security and privacy topics, to raise awareness of cyber-threats, and when applicable, to change user behaviors that might put the organization at risk (Zhang-Kennedy & Chiasson, 2021). Thus, it is imperative to assess whether these tools successfully achieve their educational goals. However, there is no widely accepted systematized evaluation method for determining the 'effectiveness' of cybersecurity educational tools. As Zhang-Kennedy and Chiasson (2021) noted, potential evaluation criteria include: (a) increased awareness and retention of information, (b) improved behavior, (c) positive user engagement, and (d) sound system usability. However, the inconsistent criteria make comparisons between tools challenging (Zhang-Kennedy & Chiasson, 2021).

Although employee information security awareness (ISA) is a relatively new field of research, many scholars have invested considerable efforts to analyze implemented information security measures and factors that affect employee performance on ISA. For instance, Khando et al. (2021) reviewed 64 academic papers to provide a systematic summary of ISA content development methods and how well they increase employee awareness. Tsohou et al. (2008) identified 48 ISA studies and conducted an analysis on assessment approaches to raising cybersecurity awareness. Haeussinger and Kranz (2017) reviewed 44 articles, while Jaeger (2018) reviewed 40 studies, in their studies of factors affecting ISA at the institutional, individual, and socio-environmental levels.

In earlier studies, Lindberg (2016) reviewed 32 papers in which gamification was utilized as an ISA method to study the relationship between game elements, users' risk behavior, user motivation, and enhancing risk awareness. Lebek et al. (2013) reviewed 113 papers exploring the use of behavioral theories as ISA methods to change employees' information security behavior, while Amankwa et al. (2015) focused on 15 studies using models in three stakeholder domains (end user, institutions, and industry domains) for enhancing ISA and conducted a comparative analysis of models identified within these three domains. Bawazir et al. (2016) reviewed 17 studies and focused on using persuasive technology to enhance employee's ISA. Lastly, Rahim et al. (2015) did a literature review of previous assessments of cybersecurity awareness (i.e., 14 studies between 2000 and 2014) to better understand their methodologies, target audiences, and scope of evaluation. One of their findings is that when assessing cybersecurity awareness, categorizing users is essential to ensure the right cybersecurity messages are tailored to the right audiences (Rahim et al., 2015).

Games and gamification

A widely practiced educational approach uses games and gamification to increase security awareness and train employees and Internet users. Many scholars have studied how games may be an effective media to change behaviors and educate users about interacting in cyberspace. However, these same scholars also concluded that current cybersecurity awareness and education tools have multiple limitations (Alotaibi et al., 2016; Battistella & Gresse von Wangenheim, 2016; Connolly et al., 2012; Cullinane et al., 2015; Hendrix et al., 2016; Herr & Allen, 2015; Le Compte et al., 2015; Pastor et al., 2010).

After examining 12 academic papers and ten industry games, Alotaibi et al. (2016) concluded that the focus of industry games is general and should rely on domain-specific topics (e.g., malware, phishing). Overall, gaming shows positive results, but there is also a need for in-depth evaluation with a large sample size of participants. Battistella and Gresse von Wangenheim (2016) identified 107 games for teaching computing in higher education, including topics like software engineering, programming fundamentals, networks, and algorithms. They observed a lack of systematic development of these games in terms of instructional/game theory. According to these authors, this may be because cybersecurity subject matter experts frequently create these games. Also, even though some of these games have been evaluated by empirical studies, there is a lack of long-term studies evaluating the effects of instructional games and comparing each type.

Connolly et al. (2012) identified 129 papers reporting empirical evidence about the impacts and outcomes of computer games on users aged 14 years or above, in terms of learning, skill enhancement, and engagement. They found some empirical evidence regarding the effectiveness of game-based learning, but suggested additional random control trials to provide more rigorous evidence. In particular, researchers should perform more qualitative studies, develop a better understanding of the tasks, activities, and operations of the different games offered, examine the skills required and how they match learning outcomes, and consider how they should be integrated in students' learning experiences (Connolly et al., 2012). Cullinane et al. (2015) likewise evaluated seven existing games based on replay value, progression qualities, and interface accessibility. They found that games with strong gameplay elements ranked higher in those categories and proposed new game designs to educate minors (aged 11–14) about cybersecurity concepts.

Similar to Battistella and Gresse von Wangenheim (2016), Hendrix et al. (2016) found that most studies assessing security tools' effectiveness covered a short period of time. Also, they noted that short-term interventions are not particularly effective in affecting behavioral change. Herr and Allen (2015) concluded that while current cybersecurity games introduce some relevant concepts, none of the reviewed games were comprehensive enough to set the proper foundation required for cybersecurity professionals.

Le Compte et al. (2015) concluded that *serious games* have pedagogical effectiveness, but they have only been used in a limited number of contexts. To remedy this situation, the authors proposed a six-step framework to design games intended to increase cybersecurity awareness: (1) preliminary analysis, (2) design, (3) development, (4) game assessment, (5) deployment, and (6) player assessment. Pastor et al. (2010) analyzed the technical features of simulation systems (N = 13) developed for information security and information assurance education, training, and awareness. They concluded that most simulation systems could be used to illustrate different information assurance concepts. Still, not all security simulators were developed with information security education, training, and awareness in mind.

For more information about how these tools can be evaluated and their educational impact (evaluation methodologies and empirical evidence) are measured, we recommend the following references:

Rahim, N. H.A., Hamid, S., Mat Kiah, M. L., Shamshirband, S., & Furnell, S. (2015).A systematic review of approaches to assessing cybersecurity awareness. *Kybernetes, 44*(4), 606–622.

Zhang-Kennedy, L., & Chiasson, S. (2021).A systematic review of multimedia tools for cybersecurity awareness and education. *ACM Computing Surveys, 54*(1), 1–39. https://doi.org/10.1145/3427920

ASSESSMENT TOOLS

The Federal Financial Institution Examination Council (FFIEC) cybersecurity assessment tool

Due to the increased volume and sophistication of cyber-threats, the Federal Financial Institution Examination Council (FFIEC) developed the cybersecurity assessment tool to place its members (US financial institutions) in a better position to identify risks and evaluate their respective organizational maturity levels in protecting themselves (FFIEC, 2017). The assessment relies on the principles of the FFIEC Information Technology Examination Handbook (IT Handbook), the NIST Cybersecurity Framework, and industry-accepted best practices. More specifically, it provides institutions with a repeatable and measurable process to inform management of their institution's risks and cybersecurity preparedness (FFIEC, 2017).

To complete the assessment, management begins by assessing the institution's inherent risk profile based on five categories: (1) technologies and connection types, (2) delivery channels, (3) online/mobile products and technology services, (4) organizational characteristics, and (5) external threats management. Then, the second step consists of evaluating the institution's cybersecurity maturity level for each of five domains: (1) cyber risk management and oversight, (2) threat intelligence and collaboration, (3) cybersecurity controls, (4) external dependency management, and (5) cyber incident management and resilience (FFIEC, 2017). By completing both steps, the management team can better assess the cybersecurity maturity level of the organization and its relation to the risks they are facing (FFIEC, 2017).

Research methods to evaluate cybersecurity awareness tools

Numerous research methods do exist to evaluate cybersecurity awareness tools. However, according to Zhang-Kennedy and Chiasson (2021), these tools consist primarily of

> lab studies conducted in a controlled environment, field studies conducted with a group of participants in their environment over some time, and web-based studies conducted completely online with no in-person contact with the participants. Data collection methods include observation, interview, pre-post tests, survey, questionnaire, eye-tracking, in-tool automated metrics, Wizard-of-Oz protocol, think-aloud protocol, feedback, and note-taking. (p. 21)

Specifically, pretest and posttest study designs, including a control condition to measure learning, are not widely used to evaluate cybersecurity assessment tools. Unfortunately, most of the previous learning assessments did not control for participants' prior knowledge or compare the tool's learning effects to other educational methods, leading to a lack of evidence on the effectiveness of the tools. Instead, most researchers use survey instruments (e.g., privacy attitudinal scale) or performance tests that usually involve participants completing a series of tasks. Also, Likert scales are used to measure the level of engagement (Zhang-Kennedy & Chiasson, 2021).

Additional practical tools

Scenario exercises (e.g., tabletop exercises) help increase cyber-risk awareness and instill a sense of urgency among employees. Security professionals can focus on the mindset of potential attackers and the concept of the weakest link in the chain of defense. They can also evaluate what could potentially happen (e.g., various threats that could affect the organization) and practice response capabilities. Such a mindset can be rolled out to the entire organization through an extensive training program, making sure skills are passed on from expert to expert and from experts to all employees (Poppensieker & Riemenschnitter, 2018).

Targeted audit and penetration testing

Organizations should conduct audits and penetration testing to assess the robustness of the security controls they have in place. They should also require their third-party providers (e.g., cloud service providers) to provide complete visibility on the controls and procedures they have implemented and any exposure to incidents (Elumalai et al., 2018). In addition, an audit of third-party providers should be conducted to assess technological and physical controls (e.g., data center security controls) in place. ASIS International offers many security standards for security professionals to use to improve the organization's security posture. Some of these standards are the Information Asset Protection, Business Continuity Management, Conformity Assessment and Auditing Management Systems for Quality of Private Security Company Operations, Risk Assessment, Security Awareness, Security and Resilience in Organizations and their Supply Chains – Requirements with Guidance, and Physical Asset Protection (ASIS International, 2021).

Surveys and executive workshops

McKinsey experts recommended five key steps to their clients: (1) identify and map digital assets (data systems and applications across the business value chain) through the use of a common taxonomy for information assets, (2) assess the risks for each asset using surveys and executive workshops, (3) identify potential attackers, the availability of assets to users, and current controls and security measures in place, (4) locate where security is the weakest around *crown jewels* and identify what controls should be in place, and (5) create a set of initiatives to address high-priority risks and control gaps (Kaminski et al., 2017). Specifically regarding the use of surveys and executive workshops, Kaminski et al. (2017) argued that security and risk management professionals should base their analysis on the business importance of each asset. It is impossible to protect all assets at the same level as it would be too costly for organizations. Having a *risk-based approach* is the best way to manage risks. Organizations need to identify their crown jewels (i.e., the most critical assets in terms of value for the organization), prioritize them, and invest more resources to reduce the probability that a threat could target vulnerabilities of essential assets (Choi et al., 2017). Executives and asset owners need to be involved in these exercises. The organization may have multiple crown jewels to protect. However, they have limited resources, so strategic decisions will need to be taken to identify which critical assets will be prioritized over others.

Risk assessment

A risk assessment provides the analytical foundation for risk management, and it is a crucial step in the overall risk management process commonly used for decision-making (ASIS International and The Risk and Insurance Management Society, 2015). It is designed to consider the mission, vision, culture, and strategic and tactical objectives of the organization, and it assesses what could affect the achievement of the organization's objectives (ASIS International and The Risk and Insurance Management Society, 2015). By conducting a comprehensive risk assessment, security professionals responsible for decision-making can select from potential choices based on the best available information, then decide on the best course of action. To do so, they have to follow a structured and rigorous approach to review and analyze relevant facts, observations, and possible outcomes (ASIS International and The Risk and Insurance Management Society, 2015).

Moreover, the ISO 31000 standard can provide guidance and a level of reassurance to organizations when it comes to risk management. This standard may allow organizations to increase the likelihood of achieving objectives, improve the identification of opportunities and threats, and improve the allocation of resources for a better risk treatment (ISO, n.d.). The first step in conducting a risk assessment is to gather data. This process is important to find, recognize, and record the various risks the organization may face (ASIS International and The Risk and Insurance Management Society, 2015). In other words, this process will allow the organization to identify its risks: the causes, events, situations, and circumstances that may negatively impact its business objectives (ASIS International and The Risk and Insurance Management Society, 2015).

Impact and probability levels to assess risks

Some of the methods that may be used are (1) evidence-based methods (e.g., observations, interviews, checklist, historical data), (2) systematic team approaches in which a team of risk experts asks a structured set of questions to identify risks, or (3) inductive reasoning techniques (e.g., scanning, scenario analysis, and event tree logic diagrams) (ASIS International and The Risk and Insurance Management Society, 2015). Another method is to evaluate the potential impact to the organization if a previously identified risk does materialize. Table 8.1 illustrates an example. We can see that the risk to data was evaluated at three different impact levels: low impact, medium impact, and high impact to the organization. The same type of exercise can be done to evaluate the probability levels. These levels can be low (e.g., at least 75% of the organization's security controls are following ISO 27002), medium (e.g., 40–60% of the organization's security controls are following ISO 27002), and high (e.g., a maximum of 30% of the organization's security controls are following ISO 27002) (Sihwi et al., 2016).

Table 8.1 Impact levels table

List impact	Low impact (green)	Medium impact (yellow)	High impact (red)
Data security	Data can be viewed by people who should not have the authority to look at the data	Data can be viewed and manipulated by people who should not have the authority to look at data	Data can be viewed and manipulated by people who should not have the authority to look at the data. As a result, the data can be lost or uncovered

Source: The table is adapted from Sihwi et al. (2016, p. 57).

Table 8.2 Probability and impact

Impact		Low	Medium	High
Probability	High	1	7	9
	Medium	2	6	7
	Low	3	4	6

Source: The table is adapted from Sihwi et al. (2016, p. 58).[ii]

Table 8.2 shows the combination of the impact levels and the probability levels in the same matrix. Each risk is evaluated for its probability and impact levels using scores from 1 (i.e., high probability and low impact) to 9 (i.e., high probability and high impact). Using this kind of matrix allows security and risk management professionals to quickly identify combinations of impact and probability levels, such as low-impact/medium-probability or medium-impact/high-probability. This helps them decide where to invest time and resources to mitigate the organization's most critical risks. For instance, if an identified risk (e.g., data leakage – insider threat) has a high impact level and a medium probability of occurring, while another risk (e.g., misconfigured cloud servers, shadow IT) is evaluated at a high impact level but a low probability, the data leakage risk needs to be prioritized. In this case, more controls need to be implemented to reduce the likelihood and impact of data leakage from potential insider threats.

RELEVANT CONCEPTUAL AND RESEARCH DESIGNS

Many scholars have recently studied information security standards, rules and regulations, and efficiency in cybersecurity awareness programs and tools. This section provides an overview of some relevant conceptual and research designs within the literature on data privacy, training and awareness, and the applicability of cybersecurity frameworks and compliance standards.

Rahaman et al. (2020) took a measurement approach to evaluate the PCI DSS certification process for e-commerce websites. They developed testbeds and tools to quantitatively measure the degree of PCI DSS compliance of PCI scanners (i.e., security companies performing external security scans and providing compliance certificates) and e-commerce merchants, but found a considerable gap between the security standard and its real-world applications. For example, none of the six PCI scanners tested were fully compliant with the PCI scanning guidelines despite issuing certificates to merchants with significant security vulnerabilities (Rahaman et al., 2020).

To further their research, Rahaman et al. (2020) built a scanning tool called PCI-CheckerLite, with which they scanned 1,203 e-commerce websites from various industries. Eighty six percent of the websites scanned had at least one PCI DSS violation that would have led to non-compliance with the standards (Rahaman et al., 2020). Without such an experiment, the clients using these e-commerce websites might wrongly assume that the websites were fully secured. Therefore, independent audit, testing, and scanning should be conducted to avoid thinking that a technological tool is safe when it has actually several vulnerabilities that attackers could exploit.

Back and Guerette (2021) aimed to investigate the effectiveness of crime management techniques and assess whether they reduce cybercrime incidents in an online setting. More specifically, this study evaluated the impact of an anti-phishing training program delivered to employees to increase their awareness and understanding of methods to protect the organization from cybercrimes (Back & Guerette, 2021). To do so, the researchers used data derived from the information technology division of a large urban research university in the US, measuring (1) whether university employees fell for phishing campaigns and (2) the security performance of university employees who completed the cybersecurity awareness program. A quasi-experimental research design was used to evaluate the effectiveness of the cybersecurity program, as a random sample selection was not possible.

From the faculty list of employees, the researchers randomly selected a group of 1,000 employees who had completed the cybersecurity awareness program between October 2018 and April 2019 (the treatment group), as well as another randomly selected group of 1,000 employees who did not complete the program (the comparison group). All the participants (N = 2,000) received one simulated phishing attempt between 15 May and 21 May 21 2019 (Back & Guerette, 2021). To measure whether a difference existed between the groups, the dependent variable was whether or not the university employee fell for the phishing campaign after completing (or not completing) the cybersecurity awareness program. The researchers used a t-test and Mann–Whitney tests to examine the differences between both groups on the dependent variable (i.e., the status of response to phishing campaign), then used a logistic regression analysis to examine associations between the dependent variable, the completion of cybersecurity awareness training, and sociodemographic background factors (Back & Guerette, 2021).

The results showed that the university's cybersecurity training had a moderate effect on the users' online behaviors when engaging with the phishing campaign email. Regression models demonstrated that the treated group was actually more likely to click a fake link or submit personal data than the comparison group (Back & Guerette, 2021). These findings show that the cybersecurity awareness instruction did not help prevent participants from engaging in at-risk behaviors in the quasi-experimental phishing campaign. In other words, the attempt to create better cyber place management (through cybercrime prevention training) did not reduce cybercrime incidents. The treatment group that participated in the cybersecurity awareness program was six times more likely to open phishing emails than the comparison group (Back & Guerette, 2021). Furthermore, some sociodemographic factors such as age, race, length of employment, and job category were associated with participants falling for phishing tests (Back & Guerette, 2021). The older generation was more resistant to cyber deception than the younger generation. The data also suggested that individuals in a higher job position and with a more extended period of employment were more likely to engage in at-risk behaviors during a phishing attack (Back & Guerette, 2021).

Other examples of related work

Ki-Aries and Faily (2017) presented a case study using the Human Computer Interaction (HCI) approach to identifying security-related human factors by incorporating personas (grounded in empirical data) into ISA design and implementation. These personas are fictitious individuals representing different types of customers who use or could use a product (Descarie, 2017). They have been successfully used in approaches to marketing, website, and interface designs, and they can also be leveraged as a tool in cybersecurity awareness programs. According to Ki-Aries and Faily (2017), the personas initially developed by Cooper (1999) offer a valuable method for identifying audience needs and security risks. This allows researchers to consider relevant, business-specific human factors in the security awareness needs of people interacting within an organization (Ki-Aries & Faily, 2017).

Moreover, the use of personas enables a more tailored approach to awareness programs. As Ki-Aries and Faily (2017) argued in their paper, the creation and application of personas can address business-specific human factors within awareness activities and demonstrate how personas may be integrated into an ongoing cycle of security awareness. They recommend six steps in developing and implementing an awareness program: (1) needs and goals, (2) personas, (3) analysis, (4) design and development, (5) implement, and (6) review. Such a program should be embedded into business-as-usual activities with 90-day cycles of awareness themes, to ensure a more frequent up-to-date approach to addressing relevant security risks through security awareness (Ki-Aries & Faily, 2017).

Both practitioners and scholars should consider other interesting research papers and studies in enhancing the development of evidence-based approaches in cybersecurity. Zhang-Kennedy and Chiasson (2021) identified 119 tools about cybersecurity and privacy (created between January 2000 and June 2019) to guide future research efforts: 54 digital games, 34 films and animations, ten tabletop games, nine learning modules, nine comics, and three other tools categorized in other types of media. These scholars found that (1) online games and short animated films are the most prevalent media for teaching cybersecurity, (2) only one-third of the tools in their sample had been evaluated, (3) there is considerable variability in study methodologies, leading to a lack of comparison and generalization of the results, and (4) there is a scarcity of long-term evaluations of tools comparing their effectiveness (Zhang-Kennedy & Chiasson, 2021). Lastly, in his study, Sönmez (2019) argued that ISG frameworks other than ISO/

IEC 27004:2016 are not adequate for measuring effectiveness, so there is a need for a metric-based framework to measure the effectiveness of security processes and tasks.

CONCLUSION

Cybersecurity is both a technical problem and a human problem, significantly impacted by non-expert end users who interact with data, online content, and various internal and external stakeholders – complicating the role of cybersecurity professionals in protecting critical assets. Thus, improving non-expert end users' knowledge and awareness should be considered a crucial step toward cybersecurity (Zhang-Kennedy & Chiasson, 2021). Moreover, organizations need to implement robust governance procedures. They need to recruit employees with both technical and cyber skills, connect data governance with technology, and protect the business's reputation (Carataş et al., 2019). Cyber breaches occur mainly because of people committing human errors. Therefore, it is imperative to mitigate the risks and enhance awareness of human risk management.

Risk management and security professionals – accountable to protect the organization – need to (a) think from the attacker's perspective, (b) evaluate the risk exposures, (c) assess the worst incident and potential loss that could be provoked by cyber-incidents, and (d) invest in risk mitigation strategies for the most valuable assets (i.e., crown jewels) (Carataş et al., 2019). Furthermore, cybersecurity scholars often mention that the data they use in their research is obsolete due to privacy concerns since organizations are not inclined to provide access to confidential and proprietary data. If the proper security measures could be implemented to protect data, organizations would greatly benefit from allowing researchers to assist them in measuring the effectiveness of the standards they use, along with the cybersecurity awareness tools and policies they implement within their operations. Without such evaluations, it is impossible to know if the tools/policies are working correctly and if they bring value to the organization. So, instead of simply buying new tools or implementing new policies, organizations should carefully assess the effectiveness of such measures and rely on evidence to influence their security investment choices.

Standards and regulations are not enough to improve cybersecurity. Monitoring solutions are also necessary, but awareness will always be essential for preventing cyber-threats. However, the delivery of awareness content should be engaging, tailored to employees, and ongoing, with a range of relevant topics that are targeted, actionable, and doable so users can learn and adapt proper behavior depending on their roles within or outside the organization (e.g., consultants and third-party stakeholders) (Ki-Aries & Faily, 2017). An organization's self-assessment of its compliance with security standards is an excellent way to improve its security posture, assuming security professionals learn from their current vulnerabilities and constantly improve risk management procedures. However, evidence of compliance should also be assessed by an objective and independent team, who can conduct tests and use various sample types to demonstrate whether the organization indeed follows comprehensive standards. Rahaman et al. (2020) noted that there is often a big gap between the specifications and the real-world environment. Therefore, more evidence-based studies should be conducted to know what works and what does not regarding data privacy, the efficacy of information security standards and regulations, and cybersecurity awareness programs.

NOTES

i These 14 security categories are (1) information security policies, (2) organization of information security, (3) human resource security, (4) asset management, (5) access control, (6) cryptography, (7) physical and environmental security, (8) operations security, (9) communications security, (10) system acquisition, development, and maintenance, (11) supplier relationships, (12) information security incident management, (13) information security aspects of business continuity management, and (14) compliance with internal requirements such as policies and with external requirement such as law.

ii Each risk in Table 8.2 can be categorized into one of the nine categories provided by Sihwi et al. (2016): HH (9) high probability and high impact, MH (6) medium probability and high impact, MM (7) medium probability and medium impact, HM (8) high probability and medium impact, LH (5) low probability and high impact, LM (4) low probability and medium impact, LL (3) low probability and low impact, ML (2) medium probability and low impact, and HL (1) high probability and low impact.

REFERENCES

Abrams, L. (2021). *Hacker claims to steal data of 100 million T-Mobile customers*. https://www.bleepingcomputer.com/news/security/hacker-claims-to-steal-data-of-100-million-t-mobile-customers/

Alotaibi, F., Furnell, S., Stengel, I., & Papadaki, M. (2016). A review of using gaming technology for cyber-security awareness. *International Journal of Information Security Research (IJISR)*, 6(2), 660–666.

Amankwa, E., Loock, M., & Kritzinger, E. (2015). Enhancing information security education and awareness: Proposed characteristics for a model. In *2015 Second International Conference on Information Security and Cyber Forensics (InfoSec)* (pp. 72–77). https://doi.org/10.1109/InfoSec.2015.7435509

Arora, S., Yttri, J., & Nilsen, W. (2014). Privacy and security in mobile health (mHealth) research. *Alcohol Research: Current Reviews*, 36(1), 143–150.

ASIS International. (2021). *Standards & guidelines*. https://www.asisonline.org/publications–resources/standards–guidelines/

ASIS International and The Risk and Insurance Management Society. (2015). *Risk assessment*. https://www.asisonline.org/publications–resources/standards–guidelines/ra/introduction/

Back, S., & Guerette, R. T. (2021). Cyber place management and crime prevention: The effectiveness of cybersecurity awareness training against phishing attacks. *Journal of Contemporary Criminal Justice, 37*(2), 427–451.

Battistella, P. E., & Gresse von Wangenheim, C. (2016). Games for teaching computing in higher education – A systematic review. *IEEE Technology and Engineering Education (ITEE), 1*(3), 1–23.

Bawazir, M. A., Mahmud, M., Molok, N. N. A., & Ibrahim, J. (2016). Persuasive technology for improving information security awareness and behavior: Literature review. In *2016 6th International Conference on Information and Communication Technology for The Muslim World (ICT4M)* (pp. 228–233). https://doi.org/10.1109/ICT4M.2016.054

Boehm, J., Merrath, P., Poppensieker, T., Riemenschnitter, R., & Stähle, T. (2018). *Cyberrisk measurement and the holistic cybersecurity approach: Perspectives on transforming cybersecurity*. McKinsey & Company. https://www.mckinsey.com/~/media/McKinsey/McKinsey%20Solutions/Cyber%20Solutions/Perspectives%20on%20transforming%20cybersecurity/Transforming%20cybersecurity_March2019.ashx

Bonner, E., O' Raw, J., & Curran, K. (2011). Implementing the payment card industry (PCI) data security standard (DSS). *Telkomnika, 9*(2), 365–376. https://doi.org/10.12928/telkomnika.v9i2.709

Carataş, M., Spătariu, A., & Gheorghiu, C. (2019). Privacy and cybersecurity insights. *Ovidius University Annals: Economic Sciences Series, 19*(2), 242–246.

Casetext. (2021). *N.Y. Comp. Codes R. & Regs. tit. 23 § 500.17*. https://casetext.com/regulation/new-york-codes-rules-and-regulations/title-23-financial-services/chapter-i-regulations-of-the-superintendent-of-financial-services/part-500-cybersecurity-requirements-for-financial-services-companies/section-50017-notices-to-superintendent

Chavalit, V., & Hohler, L. (2020). Data protection in a GDPR world. *Internal Auditor, 77*(3), 35–39.

Choi, J., Kaplan, J., Krishnamurthy, C., & Lung, H. (2017). *Hit or myth? Understanding the true cost of cybersecurity programs*. McKinsey & Company. https://www.mckinsey.com/~/media/McKinsey/McKinsey%20Solutions/Cyber%20Solutions/Perspectives%20on%20transforming%20cybersecurity/Transforming%20cybersecurity_March2019.ashx

Cooper, A. (1999). *The inmates are running the asylum*. Sams.

Connolly, T. M., Boyle, E. A., MacArthur, E., Hainey, T., & Boyle, J. M. (2012). A systematic literature review of empirical evidence on computer games and serious games. *Computers & Education, 59*(2), 661–686. https://doi.org/10.1016/j.compedu.2012.03.004

Crozier, D., & Law, T. (2019). Understanding the payment card industry data security standard. *Canadian Travel Press, 51*(28), 5.

CSO. (2021). *Global intelligence report: State of cybersecurity in 2021*. https://images.idgesg.net/assets/2021/07/idg-cso-gir-final20july202021.pdf

Cullinane, I., Huang, C., Sharkey, T., & Moussavi, S. (2015). Cyber security education through gaming cybersecurity games can be interactive, fun, educational and engaging. *Journal of Computing Sciences in Colleges, 30*(6), 75–81. https://dl.acm.org/doi/10.5555/2753024.2753042

De Groot, J. (2020a). *What is the general data protection regulation? Understanding & complying with GDPR requirements in 2019.* https://digitalguardian.com/blog/what-gdpr-general-data-protection-regulation-understanding-and-complying-gdpr-data-protection

De Groot, J. (2020b). *What is the NYDFS cybersecurity regulation? A cybersecurity compliance requirement for financial institutions.* https://digitalguardian.com/blog/what-nydfs-cybersecurity-regulation-new-cybersecurity-compliance-requirement-financial

Descarie, F. (2017). *Les personas: Un outil de marketing inspirant et ludique.* https://www.infopresse.com/opinion/francois-descarie/2017/8/25/les-personas-un-outil-marketing-inspirant-et-ludique

Elumalai, A., Kaplan, J., Newborn, M., & Roberts, R. (2018). *Making a secure transition to the public cloud.* McKinsey & Company. https://www.mckinsey.com/~/media/McKinsey/McKinsey%20Solutions/Cyber%20Solutions/Perspectives%20on%20transforming%20cybersecurity/Transforming%20cybersecurity_March2019.ashx

FFIEC. (2017). *Cybersecurity assessment tool.* https://www.ffiec.gov/pdf/cybersecurity/FFIEC_CAT_May_2017.pdf

Fruhlinger, J. (2020). *Equifax data breach FAQ: What happened, who was affected, what was the impact?* https://www.csoonline.com/article/3444488/equifax-data-breach-faq-what-happened-who-was-affected-what-was-the-impact.html

Galli, S. (2018). NYDFS cybersecurity regulations: A blueprint for uniform state statute. *North Carolina Banking Institute, 22,* 235–256.

Garcia, M., Forscey, D., & Blute, T. (2017). Beyond the network: A holistic perspective on state cybersecurity governance. *Nebraska Law Review, 96*(2), 252–280.

Gilchrist, A. (2017). *IoT security issues* (1st ed.). DeG Press.

Gressin, S. (2018). *The Marriott data breach.* https://www.consumer.ftc.gov/blog/2018/12/marriott-data-breach

Haeussinger, F., & Kranz, J. (2017). Antecedents of employee's information security awareness - review, synthesis, and directions for future research. In *Proceedings of the 25th European Conference on Information Systems (ECIS)* (pp. 1–19). https://aisel.aisnet.org/ecis2017_rp/12

Hendrix, M., Al-Sherbaz, A., & Bloom, V. (2016). Game based cyber security training: Are serious games suitable for cyber security training? *International Journal of Serious Games, 3*(1), 53–61. https://doi.org/10.17083/ijsg.v3i1.107

Herr, C., & Allen, D. M. (2015). *Video games as a training tool to prepare the next generation of cyber warriors.* Software Engineering Institute. https://resources.sei.cmu.edu/asset_files/Presentation/2015_017_001_442344.pdf

HIPAA Journal. (2021). *HIPAA compliance checklist.* https://www.hipaajournal.com/hipaa-compliance-checklist/

ISO. (2013). *Information technology – Security techniques – Code of practice for information security controls.* https://www.iso.org/obp/ui/#iso:std:iso-iec:27002:ed-2:v1:en

ISO. (n.d.). *ISO 31000 risk management.* https://www.iso.org/iso-31000-risk-management.html

IT Governance. (2021). *ISO 27001 vs. ISO 27002: What's the difference?* https://www.itgovernance.co.uk/blog/understanding-the-differences-between-iso-27001-and-iso-27002

Jaeger, L. (2018). Information security awareness: Literature review and integrative framework. In *Proceedings of the 51st Hawaii International Conference on System Sciences* (pp. 4703–4712). https://scholarspace.manoa.hawaii.edu/bitstream/10125/50482/paper0595.pdf

Jibilian, I., & Canales, K. (2021). *The U.S. is readying sanctions against Russia over the SolarWinds cyber attack. Here's a simple explanation of how the massive hack happened and why it's such as big deal.* https://www.businessinsider.com/solarwinds-hack-explained-government-agencies-cyber-security-2020-12

Kaminski, P., Rezek, C., Richter, W., & Sorel, M. (2017). *Protecting your critical assets: Not all systems and data are created equal.* McKinsey & Company. https://www.mckinsey.com/~/media/McKinsey/McKinsey%20Solutions/Cyber%20Solutions/Perspectives%20on%20transforming%20cybersecurity/Transforming%20cybersecurity_March2019.ashx

Khando, K., Gao, S., Islam, S. M., & Salman, A. (2021). Enhancing employees' information security awareness in private and public organizations: A systematic literature review. *Computers & Security, 106,* 102267. https://doi.org/10.1016/j.cose.2021.102267

Ki-Aries, D., & Faily, S. (2017). Persona-centred information security awareness. *Computers & Security, 70,* 663–674. https://doi.org/10.1016/j.cose.2017.08.001

Lebek, B., Uffen, J., Breitner, M. H., Neumann, M., & Hohler, B. (2013). Employees' information security awareness and behavior: A literature review. In *2013 46th Hawaii International Conference on System Sciences* (pp. 2978–2987). https://doi.org/10.1109/HICSS.2013.192.

Le Compte, A., Elizondo, D., & Watson, T. (2015). A renewed approach to serious games for cyber security. In *Proceedings of the Conference on Cyber Conflict: Architectures in Cyberspace (CyCon'15)* (pp. 203–216). https://doi.org/10.1109/CYCON.2015.7158478

Lee, W. W., Zankl, W., & Chang, H. (2016). *An ethical approach to data privacy protection.* https://www.isaca.org/resources/isaca-journal/issues/2016/volume-6/an-ethical-approach-to-data-privacy-protection

Lee Williams, J. (2016). Privacy in the age of the Internet of things. *Human Rights, 41*(4), 14–22.

Lindberg, D. (2016). *Gamified systems for security awareness. A literature review.* University of Skövde. http://www.diva-portal.org/smash/get/diva2:945412/FULLTEXT01.pdf

Monev, V. (2020). Organisational information security maturity assessment based on ISO 27001 and ISO 27002. In *2020 International Conference on Information Technologies (InfoTech)* (pp. 1–5). https://doi.org/10.1109/InfoTech49733.2020.9211066

Moschovitis, C. (2018). *Cybersecurity program development for business; The essential guide.* Wiley.

National Institute of Standards & Technology (NIST). (2012). *NIST special publication 800-30: guide for conducting risk assessments.* https://nvlpubs.nist.gov/nistpubs/Legacy/SP/nistspecialpublication800-30r1.pdf

National Institute of Standards & Technology (NIST). (2017). *About NIST.* https://www.nist.gov/about-nist.

National Institute of Standards & Technology (NIST). (2018). *Framework for improving critical infrastructure cybersecurity – Version 1.1 (April 16, 2018).* https://www.nist.gov/cyberframework/framework

Pastor, V., Díaz, G., & Castro, M. (2010). State-of-the-art simulation systems for information security education, training, and awareness. In *IEEE EDUCON 2010 Conference, Education Engineering (EDUCON)* (pp. 1907–1916). https://doi.org/10.1109/EDUCON.2010.5492435

PCI Security Standard Council. (2021a). *About us*. https://www.pcisecuritystandards.org/about_us/

PCI Security Standards Council. (2021b). *Maintaining payment security*. https://www.pcisecuritystandards.org/pci_security/maintaining_payment_security

Pomerleau, P. L. (2019). *Countering the cyber threats against financial institutions in Canada: A qualitative study of a private and public partnership approach to critical infrastructure protection*. Available from ProQuest Dissertations & Theses Global. (2320957957). https://about.proquest.com/products-services/pqdtglobal.html

Pomerleau, P. L., & Lowery, D. (2020). *Countering the cyber-threats to financial institutions*. Springer.

Poppensieker, T., & Riemenschnitter, R. (2018). *A new posture for cybersecurity in a networked world. Perspectives on transforming cybersecurity*. McKinsey & Company. https://www.mckinsey.com/~/media/McKinsey/McKinsey%20Solutions/Cyber%20Solutions/Perspectives%20on%20transforming%20cybersecurity/Transforming%20cybersecurity_March2019.ashx

Rahaman, S., Wang, G., & Danfeng, Y. (2020). Security certification in the payment card industry: Testbeds, measurements, and recommendations. In *Proceedings of the 2019 ACM SIGSAC Conference on Computer and Communications Security* (pp. 481–498). Association for Computing Machinery. https://doi.org/10.1145/3319535.3363195

Rahim, N. H. A., Hamid, S., Mat Kiah, M. L., Shamshirband, S., & Furnell, S. (2015). A systematic review of approaches to assessing cybersecurity awareness. *Kybernetes, 44*(4), 606–622.

Rebollo, O., Mellado, D., Sanchez, E. L., & Fernández-Medina, E. (2014). *Comparative analysis of information security governance frameworks: A public sector approach*. https://www.researchgate.net/publication/232252326_Comparative_Analysis_of_Information_Security_Governance_Frameworks_A_Public_Sector_Approach

Shaw, R. S., Chen, C. C., Harris, A. L., & Huang, H.-J. (2009). The impact of information richness on information security awareness training effectiveness. *Computers & Education, 52*(1), 92–100. https://doi.org/10.1016/j.compedu.2008.06.011

Sihwi, S. W., Andriyanto, F., & Anggrainingsih, R. (2016). An expert system for risk assessment of information system security based on ISO 27002. In *2016 IEEE International Conference on Knowledge Engineering and Applications (ICKEA)* (pp. 56–61). https://doi.org/10.1109/ICKEA.2016.7802992

Sönmez, F. Ö. (2019). A conceptual model for a metric-based framework for the monitoring of information security tasks' efficiency. *Procedia Computer Science, 160*, 181–188. https://doi.org/10.1016/j.procs.2019.09.459

Swinhoe, D. (2021). *The biggest data breach fines, penalties, and settlement so far*. https://www.csoonline.com/article/3410278/the-biggest-data-breach-fines-penalties-and-settlements-so-far.html

Tsohou, A., Kokolakis, S., Karyda, M., & Kiountouzis, E. (2008). Investigating information security awareness: Research and practice gaps. *Information Security Journal: A Global Perspective, 17*(5/6), 207–227. https://doi.org/10.1080/19393550802492487

Tungall, A. T. (2021). *The 57 biggest data breaches (Updated for 2021)*. https://www.upguard.com/blog/biggest-data-breaches

U.S. Department of Health & Human Services. (n.d.-a). *Health information privacy*. https://www.hhs.gov/hipaa/index.html

U.S. Department of Health & Human Services. (n.d.-b). *Summary of the HIPAA privacy rule*. https://www.hhs.gov/hipaa/for-professionals/security/laws-regulations/index.html

U.S. Department of Health & Human Services. (n.d.-c). *Summary of the HIPAA privacy rule*. https://www.hhs.gov/sites/default/files/ocr/privacy/hipaa/understanding/summary/privacysummary.pdf

Williams, J. (2016). Privacy in the age of the Internet of things. *Human Rights, 41*(4), 14–22.

Wolford, B. (2021). *What is GDPR, the E.U.'s new data protection law*. https://gdpr.eu/what-is-gdpr/

Zhang-Kennedy, L., & Chiasson, S. (2021). A systematic review of multimedia tools for cybersecurity awareness and education. *ACM Computing Surveys, 54*(1), 1–39. https://doi.org/10.1145/3427920

Chapter 9

Risk and threat intelligence

The effectiveness of online threat intelligence in guiding financial institutions' incident response to online banking account takeovers

INTRODUCTION

The Internet Crime Complaint Center (2020) defines a personal data breach as a security event in which an individual's sensitive, protected, or confidential data is copied, transmitted, viewed, stolen, or used by an unauthorized individual in an untrusted environment. In 2020, the annual losses from personal data breach incidents reported by victims were more than US \$194 million, a 61.6% increase from the yearly losses reported by victims of this crime in 2019 (Internet Crime Complaint Center, 2020). A bank account takeover (ATO) is a type of personal data breach incident in which cybercriminals gain unauthorized access to a customer's bank account and use the account for illegal financial transactions. Shein (2020) reported that online criminals' efforts to take over bank accounts to steal money from customers, financial institutions, and merchants increased by 282% between 2019 and 2020 (Shein, 2020). The main reason for the soaring popularity of ATO scams among cybercriminals is embedded in the relative ease with which they can lure bank account customers to comply with various suspicious requests, thereby gaining access to targets' personally identifiable information (PII) (Buzzard & Kitten, 2021).

Due to this new reality, financial institutions have to find practical solutions which will allow them to respond to ATO incidents efficiently and rapidly, so they can mitigate the harm to their customers (Columbus, 2020; Reynolds, 2020). Methods employed by financial institutions to manage ATO incidents involve both reactive and proactive solutions. Reactive solutions include response to fraud detection system alerts identifying a suspicious transaction in a customer account, a discovery of a fraudulent transaction in a customer account during an audit review, a law enforcement investigation, or a complaint from a victimized customer regarding suspicious activity in his/her account (Simha & Satyanarayan, 2016). On the proactive front, data analytics and machine learning technologies are being used to detect anomalies in customers' behavioral patterns with their accounts (Pomerleau & Auger-Perreault, 2020), along with various threat intelligence feeds (e.g., fraud and cyber indicators), which are used to improve organizational understanding of emerging and existing

DOI: 10.1201/9781003201519-9

threats. However, research is scarce regarding the effectiveness of proactive approaches in general, and threat intelligence in particular, in countering bank ATO incidents and mitigating consequences to victims.

Drawing on insights from the situational crime prevention (SCP) perspective (Cornish & Clarke, 2003), we examined whether open-source intelligence found over text message applications (i.e., encrypted communication platforms) constitutes a valid source of threat intelligence for financial institutions, and whether it could be used to guide financial institutions' efforts to respond to these incidents by denying online offenders' benefits after offenders take over those accounts. To answer these questions, we partnered with a large Canadian financial institution to conduct a case study in which we shared intelligence regarding stolen bank accounts, found on various encrypted darknet markets, with the bank's fraud prevention team. This unique work demonstrates the advantages embedded in joint research efforts of scholars and practitioners, as well as the usefulness of these efforts in guiding effective incident response around the issue of online bank ATO.

BACKGROUND

Bank ATO and financial institutions response

An ATO is a form of data breach in which cybercriminals gain unauthorized access to a legitimate user's account. As such, any company's valid user accounts (e.g., telecommunications, banking, government emergency funds) are at risk of an ATO and could be targeted by online criminals in their quest to commit fraudulent activities (e.g., adding a payment to a mule account, wiring money internationally, making a payment to a credit card, creating a fake check image, or taking over a mobile phone account via a sim swap). Still, online banking accounts are at higher risk of ATO due to the financial opportunities they represent to offenders. The most common approaches employed by online offenders for taking over victims' bank accounts include phishing, spear-phishing (i.e., targeted phishing attacks against specific individuals), and malware attacks.

During phishing and spear-phishing attacks, fraud victims receive emails that appear to come from a trusted organization (e.g., their financial institution). They will be asked to click on a link within the email and enter their username, password, and security questions (i.e., additional questions used to authenticate the customers). However, the link provided in the phishing email will bring the victims to a scam page (fake website) that appears legitimate, on which they will be lured to provide their credentials to the account. Once provided on the scam page, the target's credentials are recorded into the cybercriminals' database and could then be sold on the darknet or various online encrypted platforms. When using malware attacks, online criminals entice targets to install malicious software on their computers. Once installed on a target computer, the malware can record the target's keystrokes while logging into various websites (including online banking websites), harvest the target's credentials, and add them to a database owned by cybercriminals.

Upon obtaining the victim's credentials to their bank accounts, online offenders visit the relevant website, log in the victim's accounts with their username and password, and take over their accounts. Once they gain control, the offenders can change the account settings and use a digital payment method to make a large withdrawal (Sundstrom, 2020). Alternatively, some cybercriminals use the bank accounts to orchestrate money laundering schemes or sell the compromised account credentials (e.g., through phishing and social engineering schemes) in exchange for cryptocurrency payments.

SITUATIONAL CRIME PREVENTION

Financial institutions worldwide attempt to prevent and respond to these threats by taking a more proactive approach for preventing and mitigating (i.e., reducing the harm from the criminal event to the victim after the event takes place) bank ATOs. Many of these approaches could qualify as SCP techniques (Clarke & Felson, 1993).

SCP stipulates that crime can be deterred by making strategic changes to an environment (Brooks, 2020). This theoretical framework combines various theoretical perspectives, including the routine activity perspective (Cohen & Felson, 1979) and the rational choice theory (Brewer et al., 2019; Shariati & Guerette, 2017). The underlying premise of this perspective suggests that criminals are rational human beings who weigh the costs and benefits of their behaviors before they initiate a criminal event (Clarke, 1995). As such, to reduce potential criminal activity, the SCP proposes the design and manipulation of the environment to nudge potential offenders away from initiating a criminal event (Brewer et al., 2019). Specifically, the SCP aims to identify criminogenic situations which support the development of criminal events in specific places, then to propose a list of techniques which will design out the impact of these criminogenic circumstances from the environment (Clarke, 1997; Shariati & Guerette, 2017).

Accordingly, Clarke recommended the adoption of crime-specific prevention strategies (e.g., strategies targeting theft, robbery, burglary, vandalism, etc.) that fall into five categories: *increase offenders' efforts, increase offenders' risks, reduce offenders' rewards, reduce provocations,* and *remove excuses* (Cornish & Clarke, 2003). For each category, Cornish and Clarke (2003) identified five categories of techniques (see Table 9.1) that are designed to deter criminals from engaging in crime by reducing the development of criminal opportunities. These five categories include a total of 25 techniques that have proven helpful in reducing different types of crime, including robbery (Crow & Bull, 1975; Duffala, 1976; Jeffrey et al., 1987; Scott et al., 1985), vandalism

(Sloan-Howitt & Kelling, 1990), teenagers' joyriding (Bell & Burke, 1992), and shoplifting (Farrington, 1993). For a comprehensive review of the effectiveness of SCP techniques in preventing different types of crimes, see Crawford and Evans (2017), Guerette and Bowers (2009), and Cozens et al. (2005).

The emergence and escalation of cybercrime incidents during the past 15 years have forced criminologists, computer scientists, and information scientists around the world to review the applicability of the SCP perspective to different types of online crimes (Beebe & Rao, 2005; Brookson et al., 2007; Coles-Kemp & Theoharidou, 2010; Hartel et al., 2010; Hinduja & Kooi, 2013; Morris, 2004; Newman & Clarke, 2003; Reyns, 2010; Willison & Siponen, 2009). Interestingly, the applicability of the SCP perspective has been assessed in the context of different type of online crimes: Coles- Kemp and Theoharidou (2010) focused on insider threats to information security, Newman and Clarke (2003) on online embezzlement, Morris (2004) on fraud and malicious software, Reyns (2010) on cyber-stalking, and Brookson et al. (2007) on hacking and online fraud. Drawing on these papers and the discussion by Brewer et al. (2019) of SCP in the context of cyber-dependent crimes, we claim that this approach could also be useful in the context of official efforts to prevent, mitigate, and respond to online bank ATOs. Table 9.1 presents a list of specific techniques that may reduce the opportunities for the occurrence and progression of ATOs, aligned with the SCP techniques of Cornish and Clarke (2003).

Denying benefits as a proactive incident response to ATO incidents

Although most SCP tactics are preventive in nature, we believe that at least two of these techniques – disrupting markets and denying benefits to offenders – are also relevant for guiding incident response to ATO incidents. Market disruptions include the implantation, by law enforcement or private investigators, of means to interfere with the illicit supply chain. In this sense, a common market disruption tactic includes police crackdowns on areas in which the underground economy flourishes (Cornish & Clarke, 2003). Similarly, denying offenders' gratifications and benefits from initiating crime may reduce the probability that a criminal event will develop and progress. An example of denying offenders' benefits from shoplifting is attaching ink tags to merchandise (Cornish & Clarke, 2003). Reflecting upon these SCP tactics in the context of ATO incidents, we assert that to guide an effective response to ATO incidents, both tactics should be implemented while considering the broader cybercrime ecosystem (Maimon & Louderback, 2019), which includes illicit online underground markets.

Illicit online markets exist both on *the surface web* and in *darknet environments* (Kremling & Parker, 2017). The surface web has all the websites and computers that are accessible to the general public. In contrast, the darknet is composed of overlay networks that offer extra anonymity to their users, and

Table 9.1 SCP techniques in the context of bank ATO

Increase efforts	Increase risks	Reduce rewards	Reduce provocations	Remove excuses
Harden targets	*Extend guardianship*	*Conceal targets*	*Reduce frustrations*	*Set rules*
• Use of strong passwords • Antivirus • Patching • Fraud awareness	• Report suspect activity (email, files) • Dark web monitoring	• Demilitarized zones	—	• Information security policies • Fraud prevention strategies
Control access	*Assist natural surveillance*	*Remove targets*	*Avoid disputes*	*Post instructions*
• Intrusion detection system • Intrusion prevention system • Firewall • Remote VPN • Double authentication	• Network traffic visualization tool	• Restrict the number of computers connected to the Internet	—	• Public awareness
Screen exits	*Reduce anonymity*	*Identify property*	*Reduce arousal*	*Alert conscience*
• IP-based restrictions • Firewall	• Blacklist IPs/Emails/URLs	—	—	• Post warnings
Deflect offenders	*Utilize place mangers*	*Disrupt markets*	*Neutralize peer pressure*	*Assist compliance*
• Production honeypots • Offsite storage	• Report suspect activity (email, files)	• Online police crackdowns	—	• Security education of computer users and customers
Control tools	*Strengthen formal surveillance*	*Deny benefits*	*Discourage imitation*	*Control disinhibitors*
• Software installation restrictions • Changes to the accounts	• Auditing reviews • Monitor employees' computers • Monitor customers' accounts	• Encrypt files and data • Block victimized accounts • Prevent fraud transaction	• Prompt software patching	—

it can only be accessed using specific software and communication protocols (Robertson et al., 2017). For that reason, criminals see darknet platforms as relatively secure places to facilitate secure communication between online offenders and enablers over hidden online forums, which support the existence and prosperity of underground online markets (Maimon & Louderback, 2019). These markets offer the hardware, software, and materials needed to initiate all types of online crimes, as well as the sensitive data that was harvested from victims of hacking and fraud like social security numbers, credit card numbers, names and addresses, and online bank credentials (Maimon & Louderback, 2019).

The interaction between offenders and enablers over these darknet platforms can be done either publicly or privately (Dupont et al., 2017). Online forums and market users who employ public communication platforms often create unique public threads that aim at asking a question or advertising a service or a product. Figure 9.1 demonstrates this point by showing a screenshot of the Empire Market, which was launched on 1 February 2018. The tree-structured

Figure 9.1 An example for a product ad selling 'Credit Card CVV' on the empire darknet market.

directory in the left column shows all categories and subcategories of fraud and counterfeit items. The number after each category name indicates the total number of product ads in the category. The right column shows an ad selling 'Credit Card CVV,' which provides price, detailed descriptions, and vendor reputation. The reputation of the vendor named 'miomentor,' as promoted via this webpage, is important for his business. The 'Feedback' column shows seven example feedback reviews about the products. The ad indicates that Bitcoin, Litecoin, and Monero are accepted methods of payment. By clicking on the vendor name 'miomentor,' the user can see the vendor's profile. Most darknet markets provide similar information for products and vendors.

Importantly, with the increased anonymity offered to users of text messaging applications, more and more online offenders have adopted encrypted messaging applications, both to communicate with other offenders as well as to sell their sketchy products (Schwartz, 2020). Like darknets, text messaging applications offer a high level of encryption and, thus, protect users from identification and make evidence-gathering more difficult. Encrypted communication channels (ECP) are easy to create and explore. After creating a profile on a platform, the user creates a dedicated channel or joins those of interest. On these channels, criminals advertise and solicit products or services. A channel's text will often include a detailed description of the product(s) or service(s), along with information on the price, payment option(s), and anonymous contact information. For an example of ECP channel information, see Figure 9.2.

Figure 9.2 An example for a product ad selling fake checks on the text messaging app ICQ.

Disrupting illicit online markets may theoretically mitigate the consequences of ATO incidents to victims, since it will prevent online offenders from selling access to victims' stolen accounts. However, so far, law enforcement agencies are the major entities that are qualified and allowed to disrupt illegal online markets at scale, by cracking down and ceasing those markets. Unfortunately, we could not find empirical evidence regarding the effectiveness of police crackdowns in either reducing offenders' involvement in cyber-dependent crimes or mitigating the consequences of cybercrimes to victims. The most relevant research presents findings on the effectiveness of this practice in reducing illegal distribution of copyright-protected content (Décary-Hétu, 2014) and illegal drugs (Décary-Hétu & Giommoni, 2017) in online cybermarkets. While Décary-Hétu (2014) reported no effect of police crackdowns in reducing the illegal distribution of copyright-protected material, Décary-Hétu and Giommoni (2017) found a limited effect of this practice (both in time and scope) in reducing the distribution of illegal drugs.

Similarly, denying offenders gratification from gaining financial benefits from possessing and selling compromised bank accounts may reduce the consequences of ATO incidents to both financial institutions and their customers. Specifically, rapid detection of compromised accounts sales over illicit online markets will allow financial institutions to respond quickly to an ATO incident by blocking the compromised accounts, denying offenders financial benefits, and reducing the probability of future account sales. Unlike with illicit online market disruption, we believe that financial institutions are the most relevant actors who could implement this SCP technique. However, no research has yet determined the effectiveness of this technique in preventing ATOs and mitigating the consequences of such incidents to financial institutions and their customers.

THREAT INTELLIGENCE AND RESPONDING TO ATO INCIDENTS

Efforts to disrupt illicit online markets and deny offenders benefits from offering compromised account for sale on these platforms require the constant monitoring of such markets, the collection of relevant threat intelligence regarding offenders and their commodities, and the transformation of this intelligence to the appropriate responding parties (either law enforcement or financial institutions). Threat intelligence products and services can support those needs. All in all, cyber-threat intelligence may consist of cyber-observable express artifacts (e.g., malicious files and their signatures, processes, and network traffic); insights on more complex indicators of compromise (IoC), vulnerabilities, and attacker behavior; and potential countermeasures relevant to incident response and attribution of attacks (Mavroeidis & Bromander, 2017).

The need for various types of cyber-threat intelligence has resulted in the emergence of an abundance of threat intelligence companies and products (Gartner, 2021a), aiming to provide clients with context for security trends, intelligence regarding cyber-threat actors' behaviors, and potential vulnerabilities which require attention. Depending on its nature, cyber-threat intelligence could support both reactive and proactive operations, which could be undertaken by security operation center (SOC) teams, network administrators, and IT professionals. For example, cybersecurity teams commonly use threat intelligence to detect potential IoC.

Specifically, darknet threat intelligence is of paramount importance to many organizations due to the high prevalence of hardware and software available for purchase by any users interested in initiating online crimes. In addition to tools, the volume of sensitive data, such as social security numbers, credit card numbers, names and addresses previously harvested from victims of cyber-dependent crimes (Yip et al., 2013), as well as an abundance of fraud-related services, are available for either free or a modest fee. Thus, once receiving information from darknet threat intel sources about specific tools or methods which could allow malicious actors to victimize either the organization or its customers, the relevant parties within the organization can take preventive measures against the threats.

Due to the relevance of these tools in the context of online fraud investigations, darknet intelligence services have also been used to support fraud investigations (Villanueva, 2021). Specifically, some fraud prevention and detection tools (e.g., online fraud detection reviews and ratings by Gartner Peer Insights (Gartner, 2021b)) can strengthen a fraud team's capability by automating processes such as threat intelligence analysis (using machine learning), which can allow fraud teams to quickly turn raw data into practical information and guide effective incident responses. However, over the years, fraud management practitioners realized that it was not enough to simply receive dark web and IOC intelligence through an application programming interface (API) feed and to use machine learning capabilities to detect potential fraud activities. Indeed, cybercriminals and online fraudsters who engage in fraudulent activities interact with their peers, exchange information about compromised data, and share images, tools, and best practices in an effort to 'make a fast buck.' Thus, preventing fraud by utilizing threat intelligence requires much more than an automated feed and an alerting process. It requires understanding how malicious actors interact with each other, what they share, the methods they use for sharing, and how they intend to target an organization. Therefore, a more proactive approach that aims at actively seeking out compromised accounts is required by fraud prevention professionals.

THE CURRENT STUDY

Drawing on the notion that actionable threat intelligence could be used by financial institutions to respond to ATO incidents and that efforts to respond to these issues should be guided by proactive attempts to gather such intelligence, this study explores the volume and quality of information available on online underground markets which pertains to Canadian bank ATO incidents. Moreover, we seek to determine whether this information could be useful in guiding Canadian financial institutions' incident response to ATO cases. Thus, we pose three research questions in this research. First, we ask *how prevalent is information on compromised bank accounts over dedicated channels populated on a single text message application?* Second, we explore *how much of the information posted on dedicated random text message applications regarding compromised bank accounts is valid?* Finally, we assess *how much of this intelligence is actionable and could be used to support financial institutions' incident response during ATO incidents?*

Data and methods

To answer our first research question, we randomly chose one of the six key encrypted text message applications which are monitored daily by the Evidence-Based Cybersecurity Research Group (EBCS-RG) at Georgia State University. Specifically, the EBCS-RG collects and parses the content of more than 1,000 channels used to facilitate illicit trade on six encrypted communication channels (Telegram, Discord, Signal, Jabber, WhatsApp, and ICQ) all over the world. Since the group monitors a wide range of channels, we narrowed our observation to one encrypted text message app and monitored 23 channels which are dedicated to discussions of online fraud in Canada. Our observation took place between the dates of 15 March and 15 May 2021. During those eight weeks, we constantly counted the unique number of vendor posts which contained concrete information and screenshots of various Canadian bank accounts. For each 30-day period, we summed the number of unique accounts we found and determined which pertained to the various Canadian financial institutions.

To answer the second and third questions, we partnered with a Canadian financial institution (Bank B) and shared the relevant compromised account information we were able to find on the same platform we used to track the prevalence of compromised account information between 13 January 2021 and 15 May 2021. The financial institution participating in this research[i] was one of the largest financial institutions in Canada. To ground our partnership, a memorandum of understanding (MOU) was signed between the parties. The information gathered by the researchers was shared with the individual financial institution on a real-time or near real-time basis, as soon as it was found on various encrypted channels, 24/7. Specifically, when relevant ATO information was found, the researchers took a picture of the information and shared the images with a specific anti-fraud specialist team member at the financial institution. At no time did our team make any payments to access the information. The anti-fraud specialists who worked on this project on behalf of the financial institution were dedicated to this project. Therefore, ongoing communication through emails and phone conversations allowed the specialists to evaluate whether the information was beneficial to the financial institution in:

1. identifying whether the account was an actual existing account (s) within their holdings,

2. blocking the account(s) as a preventative measure and contacting the potential victim,
3. detecting other potential illicit activities, such as individuals acting as money mules, and reporting the transactions as per their anti-money laundering (AML) requirements, and
4. validating if the information provided allowed them to identify potential friendly fraud.[ii]

Upon receiving intelligence from our team, the financial institution anti-fraud specialists followed a standard operating procedure (SOP) to respond to the potential fraud incident, with the objective of protecting the organization and its customers against fraudulent transactions. First, account numbers, the time of the transaction on the financial product (such as a bank account or line of credit), and/or the names of the potential victims were extracted from the information (i.e., an image, video, or gif), in order to be used as pointers for finding and identifying the compromised account among the long list of bank accounts the financial institution maintains.

When an account was found within the bank's internal systems, anti-fraud specialists assessed the account's attributes in order to determine the risk associated with the compromised account. If the account information or transactions were deemed highly suspicious (e.g., account potentially opened fraudulently, mule account), the information was provided to another team (i.e., the senior investigative team) to investigate further and decide if the account would be closed (i.e., demarketing the customer). If the account information or transactions were deemed unsuspicious, the information was provided to an outbound fraud prevention team with instructions to contact the customer (i.e., the victim). This call was necessary to better understand how and where the customer's credentials could have been compromised. Also, these calls allow taking preventative actions such as resetting the customer's online banking passwords and providing fraud prevention recommendations to the customer, in the event the analysis demonstrated the customer might be a victim of identity theft. At the end of each incident response effort, we were briefed by the anti-fraud specialists to evaluate the accuracy and the validity of the intelligence we provided.

RESULTS

How prevalent is information on breached bank accounts on text message applications?

Figure 9.3 demonstrates the prevalence of potential compromised Canadian bank accounts observed over 23 channels hosted on a single encrypted communication application between 15 March and 15 May 2021. These compromised accounts were available for buyers to purchase in order to continue

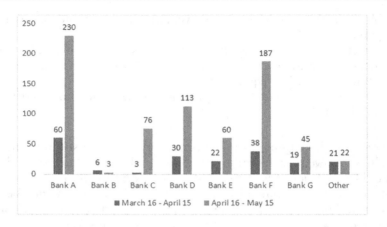

Figure 9.3 Number of compromised bank accounts at major Canadian financial institutions.

and finalize an ATO event. We mask the true identity of the Canadian financial institutions in order to avoid privacy concerns. As may be observed in Figure 9.3, Bank A (290 unique bank accounts) and Bank F (225 unique bank accounts) had a significant number of compromised accounts on sale compared to other large financial institutions for which we found potential compromised accounts. Importantly, although we found a higher representation of compromised bank accounts issued by major Canadian financial institutions, we were also able to observe compromised bank accounts, which were issued by medium and small Canadian banks. Interestingly, and as could be inferred from the graph, the sales of compromised bank accounts over the platform we monitored increased substantially. This finding illuminates the emerging trend related to bank ATO incidents.

How much of the information posted on the dark web or online encrypted applications is valid?

Although we could not assess the validity of the information we found over the platform we monitored with all the Canadian financial institutions, we were able to validate the information we found for Bank B, which we partnered with. Table 9.2 shows the preliminary results of this study after 123 consecutive days, between 13 January 2021 and 15 May 2021. For each case, we describe the date when the information was found, the available funds in the bank account, the information available in the image or video, whether the information provided to the financial institution corresponded to one of their customers, and whether the bank's fraud team was able to protect the account based on the intelligence provided.

All in all, the research team was able to observe 14 unique compromised bank accounts which belonged to Bank B customers during the five months we worked with them. Twelve of the compromised accounts were real bank

Table 9.2 Results of the case study (N = 14)

Date	Corresponds with data found on the darknet?	Account protected following tip?	Available funds in account ($)	Information available
13 January 2021	Yes	Yes	Negative balance	Seven transactions on the account
10 February 2021	Yes	Yes	$2,004.72	Check account + transit numbers + six transactions
10 February 2021	Yes	Yes	$13 908.14	Two commercial accounts
11 February 2021	Yes	Yes	$21.02	Date + two account balances
14 February 2021	Yes	Yes	$421.32	Date + account balance
15 March 2021	Yes	No	$0	Name + last four digits of two credit cards linked to the account + date + account type
16 March 2021	No	No	$96,579.27	Three products in the account summary
23 March 2021	Yes	No	$1,100.00	Account and transit number received
25 March 2021	Yes	No	$85,086.97	Specific deposit amount + few transactions
28 March 2021	Yes	No	$15,000.00	Account and transit number
13 April 2021	Yes	Yes	$2,574.92	Name, address, telephone, and email of the client
22 April 2021	Yes	No	$31,000.00	Account number
2 May 2021	Yes	Yes	Negative balance	Account balance and credit card information
13 May 2021	No	No	–	Name of payee in online transaction and amount

accounts (85.7%), and the information posted on online encrypted channels matched with one customer profile at the financial institution. The available funds in the bank accounts were the funds available in a checking or commercial account. Most of the potential victims had many products available through the same compromised online banking credentials. All the customers had at least one checking account; some also had a credit line, investments, loans, and credit cards. This information is critical because these products were also available to cybercriminals through the same online compromised credentials. Thus, the account balance could have been used to wire funds or make credit card payments to other criminals. The lines of credit could also have been used to make payments or money transfers to other bank accounts at other financial institutions worldwide, under the control of the same cybercriminals. Moreover, some of the investment account balances could have been withdrawn and deposited in the cybercriminal's bank accounts.

How much of this intelligence is actionable and could be used to support financial institutions' incident response?

The intelligence provided by our research team would not have been made available to the financial institution (e.g., through other commercial vendor threat intelligence platforms) without this project in 7 cases out of 14. In other words, the intel we provided to our partners in the financial institution was actionable in 50% of the cases. These accounts were live accounts for which no other threat intelligence vendors used by the financial institution provided the same intelligence.

Also, these account activities did not trigger the fraud prevention and detection systems. A potential explanation for this finding is that cybercriminals had access to the victims' online credentials, but they either did not make any changes to the accounts as of yet or they used proxy providers as a precaution when logging into the victim's account, to hide their IP address (Hernandez et al., 2015). These were ATOs in which cybercriminals had access to log into the accounts, but they were waiting for the right buyer to purchase the information.

How much money could an effective intelligence-based incident response to ATO save for the victim?

For the seven cases for which the accounts were protected due to the intelligence provided by our research team, the account balance available (only for the checking accounts) totaled CAD $18,930.12 in available funds. The total fraud savings, estimated at CAD $2,500 per case, were estimated at CAD $17,500. However, the full balance available the fraudsters could have used was CAD $151,117.09 (i.e., the total checking account balance available for fraud corresponding with the data found by GSU).

For cases 1 and 13 (13 January 2021; 2 May 2021), the account balances were negative when the research team provided the intelligence. Despite negative account balances, the victims in these cases had a line of credit and credit cards attached to these accounts, so the cybercriminals could have used the full line of credit. Indeed, once an account is compromised, there are various ways for fraudsters to increase the available funds, such as depositing counterfeit checks (e.g., using mobile check deposit technology) or requesting a credit limit increase. Moreover, case 1 (13 January 2021) was confirmed to be a case of ATO. At first, when the financial institution's outbound fraud prevention analyst contacted the customer by phone, he claimed that he might have been a victim of fraud. The individual confirmed he did not know where he could have been compromised in providing his online credentials. After validating the person's identity on the line, the fraud prevention agent reactivated his account so that the customer could generate a new online banking password. The next day, the researchers contacted the financial institution anti-fraud specialists to let them know that this same customer's credentials were still for sale on a channel on the same application. Then, it was confirmed through further investigation that the individual who the outbound fraud prevention analyst spoke to over the phone was implicated in this fraud.

For case 7 (16 March 2021), even though the researchers found an image of an online banking account with a substantial account balance (i.e., CAD $96,579.27) featuring the financial institution's logo, Bank B's anti-fraud specialists could not find this account within their holdings. After searching for a potential victim without success, the researchers realized that the available image might be fake. The researchers decided to contact the individual selling the account to get more information to provide to the anti-fraud specialists, so they could locate the account and block it to prevent potentially fraudulent activities. When the researchers contacted the individual selling the account credentials, they asked him to provide an updated image of the account or a video of himself logging into the account as evidence the account was still available. This request was also made to try to get access to an account number or any other information that would lead to identifying an account holder at the financial institution. However, the individual selling the account credentials did not want to provide more details. He still insisted the account was 'a good account' and asked for a payment to be made in cryptocurrency. At this point, the researchers realized they might be dealing with an individual selling a fake image. The researchers did not make any payment and decided to wait, a choice supported by the financial institutions' anti-fraud specialists. The following day, it was confirmed that the image was fake since other users of the chat software confirmed through their comments this individual was selling fake information, and he was defrauding other people within this channel.

For the estimated fraud saving amount, an average of CAD $2,500 per account was chosen as a potential conservative fraud loss since it is possible that the financial institution could have prevented the loss through other fraud prevention means. For instance, it is possible that without the intelligence provided by our research team, the financial institution could have blocked the accounts before cybercriminals would have been able to withdraw the totality of the funds available in the account. While the exfiltration of funds is not always preventable, there is often a chance for the financial institution's anti-fraud specialists to track the fraudulent beneficiary and act quickly enough to recover the funds by following the money and recalling funds. Also, the financial institution could have received intelligence through a tip from one of their threat intelligence providers, detected it with their fraud prevention and detection systems, or learned about it through the information provided by law enforcement or another financial institution at a later stage within the criminal activity of these cybercriminals. Therefore, the overall conservatively estimated total losses to Bank B in these seven cases are CAD $17,500.

DISCUSSION

A bank ATO incident consists of a cybercriminal gaining access to an existing bank account through either phishing scams or malware attacks. Once taking over the account, fraudsters change the account information (e.g., the account holder's physical address, phone numbers, emails, and online passwords on the victim's accounts) to be in a position to control the accounts and to perpetrate fraudulent transactions. This issue poses a serious challenge to financial institutions and their customers, since detecting and responding to ATOs cases may be difficult even for fraud prevention professionals. Therefore, in addition to pursing existing reactive measures to deal with this issue, we proposed that financial institutions should take a more proactive stance to respond to this issue, allowing them to mitigate the consequences of these online crimes to victims. Specifically, we hypothesized that by responding to actionable intelligence gathered from relevant online platforms, financial institutions could be in a better position to deny offenders benefits from taking over and selling those accounts (Cornish & Clarke, 2003). To test this claim, we explored whether information about compromised bank accounts, which is available on encrypted communication text message applications, is actionable enough to drive effective incident response to these issues.

Findings from this case study reveal three major insights. First, the prevalence of information regarding comprised bank accounts is growing. Specifically, the number of potentially compromised bank accounts we observed during a two-month period over a single encrypted communication platform was relatively high for some bank (at some banks, over 200 bank accounts became available for criminals during this span) and lower for others. Still, we were able to find compromised Canadian bank accounts for many Canadian banks. Second, by verifying the validity of the compromised accounts with one financial institution, we were able to determine that in 85.7% (i.e., 12 cases out of the 14 cases) of the cases, the compromised accounts indeed belong to the financial institution. In 14.3% (i.e., 2 cases out of the 14 cases), the information we forwarded to the fraud specialist team at the financial institution we worked with was deemed fraudulent or the financial institution was unable to identify an existing account. Finally, we demonstrated that the intelligence provided to our financial institution partner was useful for guiding effective incident response to bank ATO incidents in 50% of the cases (i.e., 7 cases out of the 14 cases) and denying offenders benefits from compromising the account.

In addition to supporting the adoption of actionable threat intelligence in guiding anti-fraud teams' incident response efforts in the context of ATO incidents, our findings also carry a significant theoretical contribution to the SCP perspective. Specifically, by tying together active threat intelligence and the SCP tactic of denial of benefits from online fraud, the theory becomes relevant not only in crime prevention, but also in mitigation of criminal events to the victims (Maimon & Louderback, 2019). Indeed, criminologists have been mainly occupied with finding ways to prevent crime from happening. While we agree that preventing crime is essential, we believe that trying to reduce the harm experienced by victims of crime – by attempting to restrict the potential damage caused from crime – is important as well. This study supports our point: while the online offenders who compromised the accounts had already committed a crime, once we alerted our partners in the anti-fraud team of Bank B, no further damage was caused to the victims.

Importantly, the financial institution participating in this study protected their customers' identities, preventing significant fraud losses by receiving various types of information on potential online account takeovers, thus reducing the impacts on their customers while preventing ATOs and fraudulent transactions. Online account information from many bank customers was advertised daily on the channels we monitored. As shown in Figure 9.3, the financial institution participating in this research (Bank B) did not have many accounts being sold on these encrypted channels, so it was significantly less affected by potential compromised accounts listed for sale during this study. Nevertheless, other financial institutions had multiple accounts available every week during this research. For instance, we found that another financial institution had more than 50 accounts on sale on the same day (Bank C in Figure 9.3). For this specific case, the researchers reported the situation to this particular bank for situational awareness and prevention purposes. Likewise, when the researchers found online compromised accounts for other financial institutions than the one participating in this study, the researchers provided the information to the participating financial institutions. Their specialists contacted the other financial institutions to provide them with the information through their established fraud prevention information-sharing protocols.

In addition to preventing banks' losses from ATO incidents, there is also a broader value to banks' efforts to address this issue. As Swaen and Chumpitaz (2008) mentioned, most definitions of corporate social responsibility (CSR) are based on the fact that companies have responsibilities beyond profit-seeking and respecting applicable laws where they do business. These responsibilities apply to shareholders, but they also apply to the business stakeholders with access to private corporate information (e.g., employees, suppliers, and customers) (Martínez-Ferrero et al., 2016; Swaen & Chumpitaz, 2008). As Gottschalk (2011) argued, knowledge-based organizations (e.g., those in the consulting, legal, medical, educational, and financial sectors) are highly dependent on a good reputation to attract customers and clients. A good reputation can lead to customer preference in doing business with the company, enhancing stakeholder support and loyalty (Gottschalk, 2011). However, there is still a lack of research focusing on the importance of companies' CSR toward crime prevention. In a business context, a moral and civic duty to customers can entail protecting them against potential harms, which, in our view, could include protecting them against fraud and the misuse of their personal information.

LIMITATIONS

This case study was only conducted with one financial institution (i.e., Bank B). This case study was conducted for only 123 consecutive days, from 13 January to 15 May 2021, and the observation of potential compromised Canadian bank accounts over 23 channels hosted on a single encrypted communication application lasted only two months, between 15 March and 15 May 2021. Also, another limitation of this study is that from the data gathered on darknet markets and online encrypted platforms, the researchers concluded that the financial institution participating in this study was not as targeted as other banks. Since the bank (and its customers) seems to have been less victimized (vs. customers from different banks of similar size) during the study period, the limited sample of cases we detected does not allow us to generalize the results.

CONCLUSION

The banking industry should work closely with academia to operationalize threat intelligence capabilities and deny access to cybercriminals who commit ATO fraud. Collaboration among universities, financial institutions, and law enforcement agencies should be explored further as the next step in preventing fraud, tracking the source of these data leaks, identifying where the money is going, and arresting the cybercriminals involved in these fraudulent schemes (Perianayagam et al., 2018; Pomerleau, 2019; Pomerleau & Lowery, 2020). More financial institutions should participate in similar case studies to compare the results from this study, since online fraud prevention should be perceived as an integral component of the CSR framework. Unfortunately, current third-party fraud and cyber-threat intelligence products and services do not always offer an adequate level of granularity for its users to act upon the information provided. As shown in this paper, tactical intelligence is critical to prevent fraudulent online ATOs and to take preventative actions to respond before criminals can use this information to commit fraud. An evidence-based approach should be utilized to evaluate intelligence tools and practices. Many cyber-intelligence providers only scrape the data from the darknet and some online encrypted platforms. Even though this approach may lead to identifying potentially compromised accounts, a *tailored intelligence approach* to look for a specific organization on the darknet and encrypted online platforms communications is, in our view, another valuable SCP approach to provide tactical intelligence. Such a tailored approach to intelligence gathering should be integrated into a multilayer strategy (i.e., prevention, detection, and response) to prevent online fraud.

NOTES

i. The name of the financial institution participating in the research is not provided. The main objective of this research was to assess if the information found on darknet markets may prevent fraud from occurring.
ii. Friendly fraud occurs when a legitimate customer makes a transaction and later disputes it, or when the customer is taking an active part in the fraud scheme to sell his or her credentials to cybercriminals. By doing so, cybercriminals can sell it on the darknet or online encrypted channels to potential buyers.

REFERENCES

Beebe, N. L., & Rao, V. S. (2005). Using situational crime prevention theory to explain the effectiveness of information systems security. In *Proceedings of the 2005 SoftWars Conference, Las Vegas, NV* (pp. 1–18).

Bell, J., & Burke, B. (1992). Cruising Cooper Street. In R. V. Clarke (Ed.), *Situational crime prevention: Successful case studies*. Harrow and Heston.

Brewer, R., De Vel-Palumbo, M., Hutchings, A., Holt, T. J., Goldsmith, A., & Maimon, D. (2019). *Cybercrime prevention: Theory and applications*. Retrieved from https://www.palgrave.com/gp/book/9783030310684#aboutBook

Brooks, A. (2020). *What is situational crime prevention? Investigating this crime reduction strategy*. Retrieved from https://www.rasmussen.edu/degrees/justice-studies/blog/situational-crime-prevention/#:~:text=Situational%20crime%20prevention%20is%20based,how%20it%20can%20be%20prevented

Brookson, C., Farrell, G., Mailley, J., Whitehead, S., & Zumerle, D. (2007). ICT product proofing against crime. *ETSI White Paper, 5*, 1–33.

Buzzard, J., & Kitten, T. (2021). *2021 identity fraud study: Shifting angles*. Retrieved from https://www.javelinstrategy.com/coverage-area/2021-identity-fraud-study-scams

Clarke, R. V. (1995). Situational crime prevention. *Crime and Justice, 19*, 91–150. Retrieved from http://www.jstor.org/stable/1147596

Clarke, R. V. (1997). *Situational crime prevention*. Criminal Justice Press.

Clarke, R. V., & Felson, M. (1993). *Routine activity and rational choice*. Transaction Publishers.

Cohen, L. E., & Felson, M. (1979). Social change and crime rate trends: A routine activity approach. *American Sociological Review, 44*(4), 588–608. https://doi.org/10.2307/2094589

Coles-Kemp, L., & Theoharidou, M. (2010). Insider threat and information security management. In C. Probst, J. Hunker, D. Gollmann, & M. Bishop (Eds.), *Insider threats in cyber security* (pp. 45–71). Springer. https://doi.org/10.1007/978-1-4419-7133-3_3

Columbus, L. (2020). *How e-commerce's explosive growth is attracting fraud.* Retrieved from https://www.forbes.com/sites/louiscolumbus/2020/05/18/how-e-commerces-explosive-growth-is-attracting-fraud/?sh=42abb3e06c4b

Cornish, D. B., & Clarke, R. V. (2003). Opportunities, precipitators and criminal decisions: A reply to Wortley's critique of situational crime prevention. *Crime Prevention Studies, 16*, 41–96.

Cozens, P. M., Saville, G., & Hillier, D. (2005). Crime prevention through environmental design (CPTED): A review and modern bibliography. *Property Management, 23*(5), 328–356.

Crawford, T., & Evans, K. (2017). Crime prevention and community safety. In A. Leibling, S. Maruna, & L. McAra (Eds.), *Oxford handbook of criminology* (6th ed., pp. 797–824). Oxford University Press.

Crow, W. J., & Bull, J. L. (1975). *Robbery deterrence: An applied behavioral science demonstration – Final report.* Western Behavioral Sciences Institute.

Décary-Hétu, D. (2014). Police operations 3.0: On the impact and policy implications of police operations on the warez scene. *Policy & Internet, 6*(3), 315–340.

Décary-Hétu, D., & Giommoni, L. (2017). Do police crackdowns disrupt drug cryptomarkets? A longitudinal analysis of the effects of operation onymous. *Crime, Law and Social Change, 67*(1), 55–75.

Duffala, D. C. (1976). Convenience stores, armed robbery, and physical environmental features. *American Behavioral Scientist, 20*(2), 227–246.

Dupont, B., Côté, A. M., Boutin, J. I., & Fernandez, J. (2017). Darkode: Recruitment patterns and transactional features of "the most dangerous cybercrime forum in the world". *American Behavioral Scientist, 61*(11), 1219–1243.

Farrington, D. P. (1993). Understanding and preventing bullying. In M. Tonry (Ed.), *Crime and justice: A review of research* (Vol. 17, pp. 381–458). University of Chicago.

Gartner. (2021a). *Security threat intelligence products and services reviews.* Retrieved from https://www.gartner.com/reviews/market/security-threat-intelligence-services

Gartner. (2021b). *Online fraud detection (OFD) reviews and rating.* Retrieved from https://www.gartner.com/reviews/market/online-fraud-detection-systems/vendors

Gottschalk, P. (2011). *Corporate social responsibility, governance and corporate reputation.* World Scientific.

Guerette, R. T., & Bowers, K. J. (2009). Assessing the extent of crime displacement and diffusion of benefits: A review of situational crime prevention evaluations. *Criminology, 47*(4), 1331–1368.

Hartel, P. H., Junger, M., & Wieringa, R. J. (2010). *Cyber-crime science=crime science+ information security.* Retrieved from https://research.utwente.nl/en/publications/cyber-crime-science-crime-science-information-security

Hernandez, E., Regalado, D., & Villeneuve, N. (2015). *An inside look into the world of Nigerian scammers.* Retrieved from https://www.fireeye.com/blog/threat-research/2015/07/an_inside_look_into.html

Hinduja, S., & Kooi, B. (2013). Curtailing cyber and information security vulnerabilities through situational crime prevention. *Security Journal, 26*(4), 383–402.

Internet Crime Complaint Center. (2020). *Internet crime report*. Retrieved from https://www.ic3.gov/Media/PDF/AnnualReport/2020_IC3Report.pdf

Jeffrey, C. R., Hunter, R. D., & Griswold, J. (1987). Crime prevention and computer analysis of convenience store robberies in Tallahassee. *Florida Police Journal, 34*, 65–69.

Kremling, J., & Parker, A. M. S. (2017). *Cyberspace, cybersecurity, and cybercrime.* SAGE Publications.

Maimon, D., & Louderback, R. E. (2019). Cyber-dependent crimes: An interdisciplinary review. *Annual Review of Criminology, 2*, 191–216.

Martínez-Ferrero, J., Banerjee, S., & García-Sánchez, I. M. (2016). Corporate social responsibility as a strategic shield against costs of earnings management practices. *Journal of Business Ethics, 133*(2), 305–324.

Mavroeidis, V., & Bromander, S. (2017). Cyber threat intelligence model: an evaluation of taxonomies, sharing standards, and ontologies within CTI. In *2017 European intelligence and security informatics conference (EISIC)* (pp. 91–98). IEEE. https://doi.org/10.1109/EISIC.2017.20

Morris, S. (2004). *The future of netcrime now: Part 2 – responses*. Home Office Online Report. Retrieved from https://citeseerx.ist.psu.edu/viewdoc/download?doi=10.1.1.105.9905&rep=rep1&type=pdf

Newman, G. R., & Clarke, V. R. (2003). *Superhighway robbery: Preventing e-commerce crime.* Willan Publishing.

Perianayagam, A., Nesbitt, R., & Caplan, M. (2018). *National approach to cyber intrusion; A comparison of United Kingdom and Canada.* Retrieved from https://globalriskinstitute.org/publications/national-approach-to-cyber-intrusion/

Pomerleau, P. L. (2019). *Countering the cyber threats against financial institutions in Canada: A qualitative study of a private and public partnership approach to critical infrastructure protection (Order No. 27540959).* Available from ProQuest Dissertations & Theses Global. (2320957957). Retrieved from https://about.proquest.com/products-services/pqdtglobal.html

Pomerleau, P. L., & Auger-Perreault, M. (2020) Fraud risk management: Using fraud analytics to combat external and insider threats. In L. Shapiro, & M. H. Maras (Eds.), *Encyclopedia of security and emergency management.* Springer, https://doi.org/10.1007/978-3-319-69891-5_296-1

Pomerleau, P. L., & Lowery, D. (2020). *Countering the cyber-threats to financial institutions.* Retrieved from https://link.springer.com/book/10.1007/978-3-030-54054-8

Reynolds, J. (2020). *9 reasons digital fraud is on the rise.* Retrieved from https://www.securitymagazine.com/articles/93912-reasons-digital-fraud-is-on-the-rise

Reyns, B. W. (2010). A situational crime prevention approach to cyberstalking victimization: Preventive tactics for Internet users and online place managers. *Crime Prevention & Community Safety, 12*(2), 99–118.

Robertson, J., Diab, A., Marin, E., Nunes, E., Paliath, V., Shakarian, J., & Shakarian, P. (2017). *Darkweb cyber threat intelligence mining.* Cambridge University Press.

Schwartz, M. J. (2020). *Why encrypted chat apps aren't replacing darknet markets.* Retrieved from https://www.bankinfosecurity.com/blogs/encrypted-chat-apps-arent-replacing-darknet-markets-p-2949

Scott, L., Crow, W. J., & Erickson, R. (1985). *Robbery as robbers see it.* Southland Corporation.

Shariati, A., & Guerette, R. T. (2017). Situational crime prevention. In B. Teasdale, & M. Bradley (Eds.), *Preventing crime and violence. Advances in prevention science* (pp. 261–268). Springer. https://doi.org/10.1007/978-3-319-44124-5_22

Shein, E. (2020). *Account takeover fraud rates skyrocketed 282% over last year.* Retrieved from https://www.techrepublic.com/article/account-takeover-fraud-rates-skyrocketed-282-over-last-year/

Simha, A., & Satyanarayan, S. (2016). Straight from the horse's mouth: Auditors on fraud detection and prevention, roles of technology, and white-collars getting splattered with red. *Journal of Accounting & Finance*, 16(1), 26–44.

Sloan-Howitt, M., & Kelling, G. (1990). Subway graffiti in New York City: 'Getting up' vs. 'meaning' it and 'cleaning' it. *Security Journal*, 1(3), 131–136.

Sundstrom, J. (2020). Why credit unions must root out non-monetary ATO schemes at three levels: CUs must have controls and systems to detect various ATO schemes, and emerging threats from well-organized fraud rings. *Credit Union Times*, 31(1), 1–4.

Swaen, V., & Chumpitaz, C. R. (2008). Impact of corporate social responsibility on consumer trust. *Recherche Et Applications En Marketing (English Edition) (AFM C/O ESCP-EAP)*, 23(4), 7–33.

Villanueva, R. (2021). *The digital underground and dark web – A treasure trove of actionable intelligence.* Retrieved from https://www.niceactimize.com/blog/fraud-the-digital-underground-and-dark-web-a-treasure-trove-of-actionable-intelligence-615/?utm_campaign=Oktopost-%23NICE2Share_Actimize&utm_content=Oktopost-linkedin-&utm_medium=social&utm_source=linkedin

Willison, R., & Siponen, M. (2009). Overcoming the insider: Reducing employee computer crime through situational crime prevention. *Communications of the ACM*, 52(9), 133–137.

Yip, M., Shadbolt, N., & Webber, C. (2013). Why forums? An empirical analysis into the facilitating factors of carding forums. In *Proceedings of the 5th Annual ACM Web Science Conference* (pp. 453–62). ACM.

Chapter 10

The future of evidence-based cybersecurity

INTRODUCTION

This concluding chapter offers our thoughts on the potential consequences resulting from a failure to embrace the evidence-based cybersecurity approach, both for guiding cybersecurity operations within public and private organizations and for guiding research within the academic discipline of cybersecurity. Cybersecurity will continue to evolve significantly in the coming years. Consequences for the cybersecurity industry may include a more pronounced preference to work with inexpensive tools, cynicism regarding those tools' ability to meet organizational security goals, substantial budgetary cuts to cybersecurity tool development and cybersecurity teams, and increases in the volume of successful cyberattacks, data loss, and fraudulent activities against organizations. Similarly, practitioners may lose trust in the findings reported by cybersecurity scholars, future security professionals may receive inadequate or even misguided training, and we may see even wider gaps between cybersecurity scholars and industry professionals. Finally, there will be negative societal consequences due to our dependency on the Internet, including increasing threats to supply chains for products and services, ultimately leading to significant impacts on life, property, and prosperity.

To avoid these potential outcomes, we will present a list of suggestions to better understand the cybercrime ecosystem and support efforts by policymakers and security teams to utilize the evidence-based approach in their decision-making processes, especially regarding the implementation and adoption of tools and policies. Given the known cybersecurity incidents attributed to nation-state actors, online criminal groups, and individual hackers (cf. Greenberg, 2019; Zetter, 2014), we will emphasize the relevance of evidence-based cybersecurity strategies in developing new and innovative detection and mitigation approaches. Finally, we will provide best practices and recommendations about how cybersecurity should be managed in the future.

DOI: 10.1201/9781003201519-10

THE ADVANCEMENT OF TECHNOLOGY AND THE INTERTWINING OF OUR DIGITAL AND PHYSICAL LIVES

Cyberattacks' extension into the *socio-techno realm* and the use of cyber channels as information, influence, and disinformation vectors (e.g., the 2016 and 2020 US Presidential campaigns) will continue to undermine our confidence in systems (Benzel, 2021). Our current technology era (Industry 4.0) is characterized as the nexus between physical and digital infrastructures (Brooks, 2021a). It is a constantly transforming ecosystem in which *innovation*, *agility*, and *investments* are critical to keeping pace with the speed at which new *technologies*, *social changes*, and *habits* evolve. For instance, artificial intelligence (AI), the Internet of Things (IoT), smart cities, big data, quantum technologies, and the 5G Internet will considerably impact our lives (Brooks, 2021a). According to Brooks (2021a), an unprecedented need exists to understand the implications of these technologies in economic, social, and cybersecurity terms. New technologies and automated hacking tools enable the growing threat attack surface and force governments and private companies to restructure their priorities and objectives. Cyberspace now includes various criminal enterprises and adversarial nation-states, and threat actor capabilities are becoming more targeted, persistent, and sophisticated each year (Brooks, 2021a).

Nothing in the cyber world is fully protected and invulnerable. However, technologies can significantly assist in monitoring the threat landscape and serve as protective tools. For example, new advances in AI and machine learning (ML), quantum computing, identity management/authentication, software assurance, real-time monitoring and diagnostics, and endpoint security can be assets to help deter and sometimes neutralize cybercriminals (Brooks, 2021a). However, it can also be problematic to manage expanding technological arrays. Maintaining legacy systems and utilizing many security tools to protect a vast corporate network may become an enormous task for organizations.

For instance, there are often between 'three and six dozen separate cybersecurity software applications in use' at large organizations, each of which individually contributes to the security of the overall network (Clarke & Knake, 2019, p. 244). As a result, Chief Information Security Officers (CISOs) often have to deal with the challenging situation of juggling all of the company's software, systems, and applications, including the security tools to integrate them. In addition, the CISO has to select products from more than 20 different vendor companies to properly secure the company's assets with each of the security products' best individual capabilities (Clarke & Knake, 2019).

FUTURE CYBERSECURITY THREATS TO CONSIDER

As of today, a majority of cyber-threats are about the C part of the CIA triad (*confidentiality*, *integrity*, and *availability*), since most cybercriminals steal or hack confidential information to use it for various criminal means, including using victims' personal information to commit fraud (Schneier, 2018). These confidentiality breaches can even threaten national security when the criminal's goal is to collect a large quantity of information about citizens of a country (e.g., the breach of the Office of Personnel Management in the US). Other common threats affecting the availability of systems may be distributed denial-of-service (DDoS) attacks and ransomware attacks, in which the attacker encrypts data and demands a ransom to release the information. These attacks render the organization unable to operate for some time, thus significantly affecting their day-to-day operations.

As for *integrity*, hacked information can be manipulated or corrupted. A great example of such an attack is the SolarWinds case in 2020. A group believed to be Russia's Cozy Bear gained access to government systems, as well as a large number of private organizations' systems, through a compromised update of SolarWinds' Orion software (Constantin, 2020). This incident demonstrates how software developers need to consider additional ways to protect their code integrity and to minimize the risks to customers using their products (Constantin, 2020). Another preview of future threats is the increasing number of attacks against critical infrastructures to destabilize the everyday activities of a city, region, or even the whole country. The attack on Colonial Pipeline is another incident in which hackers gained access to the corporate network by exploiting a stolen password (later found inside a batch of leaked passwords on the dark web) to use the virtual private network (VPN) account of a Colonial Pipeline employee (Turton & Mehrota, 2021).

As Schneier (2018) suggested, one way to think about the CIA triad is that confidentiality threats primarily affect privacy, but integrity and availability threats may affect individual safety. He gave this useful example:

> My car has an Internet connection. And while I am worried that someone will hack into the car and eavesdrop on my conversations through the Bluetooth connection (a confidentiality threat), I am much more worried that they will disable the brakes (an availability threat) or modify the parameters of the automatic lane-centering and following-distance systems (an integrity threat). The confidentiality threat affects my privacy; the availability and integrity threats can kill me. (p. 79)

Although the IoT is already generating new challenges for security professionals, there is a long list of threats, including highly sophisticated threats, that security practitioners and researchers should consider in the future. Some not-so-sophisticated threats should also be considered because cybercriminals will continue to orchestrate these threats efficiently. After all, some nefarious activities and tactics still generate considerable benefits for cybercriminals while at the same time significantly impacting victims. Meeting these new threats will become a pivotal moment in cybersecurity.

COMMON SPECIFIC THREATS TO CONSIDER IN THE FUTURE

Email security and social engineering

Email security and social engineering will still be threats to consider in the future as they take advantage of human behaviors. Email is often the primary method of personal and organizational communication. Unfortunately, email is also a gateway that allows access to confidential information, compromises a system, and commits fraud in most security incidents. In other words, this unsophisticated threat is here to stay. Cybercriminals take advantage of an error in judgment made by an employee or another potential victim to trick them into doing something (e.g., opening a compromised PDF document) they would not do if they knew the criminal intent behind it. Then, fraudsters sell the stolen information and the tools used to extract it in illicit marketplaces (Dupont et al., 2017).

They also leverage the data for illegal purposes, such as using social engineering and spear-phishing attacks to trick potential victims into providing confidential information, perform fraudulent transactions, or install malware on victims' computers (Butavicius et al., 2016; Pomerleau & Auger-Perreault, 2020). Whereas traditional phishing involves sending email to a massive number of individuals but expecting only a small response, in spear-phishing the attackers have personal information about their victims and can target specific individuals within an organization – often chief executive officers, executives, or accounting and finance personnel (Pomerleau & Auger-Perreault, 2020). In addition, the spear-phishing emails include relevant information about the victims, increasing the likelihood that they will click on a link and provide confidential information (Pomerleau & Auger-Perreault, 2020).

Fraudsters have also migrated to wire-transfer fraud. One type of wire-transfer fraud is the business email compromise (BEC). Cybercriminals use social engineering to trick employees into transferring funds to another country (e.g., an accounting employee in the US sending a US$1.5 million wire transfer to China). Within such a scam, they will spoof the requests to make them appear to come from an authority figure, such as a CEO or CFO (chief financial officer). In one version, for instance, the fraudster poses as a lawyer representing the CEO, asking an employee to quickly transfer the money to a country where the CEO is supposedly on a business trip (Pomerleau & Auger-Perreault, 2020).

Ransomware attacks

Ransomware attacks have been around for over two decades, but more recently ransomware has become a trending and more dangerous cybersecurity threat. The inter-connectivity of digital commerce and expanding attack surfaces (i.e., more devices connected to the Internet) have enhanced the utility of ransomware as a weapon of choice for cybercriminals (Brooks, 2021b).

Like bank robbers, cybercriminals go where the money is, and our money is now easily accessible through online means instead of sitting in a physical vault. It's also easier for cybercriminals to generate benefits from extortion, as hackers can require payments in cryptocurrencies or pre-paid cards that can be anonymously transacted and are difficult to trace (Brooks, 2021b).

Unfortunately, this type of attack will both continue and evolve in the future. After installing malware and encrypting system files, cyberattackers deliver the ransom message to the victim. The email will remain a predilected vector of choice for cyberattackers to compromise potential victims (Mohanta et al., 2018). Some criminal groups have used ransomware attacks to target critical infrastructures. For example, the BlackMatter ransomware group infiltrated the New Cooperative (a major US agriculture group) in 2021, demanding US$5.9 million to provide a decryptor, affecting the production of 40% of US grain production and the feeding schedule of 11 million farm animals (Sharma, 2021). The attack also caused collateral damages to other businesses intertwined in the New Cooperative supply chain and threatened overall food production – an outcome that would potentially affect the whole population if the company could not resume its regular activity in a short period.

The future of ransomware management will be to use ML and AI to detect environments hiding the true nature of the malware. If ransoms are paid regularly, these types of attacks will undoubtedly increase. Cybercriminals will focus on ill-protected platforms, such as IoT devices that do not run any antivirus software (Mohanta et al., 2018). However, ransomware attackers may also begin to delete files more frequently until the ransom is paid. In some cases, the threat of public disclosure is critical, such as when cyberattacks extort companies to pay or risk their files being posted publicly. This criminal technique works very well when the data (a) is embarrassing, (b) holds a high amount of valuable intellectual property, or (c) is a valuable intelligence asset (Mohanta et al., 2018).

In a world of connected smart homes and cities, cyberattacks may allow cybercriminals to control anything connected to the Internet, interrupting, or disabling vital functions like heating and cooling systems, elevators, and traffic lights (Mohanta et al., 2018). As Mohanta et al. (2018) noted, ransom demands will be equivalent to the potential damage created. Thus, large ransoms will be demanded when lives may be at risk. Cyberattackers may attempt to attack and control Internet-connected devices that have severe vulnerabilities in their communication protocols, e.g., taking a pacemaker hostage, controlling a smart car remotely, or even taking over an entire smart grid (Mohanta et al., 2018).

Single-factor authentication

Cybercriminals have been using numerous tactics and modus operandi (e.g., phishing, malware, brute force attack, hash cracking, physical attacks) to break into networks and systems that are protected only by a single-factor authentication process (Stanislav, 2015). Authentication plays a significant role in ensuring the confidentiality of data. All human authentications rely on one of the following elements: (a) something you know, (b) something you have, or (c) something you are. First, *something you know* refers to the information a user knows, such as a password. Second, *something you have* is what the user has in his possession to authenticate himself, such as a smart card or a security token (e.g., an RSA SecurID hardware token or a YubiKey). Authentication based on *something you are* is intrinsic to the user and often associated with biometrics, such as fingerprint biometrics on a mobile device or Apple Face ID. In our digital and interconnected world, the use of a single-factor authentication process (e.g., password only) is not sufficient even if password-complexity rules are applied (Stanislav, 2015).

Two-factor authentication or 2FA is the authentication process where two of the three possible authentication factors are combined. For example, using a password to connect to an online banking application using a 2FA authentication process will generate a one-time password, such as an authentication code. That one-time password will be sent to a second device other than a computer (e.g., a mobile phone), and the user must then enter it in the original application. Multifactor authentication (MFA) takes this process even further, using two or more authentication factors. Both 2FA and MFA offer better protection than a password, so they are some of the most effective ways to reduce the risk of being a victim of an account takeover (e.g., phishing scams, clicking an infected link, and providing credentials on a fake website). However, there are some risks associated with the use of 2FA that need to be considered.

A common concept in security is that the more layers of authentication you have (which is the case in MFA), the more secure your account will be (Ledesma, 2021). However, different forms of 2FA are more secure than others. For instance, SMS (i.e., using text messages) 2FA is one of the riskier forms of 2FA since SMS messages can get intercepted, and SMS carries its own inherent risks (Ledesma, 2021). One risk is the sim-swap fraud, a scam in which a fraudster impersonates a victim and falsely claims (to a telecommunications company call-center agent) that their phone has been lost or stolen. Then, the fraudster will try to activate a new sim card – that the fraudster just happens to have in his possession – thus taking over the victim's account. Other attackers try to steal one-time passwords through the use of a bot called SMSRanger, which calls potential victims posing as a legitimate contact from an organization. This tactic is popular among cyberattackers who already have access to the victim's personal information, often by purchasing a 'fullz' or complete package of an individual's personal information (KrebsonSecurity, 2021).

Using 2FA is better than only using a password to authenticate, but device prompts, email codes, and authenticator apps (e.g., Duo Mobile) are all more secure (Ledesma, 2021). Furthermore, with the advances of modern science and information technology and the reliance on the IoT, authentication will be critical to allow users to rely on various communication types (e.g., between IoT devices), using the information provided by smart objects (Harish Kumar & Deepak, 2018).

FUTURE SOPHISTICATED THREATS

Quantum computing

A digital computer has two functions, storing and processing information, using bits (i.e., 0 or 1). A bit can be anything with two distinct configurations, like a light bulb or a coin flip. In modern computing and communications, classical bits are represented by the absence or presence of an electrical signal, encoding '0' and '1' respectively (University of Waterloo, n.d.). In contrast, a *quantum bit* is any bit made out of a quantum system, such as an electron or photon. Similar to classical bits, a quantum bit (qubit) must have two distinct states, one meaning '0' and one meaning '1,' but a quantum bit can also exist in superposition states – subjected to incompatible measurements and even intertwined with other quantum bits. Having the ability to harness the powers of superposition (i.e., placing a physical system in one of many configurations or arrangements of particles or fields), interference, and entanglement (i.e., two or more qubits that allow a set of qubits to express higher correlation than is possible in classical systems) makes qubits fundamentally different and much more potent than classical bits (University of Waterloo, n.d.).

To build quantum computers and other quantum information technologies, quantum objects need to act as qubits. In recent years, scientists have learned to harness and control many physical systems to act as qubits. This allows them to match the demands of different quantum technologies to the advantages of each type of qubit (University of Waterloo, n.d.). There are many types of qubits, most commonly (a) spin, (b) trapped atoms and ions, (c) photons, and (d) superconducting circuits (University of Waterloo, n.d.). Quantum computing may change the underlying assumptions about how computers work and, more importantly, how quickly computers can perform math calculations (Grobman, 2020). In explaining how quantum computing will work and how it will change the laws of physics that we know today, Clarke and Knake (2019) offered an interesting analogy:

> Think about Dick's grandparents or Rob's great-grandparents, people born in the nineteenth century. If they were brought back to life with the knowledge they had as teenagers and were show an Airbus A380, a metal object weighing six hundred tons, they would not believe for a second that it could fly. If they then saw it fly, they would think it was magic. Nothing about a six-hundred-ton metal objects traveling at five hundred miles an hour seven miles up in the air would make any sense to them. (p. 255)

Quantum computing can bring enormous advancements to biology, chemistry, physics, and many other disciplines (Grobman, 2020). For instance, the practical application of quantum computing may allow (a) a more robust defense against future pandemics, (b) the acceleration of the development of vaccines and treatments, and (c) solving critical logistics problems (e.g., route vaccines) (Grobman, 2020). However, quantum computing can also be a dangerous tool if nation-states and foreign intelligence services can use it to break cryptographic systems. Its malicious cousin, *quantum codebreaking*, will lead to significant data security questions for every organization and every individual that uses a computer (Johnson, 2021a).

We currently rely upon cryptographic systems to secure our digital world as we know it today: web traffic, emails, downloading confidential files, installing software updates, etc. (Grobman, 2020). But using the power of quantum computing to decrypt data encrypted with existing implementations (e.g., RSA and Elliptic Curve algorithms) may bring unprecedented visibility to highly sensitive data and even national security secrets (Grobman, 2020; Johnson, 2021a). As Grobman (2020) pointed out, the RSA encryption algorithm is the standard that our modern secure network protocols and data security system rely upon. Some of these algorithms are still used by NSA's Cybersecurity Directorate to protect classified and unclassified data (Johnson, 2021a). Two of them (e.g., AES-256 and SHA-384) are still considered safe against attacks on large quantum computers (Johnson, 2021a). Thus, the concern is mainly over major public key algorithms that may be susceptible to quantum-based attacks. The National Institute of Standards and Technology (NIST) is currently leading a post-quantum cryptography standardization initiative to specify the public-key cryptography standards that should be available to protect sensitive government information after the advent of quantum computers (NIST, 2021).

Blockchain threats

Blockchain is a technology that has significantly impacted businesses, industries, and economies. There are three types of blockchains: public, private, and consortium. A public blockchain is accessible to anyone with an Internet connection. A private blockchain is an authorization blockchain where only selected members can participate, while a consortium blockchain is semi-decentralized; in other words, organizations are responsible for managing the blockchain and deciding who can exchange information or mine it (i.e., digital mining currency) (Sibai et al., 2021).

Blockchain is a unique type of distributed ledger database represented by numerous layers (i.e., (1) application layer, (2) execution layer, (3) semantic layer, (4) propagation layer, and (5) consensus layer) providing specific services (Sibai et al., 2021). For instance, the *application layer* is where application programming interfaces (APIs) and access control mechanisms are managed, the *execution layer* is where smart contracts are developed and stored, the *semantic layer* is where the transaction validation is performed, the *propagation layer* is where peer-to-peer communications are executed, and the consensus layer is where mining (e.g., Proof-of-Work) and minting (e.g., Proof-of-Stake) are performed using different consensus algorithms (e.g., Proof-of-Activity) to ensure transactions are genuine (Sibai et al., 2021).

The blockchain's success is due to its multi-role technology being applicable to various fields, including financial services, data storage, and security services (Sibai et al., 2021). Blockchains do have numerous benefits, such as increasing trust, security, and transparency; the traceability of data being shared across the network; and reducing costs (IBM, n.d.). As Kshetri (2017) noted, data in the blockchain is distributed among many interlocked computers. For hacking efforts to be successful, more than 50% of the systems in the network need to be hacked (Kshetri, 2017). However, this also generates new challenges from a security perspective, such as additional attack footprints that need to be addressed to maintain the network's security (Sibai et al., 2021).

Blockchains can be attacked through various techniques. Maleh et al. (2020) classified five categories of blockchain threats and vulnerabilities: (1) client vulnerabilities (e.g., digital signatures based on elliptic curve cryptography), (2) consensus mechanism vulnerabilities (e.g., the 51% vulnerability when a single group of users has more than 51% of the hashing power in the blockchain network), (3) mining pool vulnerabilities (e.g., the bribery attack; the attacker can validate random transactions since he paid dishonest nodes to validate them), (4) network vulnerabilities (e.g., DDoS attacks or Sybil attacks), and (5) smart contract vulnerabilities (e.g., solidity vulnerability; Ethereum smart contract coding flaws).

According to Aggarwal and Kumar (2021), some blockchain attacks are the Finney attack, race attack, 51% attack, eclipse attack, Sybil attack, DDoS, routing attack, decentralized autonomous organization (DAO) attack, and the parity multisig parity attack. These attacks become more complex as more computing power is added to the network (Aggarwal & Kumar, 2021). For example, the Sybil attack can severely impact a public blockchain (Swathi et al., 2019). This attack is perpetrated when an attacker can corrupt the blockchain by creating many pseudonymous *fake* user accounts, thus securing a disproportionately large influence within the network, and forcing legitimate entities to become a minority (Swathi et al., 2019). As a result, genuine miners may no longer process blockchain transactions appropriately, significantly decreasing the system's throughput since legitimate user blocks cannot be verified (Swathi et al., 2019). Thus, blockchain brings numerous cybersecurity benefits, but such technology and solutions are not without any risks. Therefore, in the future, exceptional attention to current and potential blockchain threats is highly recommended.

Machine Learning (ML) and Artificial Intelligence (AI)

The use of ML and AI has been growing exponentially over recent years, in many practical applications: fraud detection, education, transportation, machine translation, medical image processing, etc. (Brundage et al., 2018).

However, less scholarly attention has been paid to their potential misuse (Tao et al., 2021). In the future, security experts should prioritize learning how ML and AI may be used for nefarious means, as both technologies will take a more prominent role within our lives. As Kilpatrick (2019) noted, the same technology allowing rescuers to identify and treat an injured person could be trained to locate and harm individuals. After all, 'no security system is perfect,' and unfortunately, ML algorithms are 'quite dumb' (Kilpatrick, 2019, p. 32). People can be presented with data and realize that it is inappropriate; they can question it and discard it when it does not make sense (Kilpatrick, 2019). However, ML algorithms take data, analyze it, and draw conclusions, regardless of whether the original data makes sense or not (Kilpatrick, 2019).

A data scientist can implement rules for an algorithm to look for specific characteristics in a file. If these characteristics are identified, algorithms can treat them in certain ways based on the intended legitimate intentions. However, data scientists must also account for and design checks for every potential error (Kilpatrick, 2019). For example, a recent study by researchers at McMaster University tested the use of different words in a popular language model called GPT-3 (i.e., OpenAI's Generative Pretraining Transformer 3) (Myers, 2021). These researchers wanted to validate if GPT-3 could '*tell them a story*' if fed the first couple of words. However, the use of the phrase 'two Muslims walk into a ...' led to potentially dangerous results. For example, 66% of the text the model provided (GPT-3's responses) involved violent themes (e.g., 'two Muslims walk into a....synagogue with axes and a bomb'), a far higher percentage than for other groups (Myers, 2021).

Other researchers have uncovered additional instances of deep-rooted biases in foundation models. For example, in 2019, Google built the transformational BERT ML technique: Bidirectional Encoder Representations from Transformers. BERT was shown to associate terms such as 'programmer' with men more than women (Sullivan, 2021). These two examples show that using algorithms may lead to unpredictable results. Thus, organizations and researchers using ML and AI capabilities should employ ethics teams, carefully select training data, and use assurance quality in their models to avoid biases (Sullivan, 2021).

Unfortunately, malicious actors have already begun using automatic and algorithmic content generation to confuse bots in many areas. Deliberately injecting bad data into the stream is known as 'poisoning the well' (Kilpatrick, 2019). Bad actors can also exploit flaws in the design of autonomous systems' goals (Brundage et al., 2018). Therefore, AI-driven cyber-threats need to be considered by cybersecurity professionals and researchers. As Senouci et al. (2020) explained, these smart attacks may turn AI into weapons to attack 5G services or hack the AI algorithms used by 5G components. More specifically, attackers could use AI's improved ability to launch lethal and stealthy attacks against attractive targets such as autonomous vehicles, drones, or manufacturing machinery (Senouci et al., 2020).

Moreover, attackers could hack ML algorithms by modifying the labels of the ML classification functions and altering the training data, decreasing the accuracy of the classification rate (Senouci et al., 2020). Also, in the future, we can expect hackers and criminals to use their own ML protocols to make malicious software more difficult to detect (Kilpatrick, 2019). For example, threat actors may use ML to compromise email by cloning phrases to fool anti-viruses' algorithms or create deepfakes that may become the next big wave of digital crime (Poremba, 2021).

Deepfakes

Deepfakes combine deep learning and a fake video, using deep learning algorithms to assemble images into a piece of content that people will believe to be truthful (Cunningham, 2020). There are also applied deepfakes such as DeepMasterPrints, digital fingerprints that AI engines can create to fool electronic devices like fingerprint scanners and smartphones. Attackers could use these fingerprints as authentication to access a smartphone or gain physical access to restricted areas (Cunningham, 2020). The concept of a MasterPrint focuses on using a partial fingerprint image and combining it with neural network ML to brute-force authentication mechanisms (Cunningham, 2020). Hacking voices using ML (i.e., deepvoice) is another technique cybercriminals are using to manipulate audio content or create a fake voice (Cunningham, 2020). Aside from video and audio content, the third medium bad actors may use is textual information (readfakes). This consists of news feeds, blogs, articles, or any textual information manipulated and used for malicious purposes and disinformation campaigns (Cunningham, 2020).

STATE-LEVEL HACKERS AND NATION-STATE ATTACKS

Nation-states have historically supported and attempted to control the powers of the Internet by harnessing hacking and hackers as resources, often for the expression of state power (Follis & Fish, 2020). For instance, North Korean hackers have carried out a systematic effort to target financial institutions all over the world (Buchanan, 2020). According to Buchanan (2020), their methods are bold, though not consistently successful, and their most profitable operations have manipulated how major financial institutions connect to the international banking system. By duping users of this system into thinking the hackers are legitimate users, they have (a) enabled the transfer of tens of millions of dollars into accounts they control, (b) tampered with log files and bank transaction records, and (c) prompted an enormous number of security alerts and upgrades in international financial institutions (Buchanan, 2020). These North Korean hackers have also disrupted hundreds of thousands of computers worldwide to hold valuable data for ransom, and they learned from both successes and failures to modify and combine their tricks, evolving their operations to be more effective (Buchanan, 2020).

As explained by Buchanan (2020), North Korean operatives found a better way to rob banks; they did not have to break through reinforced concrete or tunnel under vaults to get at the money, and they did not need to use force or threats. Instead, they duped the bank's computers into giving it away. To do this, they set their sights on a core system in international business called the Society for Worldwide Interbank Financial Telecommunication, or SWIFT. Many financial institutions in the SWIFT system have particular user accounts for custom SWIFT software, which they use to communicate with other banks worldwide (Buchanan, 2020). As an example, in the Bangladesh Central Bank Reserve hack case in 2016, stolen funds were transferred to various accounts in the Philippines, resulting in a US$100 million loss (Pomerleau, 2019; World Bank, 2017).

Another high-profile example is the *United States of America vs. Park Jin Hyok* case (2018). The case helps clarify how nation-states may be orchestrating attacks against financial institutions. The members of the Lazarus Group, working on behalf of the government of the Democratic People's Republic of Korea (DPRK) – commonly referred to as North Korea – defrauded the Central Bank of Bangladesh (Pomerleau, 2019). This case demonstrates how the group gained access to banking systems from financial institutions in Vietnam, the Philippines, Africa, Asia, Europe, and North America between 2015 and 2018, to commit significant wire frauds (United States District Court for the Central District of California, 2018). In these incidents, the hackers used social engineering techniques and spear-phishing emails to lure banking employees into breaching their employer's network security. In addition, the evidence shows these hackers were responsible for authoring the malware used in the May 2017 international ransomware cyberattack named WannaCry 2.0 that infected computers around the world (United States District Court for the Central District of California, 2018).

In 2018 alone, a total of seven banks were attacked using international money transfer schemes such as SWIFT, including the State Bank of Mauritius, Bank Islami in Pakistan, Cosmos Cooperative Bank in India, Banco de Chile, and three Mexican banks (Pomerleau, 2019). In February 2019, the bank of Valletta, located in the Republic of Malta, was also the victim of a cyberheist, forcing the bank to temporarily shut down all its operations after it identified the breach (Muncaster, 2019). The bank discovered that the hackers had made fraudulent electronic transactions using international money transfers totaling €13 million (Corfield, 2019).

In 2021, a report published by Eisenbach et al. (2021), citing data from the Boston Consulting Group (2019) Global Wealth report, stated that financial service firms experience 300 times more cyberattacks per year than other types of firms. Most of the malicious breaches in 2020 with a known source were conducted by financially motivated criminal actors (67%). Still, the rest were split equally among nation-state actors and hacktivists and were, on average, at least as costly to the victim. Even though the financial sector had the shortest average timespan of breaches, its average time to identify a breach was more than half a year (Eisenbach et al., 2021). Further, the lifetime of the malicious violations was, on average, 30% longer than in other industries (Eisenbach et al., 2021).

Attacks are increasingly perpetrated by Advanced Persistent Threat (APT) actors (Layton, 2021). These sophisticated, sustained attacks are meant to infiltrate networks and conduct long-term operations, such as spying or data exfiltration. Unlike an opportunistic cyberattack, where the perpetrator seeks to get in and get out of the system for some immediate payoff, an effective APT evades a system's security and remains undetected for a prolonged period (Layton, 2021).

LIST OF SUGGESTIONS AND RECOMMENDATIONS

The following section provides a list of suggestions that factor in the cybercrime ecosystem, to support security teams and policymakers' efforts to utilize the evidence-based approach in their decisions about the implementation and adoption of cybersecurity tools and policies.

Rethink investment in cybersecurity

Since significant financial resources are invested in cybersecurity, organizations should measure the efficiency of their tools, systems, and policies to invest resources where they are the most needed. According to Gartner (2021), worldwide spending on *information security and risk management technology and services* is forecast to grow 12.4% in 2021, reaching US$150.4 billion, while the investment in this same category was only of 6.4% in 2020. The security segment that will see the most significant increase in spending is *cloud security*, increasing 41.2% year over year (Gartner, 2021). In addition, the firm Momentum Cyber (Page, 2021) reported that there had been US$11.5 billion in total venture capital financing into cybersecurity start-ups in the first half of 2021, compared to US$4.7 billion during the same period a year earlier. The volume of these investments highlights the global urgency for acquiring new cybersecurity capabilities and the need for new technologies and approaches (Brooks, 2021b).

While spending increases, the cost of data breaches increases at the same time. Statistics from IBM (2021) show the average cost of a data breach has increased by nearly 10% year over year, from US$3.86 million in 2020 to US$4.24 million in 2021. For 11 consecutive years, healthcare had the highest industry cost of a breach, with an average total cost of US$7.13 million in 2020 and US$9.23 million in 2021 (IBM, 2021). In terms of why these breaches occurred, the most common initial vector of attack (present in 20% of all incidents) was compromised credentials. BEC represented only 4%

of the breaches but had the highest average total costs at US$5.01 million, while phishing's average total costs were US$4.65 million, malicious insiders US$4.61 million, social engineering US$4.47 million, and compromised credentials US$4.37 million (IBM, 2021).

We believe that innovation and drastic changes to policies will be necessary on various fronts to combat these trends. These changes should apply to law enforcement, academics, and public and private organizations. Without significant changes to the way that cybersecurity is managed and attention to the rapid growth of new technology (e.g., IoT, quantum computing, the 5G Internet), the risk landscape will increase, and it will be difficult to change our policies at the same pace that new technologies and risks evolve. Thus, actions need to be taken now to prepare for the future.

Law enforcement

Law enforcement should use evidence-based cybersecurity to evaluate the efficiency of their policies and criminal investigation projects targeting repeated offenders. For decades, it has been known that crime hot spots are areas (e.g., of a city) with high crime intensity. For instance, it has been demonstrated that 10% of criminals are responsible for more than half of all crimes (Blumstein et al., 1986; Lum & Koper, 2017). Similar to strategies applying in the physical world, criminal operations and investigations in cyberspace should target the 10% of criminals responsible for most cybercrime activities. More policing needs to be done online, and the same efforts and resources invested in the physical world should apply to cyberspace. Also, empirical studies should evaluate online policing operations to assess which investigation tactics and strategies best reach predetermined investigation objectives.

Academics

Academics should teach evidence-based cybersecurity courses so that university students and future leaders understand how to evaluate policies, tools, and cybersecurity practices in the real world. Faculty members who deliver these curriculums should also have practical experience in the field and evaluate cybersecurity from a multidisciplinary perspective (Blair et al., 2019). As Blair et al. (2019) persuasively argued, 'Without having had some set of experiences that helps them understand and appreciate the skills needed to effectively work with people who have very different disciplinary expertise, it is unlikely that faculty members will be able to succeed in developing those skills in their students' (p. 64). Indeed, academic professionals across disciplines will have to agree that cybersecurity needs to consider many areas, domains, and practices to fulfill the mission of protecting critical assets adequately – in the face of a constantly changing world with *ever-changing human and autonomous adversaries*. Indeed, cybersecurity should be perceived not as a single field of study but as a *meta discipline* (Blair et al., 2019).

GOVERNMENTS AND PRIVATE ORGANIZATIONS

Education

Evidence-based cybersecurity education, starting with training and awareness at a very young age, should be prioritized in schools so that children are aware of what can happen online and better protect themselves. Cybersecurity should be a subject included in school curricula at elementary, middle school, and high school levels. For instance, children should learn how to detect phishing emails and social engineering techniques, how to use a strong password, the importance of double authentication, how malware and viruses may affect systems, and how some types of cyberattacks work, so these students can avoid becoming victims later. Just as it is now essential to teach computer science and coding at a young age, it is also critical to teach cybersecurity to teenagers and future adults.

Unfortunately, there is no governance of the Internet, and there is currently a minimal academic cybersecurity curriculum in K-12 schools and universities around the world. While our lives (and our devices) are always online, there is no evidence-based training and education provided to students and citizens about securely using online platforms, tools, and the Internet. Cybersecurity is now a societal problem, and it is long past time to implement measures and invest resources to address it.

Multidisciplinary cybersecurity teams

When it comes to the future of cybersecurity management, we strongly agree with Blair et al. (2019) that cybersecurity is interdisciplinary at the individual level, but it must be multidisciplinary at the team level. Future cyber-threats will be so wide in scope (e.g., nation-states, individual hackers, industrial spies targeting academia, critical infrastructure attacks, and threats affecting small and medium organizations) that risk-based decisions will not be possible if companies and governments focus solely on technical vulnerabilities. Only a holistic approach to managing cybersecurity will allow them to adequately address the risks and impacts of cybersecurity policies on people and processes (Blair et al., 2019). Cybersecurity professionals should be involved in all business processes to ensure risks are adequately managed and that business solutions, products, and services are designed and developed considering the full array of threats that may affect actual and future customers and thus the organization's reputation and bottom line (Blair et al., 2019).

Public and private organizations must rely on multidisciplinary cybersecurity teams, representing considerable expertise and varied disciplinary backgrounds, to achieve the best potential security outcomes. Both individual team members and the group as a whole will need to adapt, use, and integrate automation and emerging technologies at the intersection of human and machine collaborations (Blair et al., 2019). In the future, cybersecurity teams will combine in-house experts with outside contractors to support internal operations in terms of additional skillsets or on-demand resources, while also leveraging specific expertise for short or long periods to assist organizations in protecting themselves.

Some of these professionals will have technical expertise (e.g., computer science, network engineering, information systems, mathematics, cryptography, ML, and AI). Others will complement the team with substantive knowledge and abilities in cybersecurity principles and practices (e.g., laws, criminology, political science and international relations, cognitive science and psychology, business, leadership, and management) (Blair et al., 2019). For example, cognitive scientists and psychologists specializing in cybersecurity will address human factors, human behaviors, and team communications. Cybersecurity lawyers will provide legal and ethical advice regarding privacy, intelligence, surveillance, information sharing within public and private partnerships, intellectual property, and potential legal liabilities involving third-party relationships. Political science and international relations experts will concentrate on strategies and policies in terms of defense and deterrence, to escalation and influence online campaigns (Blair et al., 2019).

Meanwhile, businesspeople who understand their clients and have expertise in customer service will work closely with cybersecurity professionals to ensure business processes and security are adequately managed and allow customers to make their transactions securely. Above all, cyber leadership in management will be critical. It is not the sole responsibility of the CISO to influence and lead security initiatives within an organization. Security will become everyone's responsibility, and cybersecurity will be integrated into all functions and roles as security is intertwined with each process, service, and product.

Threat hunting tools and techniques

In the future, a proactive approach to risk management will be critical in cybersecurity. Instead of waiting for specific threats that may or may not materialize, cybersecurity professionals and organizations will need to look for threats on a full-time basis. Various techniques for threat hunting already exist (e.g., penetration testing, ethical hacking, threat hunting on the darknet, red teaming), but organizations rarely use them as effectively as they could. We already know that malicious actors can successfully penetrate organizational systems or networks. Thus, threat hunters should examine IT environments using behavioral analysis to find any unusual patterns indicative of an attack (Ozkaya, 2021). Threat hunting should also be conducted outside of the organization. Collins (2018) defined threat hunting as 'an advanced security analysis process that leverages deep knowledge of a network or organization to catch subtler, more deeply embedded attackers than a security operations center (SOC) finds' (p. 1).

Threat intelligence data is drawn from multiple sources, including tactical and technical intelligence from internal and external sources (Ozkaya, 2021).

Intelligence about potential threats may come from threat intelligence partners, law enforcement, intelligence agencies, regulators, knowledge databases like MITRE ATT&CK (The Mitre Corporation, 2021), cyber-threat intelligence sharing platforms to provide information on attackers' tactics, techniques, and procedures (TTPs), security monitoring tools (e.g., security information and event management (SIEM), data loss prevention (DLP), and endpoints), and the security operation center. Threat intelligence should also go beyond acquiring new intelligence, instead analyzing it to recommend appropriate countermeasures against emerging threats (Sauerwein et al., 2021).

For instance, forums and online encrypted channels are portals to underground markets. Cybersecurity professionals and researchers need to be present in these markets to know what threat actors are discussing, planning, buying, and selling, as well as the vulnerabilities they wish to exploit. As Troia (2020) argued, forum research should not be limited to dark web hacker forums as threat actors also spend time on non-hacker forums. However, without experience in these markets, it might be highly time-consuming to search for vulnerabilities. Additionally, one threat actor may lead to many forums and channels. Other threat actors and new criminal activities will be identified from a single threat actor activity, rendering link analysis essential to gather intelligence on these groups.

Murphy (2021) pointed out that Telegram has emerged as a new dark web for cybercriminals. Many of these markets require investing money (e.g., in cryptocurrencies) to access some criminal channels or to purchase step-by-step instructions on how to attack one company. In many countries, it is not recommended by law enforcement to finance illicit activities online (i.e., to pay criminals) to get access to information or compromised data, even when it is for prevention purposes. This situation can make it extremely difficult for cybersecurity professionals to protect their organizations by accumulating intelligence on threat actors or other forms of threats (e.g., software vulnerability leaked on encrypted channels), so they can apply concrete threat reduction measures. Most of the time, it is not necessary to pay cybercriminals to get access to various forms of threat intelligence. However, it is essential to partner with specialized firms that know where to look and that have already established trust and relationships with some of these threat actors (see Vidocq, 2021 for more information).

Learning from mistakes

Ozkaya (2021) argued that security incidents are on the rise because organizations are not learning from their mistakes (or from mistakes by other companies) that led to cyberattacks. There are many cases of similar types of attacks being used to compromise a large number of organizations. If several attacks occur, the unaffected companies may be inclined to do nothing to improve their security posture, since they were not victims (Ozkaya, 2021). For instance, a report of a specific organization falling victim to a hacker does not typically cause other organizations to train their employees about phishing. However, this attitude is why attacks such as phishing are likely to succeed again and again.

The same mindset of learning from others' victimization processes should apply to any type of cybersecurity-related incidents, including insider threats, data leakage, fraud, and ransomware attacks. Post-mortem analysis of these incidents should be conducted to help cybersecurity professionals analyze whether their organization could become a victim of such an attack. Moreover, table-top exercises, both at the individual level (within one organization) and at the industry level, should be conducted every year, so organizations and employees can practice various cyber-threat scenarios identified as potential risks to their organizations.

Homomorphic encryption and privacy

The current problem with encrypted data is that it must be decrypted to work with it, rendering the data vulnerable to the very things companies are trying to protect against by encrypting it (Marr, 2019). A new potential solution is the use of homomorphic encryption. As Marr (2019) explained, there are three main types of homomorphic encryption: (1) partially homomorphic encryption (which keeps sensitive data secure by only allowing select mathematical functions to be performed on encrypted data); (2) somewhat homomorphic encryption (which supports limited operations that can be performed only a set number of times), and (3) fully homomorphic encryption (the gold standard of homomorphic encryption that keeps information secure and accessible). In the future, homomorphic encryption might eventually be the answer for organizations that need to process information while still protecting privacy and security. This type of encryption makes it possible to analyze or manipulate encrypted data without revealing it to anyone (Marr, 2019). In addition, it allows different organizations to use advanced analytics and ML techniques on encrypted data (Woodie, 2021).

Homomorphic encryption is a security tool that will positively impact industries with sensitive personal data, such as financial services or healthcare, where privacy is paramount (Marr, 2019). Most importantly, homomorphic encryption (a) can protect the sensitive details of the actual data, (b) still allows the data be analyzed and processed, and (c) is safe from break-ins from quantum computers (Marr, 2019). Similar to other forms of encryption, homomorphic encryption uses a public key to encrypt the data. However, unlike other forms of encryption, it uses an algebraic system to allow functions to be performed on the data. At the same time, it's still encrypted, and only the individual with the matching private key can access the unencrypted data (Marr, 2019). This approach allows the data to be and remain secure and private even when someone is using it. One very relevant way homomorphic encryption can be used is to ensure democratic elections are secure and transparent. More specifically, votes could be counted while keeping the voters' identities private; third parties could verify the results and voting data would be protected from manipulation (Marr, 2019). Another application would be for financial institutions to share information to prevent financial crimes.

The biggest challenge to the widescale adoption of homomorphic encryption is that using older technology it was slow to compute, so it was not practical to use it in many applications (Marr, 2019). For instance, in 2009 multiplying two bits homomorphically took half an hour, but today the same task can be performed in nanoseconds (Wiggers, 2021). Companies such as IBM, Microsoft, Oracle, and Duality Technologies are working diligently to speed up this process by decreasing the computational overhead required for homomorphic encryption. For example, Duality Technologies is developing privacy-centric and secure collaboration tools using homomorphic encryption. Duality also has a contract with the US Department of Defense (Lunden, 2021).

The Zero Trust approach

Most current infrastructures, both in governments and private organizations, are built on a failed perimeter-based security model (Cunningham, 2020). As many researchers and practitioners argue (Cunningham, 2020; Rose et al., 2020; Samaniego & Deters, 2018; Sibai et al., 2021; Walker, 2021), a new strategy based on trust management must be adopted, enabling a better response to new threats while reducing vulnerabilities, deterring attackers, and securing systems with a practical focus. The terms *Zero Trust Network* and *Zero Trust Architecture* both refer a model created in 2010 by John Kindervag while working as a principal analyst at Forrester Research Inc (Pratt, 2018).

The Zero Trust concept applies to two primary areas: authentication and authorization (Rose et al., 2020). This model considers that no system can be secured unless all interconnecting devices accessing the infrastructure are secured (Cunningham, 2020). Samaniego and Deters (2018) claimed that the only way to manage IoT networks expected to be formed of millions of 'things,' all connected through the Internet, is not to trust anything. Thus, security professionals should ask several questions about each device: (1) What is the level of confidence about the subject's identity for this unique request? (2) Is access to the resource allowable given the level of confidence in the subject's identity? (3) Does the device used for the request have the proper security posture? (4) Are there other factors that should be considered that would change the confidence level (e.g., time, location of subject, subject's security posture) (Rose et al., 2020)? The critical aspect of this security strategy is well described by Cunningham (2020): 'Consider every network, device, user, account, access, or other related item compromised until proven otherwise. Everything is a threat, all the time. Nothing should be allowed to operate by default, and any and all access must be explicitly proven valid before it can take place' (p. 186).

Public and private partnerships

As Kolbe (2021) argued, private organizations cannot be expected to defend against cyberattacks from nation-state actors by themselves, just as they would be unable to defend against a conventional military attack. The SolarWinds supply chain cyber operation in 2020 demonstrated the collective vulnerability between the government and private sector, as an adversary identified and exploited weak links in the supply chain (Zabierek et al., 2021). Thus, reducing the cyber risk posed by state or non-state adversaries requires a multi-layered defense to understand the threat, harden defenses, deter attacks, and mitigate damages when an attack occurs (Zabierek et al., 2021).

Effective and practical intelligence is not just a product or a report. It has to become a system that can provide an early warning before an attack and situational awareness during an attack (Zabierek et al., 2021). Unfortunately, private organizations may have critical insight into attacks on their networks but may not reveal their vulnerabilities for fear of damaging their reputation or stock price. Government agencies may likewise have critical intelligence on threat actors, methods, and targets, but they often choose not to reveal them to protect classified sources and methods (Zabierek et al., 2021). Similar to Zabierek et al. (2021), Pomerleau (2019) and Pomerleau and Lowery (2020) noted that the private sector does not have the necessary intelligence collection authorities and capabilities to protect its network and infrastructure. On the other hand, the government does possess these necessary attributes, but it does not always have the expertise in the cyber-threats affecting private industries (Boes & Leukfeldt, 2017; Borghard, 2018).

It is now imperative to develop an integrated, networked approach to collaborative defense, intelligence analysis, and intelligence sharing between the government and the private sector (Johnson, 2021b; Pomerleau, 2019; Pomerleau & Lowery, 2020; Zabierek et al., 2021). Sharing between the private and public sectors is often case-by-case and incident-based, saved for limited, voluntary coordination between actors. Furthermore, the structures and policies are not in place to facilitate sharing and collaboration (Zabierek et al., 2021). A cyber-threat (e.g., a data breach) is certainly different from the threat of acute terror attacks on our homeland. But the current cyber-threat (e.g., cyber-attacks on critical infrastructures) is particularly pressing and unique compared to previous challenges faced by many nations worldwide. People, businesses, and government are already under attack – and as Zabierek et al. (2021) noted, they are ill-prepared to tackle imminent present and future attacks and have been for much of the last decade.

For this reason, cybersecurity should be seen as a national security problem. In the words of Lt. General Stanley McChrystal, 'it takes a network to defeat a network' (McChrystal et al., 2015). Policymakers need to recognize that looking at domestic cyberattacks solely through a law enforcement lens limits the ability to put these attacks in the context of national security. Moreover, solely relying on the private sector to carry the nation's security burden is untenable. This crisis presents an opportunity to reimagine and redesign a new approach to how we collectively tackle cybersecurity

(Zabierek et al., 2021). As Pomerleau (2019) argued, in the future, information exchange, knowledge-generating, problem-solving networks, and coordination networks – in line with the network typology developed by Whelan and Dupont (2017) – will become prominent types of security networks, and they must operate at the international level.

The challenge in our current cybersecurity posture involves both policies and structures. Policies are the building blocks of how the system will respond to the needs of a cyber-secure country in the coming years (Zabierek et al., 2021). The increasing sophistication of state and non-state cyberactors, taking advantage of uncoordinated policies' weaknesses, can act without any respect to strict protocols and laws, knowing that the response time by security actors will be significantly postponed (Alperovitch, 2021). Moreover, security professionals who need to make critical decisions to protect infrastructures are not fully empowered to make timely, measured decisions (Zabierek et al., 2021).

To be in a position to operate at the same level of cyberattackers and to operationalize the mindset of security networks, we need an organizational model that is responsive to domestic cybersecurity operations and that is geared toward increasing our resiliency and defense structure – now more than ever (Johnson, 2021b; Pomerleau & Lowery, 2020; Zabierek et al., 2021). More specifically, we must reimagine and design a collaborative defense architecture in which cyber operations are (1) coordinated in planning and execution and (2) driven by analysis and rapid sharing of threat intelligence between networked nodes, ensuring that a common situational awareness is in place across the entire system (Zabierek et al., 2021).

Recommended references

U.S. Cyberspace Solarium Commission, (2020). *United States of America Cyberspace Solarium Commission*. https://www.solarium.gov/report

Zabierek, L., Bueno, F., Sady-Kennedy, A., Kanyeka, N., & Kennis, G. (2021). *Toward a collaborative cyber defense and enhanced threat intelligence structure*. Belfer Center Harvard Kennedy School. https://www.belfercenter.org/publication/toward-collaborative-cyber-defense-and-enhanced-threat-intelligence-structure

AN EVIDENCE-BASED CYBERSECURITY APPROACH TO DEVELOPING NEW AND INNOVATIVE DETECTION AND MITIGATION APPROACHES

Maimon (2020) argued that although past cybersecurity research has focused on technical aspects of security tools, future research should shift to the humans who operate within the cybercrime ecosystem. Several academic scholars (Kraemer-Mbula et al., 2013; Moore et al., 2009) have likewise suggested that the interactions among cybercriminals, enablers (i.e., individuals who support the online criminal operations), targets, and guardians (i.e., law enforcement agencies and system administrators) form a unique ecosystem, in which the activities of each actor influence the behaviors of other actors. Thus, rigorous scientific research designs should include field experiments, longitudinal surveys, and observations, and these research designs should be deployed to generate evidence that can: (a) identify online threats and vulnerabilities and educate targets of cybercrime, (b) guide policy development and guardians' efforts to secure cyberspace, and (c) drive the design and configuration of computing environments that can effectively mitigate the consequences of cybercrime events (Maimon, 2020).

Another crucial component of the evidence-based cybersecurity approach is translating research findings into a format that is accessible and easy to digest for cybersecurity professionals in the field (Maimon, 2020). For example, a CISO and his or her team who are deciding which tools and policies to deploy, in order to reduce their organization's risk of cybercrime, should have access to recent research findings providing a clear picture regarding the effectiveness of various tools/policies in achieving their goals, to guide their decision-making process (Maimon, 2020). In other words, the overarching goal of the evidence-based cybersecurity approach is to allow cybersecurity practitioners easy access to relevant scientific research that may address cybercrime and cybersecurity problems pertinent to their organization (Maimon, 2020). Moreover, measuring what works and what does not in terms of success methods should be a priority for CISOs. As Pease (2021) argued, organizations establish and use many helpful technical metrics, but these metrics may not be in line with the objectives of the security team. Some simple metrics to measure success (e.g., threat hunting) could include the (1) mean time to detect (i.e., how long did it take to detect the attacker), (2) mean time to respond (i.e., how long did it take for the security team to respond), and (3) rate of recidivism (i.e., how long after the attackers were evicted did they try again) (Pease, 2021).

According to Benzel (2021), a cybersecurity experimentation strategy should be driven by five fundamental principles: (1) support experimentation and testing, (2) enable the creation of repeatable, science-based research that peers can validate, (3) generate research results that can be leveraged to make the whole greater than the sum of its parts, (4) foster methodologies and tools to guide experimenters toward a new and scientific cybersecurity discipline, and (5) provide an open environment for researchers, industries, and academic experts to build on one another's achievements. One way to do so would be for governments to fund research programs and provide grants to academia and institutions for basic and applied cybersecurity research (Brooks, 2021a). Another way would be to invest more resources in cybersecurity R&D, e.g., a cross-disciplinary range of cybersecurity experimentation and testing methods and tools (Benzel, 2021). These investments would help create the next generation of ideas and inventions, since investments in science and technology for cybersecurity in agencies, the private sector, and national labs are indispensable for securing the future (Brooks, 2021a).

CONCLUSION

Cybersecurity is no longer solely a computer science and engineering discipline. The cyber component touches every sphere of our lives. Thus, cybersecurity is a field of study – a meta discipline – that needs to consider other areas, domains, and practices to fulfill its mission of protecting critical assets adequately.

Cyber-threats are proliferating and morphing rapidly, and they will become exponentially more dangerous with the development of new technologies unless drastic actions are undertaken at the policy and practical levels. Nations worldwide will need to become more resilient and assist both their organizations and citizens in learning how to protect themselves against novel cyber-threats. Unfortunately, we still have little empirical and systematic knowledge on how cybersecurity research gets translated into practice. This is why the evidence-based cybersecurity approach should be the vehicle in demonstrating how evidence, research, and science should apply to cybersecurity management going forward. Public and private organizations, as well as practitioners and researchers, should work closely together in translating research into practice. At the strategic and operational levels, innovative strategies should be employed to remove current challenges and barriers while leveraging the opportunities we now have to create a better cyber ecosystem.

REFERENCES

Aggarwal, S., & Kumar, N. (2021). Attacks on blockchain. *Advances in Computer, 121*, 399–410. https://doi.org/10.1016/bs.adcom.2020.08.020

Alperovitch, D. (2021). *America is being held for ransom. It needs to fight back.* https://www.nytimes.com/2021/09/20/opinion/ransomware-biden-russia.html

Benzel, T. (2021). Cybersecurity research for the future: Considering the wide range of technological and societal trade-offs associated with cybersecurity. *Communications of the ACM, 64*(1), 26–28. https://doi.org/10.1145/3436241

Blair, J. R. S., Hall, A. O., & Sobiesk, E. (2019). Educating future multidisciplinary cybersecurity teams. *Computer, 52*(3), 58–66. https://doi.org/10.1109/MC.2018.2884190.

Blumstein, A., Cohen, J., Roth, J. A., & Visher, C. (1986). *Criminal careers and "Career Criminals," Vol I.* National Academies Press.

Boes, S., & Leukfeldt, E. R. (2017). Fighting cybercrime: A joint effort. In R. Clark, & S. Hakim (Eds.), *Cyber-physical security: Protecting critical infrastructure at the state and local level* (pp. 185–203). Springer.

Borghard, D. E. (2018). *Protecting financial institutions against cyber threats: A national security issue.* https://carnegieendowment.org/files/WP_Borghard_Financial_Cyber_formatted_complete.pdf

Boston Consulting Group. (2019). *Global wealth 2019: Reigniting radical growth.* https://image-src.bcg.com/Images/BCG-Reigniting-Radical-Growth-June-2019_tcm9-222638.pdf

Brooks, C. (2021a). *Investment in research & development required for a safer cybersecurity future.* https://cybertheory.io/investment-in-research-development-required-for-a-safer-cybersecurity-future/

Brooks, C. (2021b). *Ransomware on a rampage: A new wake-up call.* https://www.forbes.com/sites/chuckbrooks/2021/08/21/ransomware-on-a-rampage-a-new-wake-up-call/?sh=1c8100152e81

Brundage, M., Avin, S., Clark, J., Toner, H., Eckersley, P., Garfinkel, B., & Amodei, D. (2018). The malicious use of artificial intelligence: Forecasting, prevention, and mitigation. *arXiv preprint arXiv:1802.07228.*

Buchanan, B. (2020). *The hacker and the state: Cyber attacks and the new normal of geopolitics.* Harvard University Press.

Butavicius, A. M., Parson, K., Pattinson, R. M., & McCormac, A. (2016). *Breaching the human firewall: Social engineering in phishing and spear-phishing emails.* https://www.semanticscholar.org/paper/Breaching-the-Human-Firewall%3A-Social-engineering-in-Butavicius-Parsons/b58de02e690f07853e88cc93e93e5b71fdf9b493

Clarke, R., & Knake, A. (2019). *The fifth domain; Defending our country, our companies, and ourselves in the age of cyber threats.* Penguin.

Collins, M. (2018). *Threat hunting: A guide to proactive network defense* (1st ed.). O'Reilly Media.

Constantin, L. (2020). *SolarWinds attack explained: And why it was so hard to detect.* https://www.csoonline.com/article/3601508/solarwinds-supply-chain-attack-explained-why-organizations-were-not-prepared.html

Corfield, G. (2019). *Hackers KO Malta's bank of Valletta in attempt to nick €13m.* https://www.theregister.co.uk/2019/02/13/bank_of_valletta_13m_euro_hackers_shutdown/

Cunningham, C. (2020). *Cyber-warfare – truth, tactics, and strategies: Strategic concepts and truths to help you and your organization survive on the battleground of cyber-warfare.* Packt Publishing.

Dupont, B., Côté, M. A., Boutin, I. J., & Fernandez, J. (2017). Darkode: Recruitment patterns and transactional features of "the most dangerous cybercrime forum in the world". *American Behavioral Scientist, 61*(11), 1219–1243. https://doi.org/10.1177/0002764217734263

Eisenbach, T. M., Kovner, A., & Junho Lee, M. (2021). *Cyber risk and the U.S. financial system: A pre-mortem analysis.* Federal Reserve Bank of New York. https://www.newyorkfed.org/research/staff_reports/sr909

Follis, L., & Fish, A. (2020). *Hacker states.* The MIT Press.

Gartner. (2021). *Gartner forecasts worldwide security and risk management spending to exceed $150 billion in 2021.* https://www.gartner.com/en/newsroom/press-releases/2021-05-17-gartner-forecasts-worldwide-security-and-risk-managem

Greenberg, A. (2019). *Sandworm: A new era of cyberwar and the hunt for the Kremlin's most dangerous hackers.* Doubleday.

Grobman, S. (2020). Quantum computing's cyber-threat to national security. *PRISM Security Studies Journal, 9*(1), 53–66.

Harish Kumar, N., & Deepak, G. (2018). User authentication for IOT objects: A two factor approach using biometrics and perceptual hashing. In *2018 International Conference on Networking, Embedded and Wireless Systems (ICNEWS)* (pp. 1–3). https://doi.org/10.1109/ICNEWS.2018.8904012

IBM. (2021). *Cost of data breach report 2021*. https://www.ibm.com/security/data-breach

IBM. (n.d.). *Building trust and boosting the bottom line*. https://www.ibm.com/topics/benefits-of-blockchain

Johnson, D. B. (2021a). *How the NSA is getting ready for the (coming) quantum codebreaking revolution*. https://www.scmagazine.com/analysis/encryption/how-the-nsa-is-getting-ready-for-the-coming-quantum-codebreaking-revolution

Johnson, D. B. (2021b). *Congress wants (another) cyber collaboration center for info sharing. Will it succeed where others have failed?* https://www.scmagazine.com/analysis/threat-intelligence/congress-wants-another-cyber-collaboration-center-around-information-sharing-will-it-succeed-where-others-have-failed

Kilpatrick, H. (2019). Malicious use of artificial intelligence in cybersecurity. *Pipeline & Gas Journal, 246*(2), 32.

Kolbe, P. (2021). Forward. In L. Zabierek, F. Bueno, A. Sady-Kennedy, N. Kanyeka, & G. Kennis (Eds.), *Toward a collaborative cyber defense and enhanced threat intelligence structure* (pp. 1–37). Belfer Center Harvard Kennedy School.

Kraemer-Mbula, E., Tang, P., & Rush, H. (2013). The cybercrime ecosystem: Online innovation in the shadows? *Technological Forecasting and Social Change, 80*, 541–555.

KrebsonSecurity. (2021). *The rise of one-time password interception bots*. https://krebsonsecurity.com/2021/09/the-rise-of-one-time-password-interception-bots/

Kshetri, N. (2017). Blockchain's roles in strengthening cybersecurity and protecting privacy. *Telecommunications Policy, 41*(10), 1027–1038. https://doi.org/10.1016/j.telpol.2017.09.003

Layton, R. (2021). *Hackers are targeting U.S. banks, and hardware may give them an open door*. https://www.forbes.com/sites/roslynlayton/2021/03/17/hackers-are-targeting-us-banks-and-hardware-may-give-them-an-open-door/?sh=6ec957a14dcc

Ledesma, J. (2021). *What is two-factor authentication (2FA) and why should you use it?* https://www.varonis.com/blog/two-factor-authentication/

Lum, C. M., & Koper, C. S. (2017). *Evidence-based policing: Translating research into practice*. Oxford University Press.

Lunden, I. (2021). *Duality nabs $30M for its privacy-focused data collaboration tools, built using homomorphic encryption*. https://techcrunch.com/2021/10/05/duality-nabs-30m-for-its-privacy-focused-data-collaboration-tools-built-using-homomorphic-encryption/

Maimon, D. (2020). Relevance of evidence-based cybersecurity in guiding the financial sector's and efforts in fighting cybercrime. In P. L. Pomerleau, & D. Lowery (Eds.), *Countering cyber threats to financial institutions* (pp. 9–28). Palgrave Macmillan. https://doi.org/10.1007/978-3-030-54054-8_2

Maleh, Y., Shojafar, M., Alazab, M., & Romdhani, I. (2020). *Blockchain for cybersecurity and privacy*. CRC Press. https://doi.org/10.1201/9780429324932

Marr, B. (2019). *What is homomorphic encryption? And why is it so transformative?* https://www.forbes.com/sites/bernardmarr/2019/11/15/what-is-homomorphic-encryption-and-why-is-it-so-transformative/?sh=22795c4e7e93

McChrystal, S. A., Collins, T., Silverman, D., & Fussell, C. (2015). *Team of teams: New rules of engagement for a complex world*. Portfolio/Penguin.

Mohanta, A., Hahad, M., & Velmurugan, K. (2018). *Preventing ransomware: Understand, prevent, and remediate ransomware attacks*. Packt Publishing.

Moore, T., Clayton, R., & Anderson, R. (2009). The economics of online crime. *Journal of Economic Perspectives, 23*, 3–20.

Muncaster, P. (2019). *Hackers target Maltese bank in €13m cyber heist.* https://www.infosecurity-magazine.com/news/hackers-target-maltese-bank-in-15m/

Murphy, A. (2021) *Telegram emerges as a new dark web for cyber criminals.* https://www.ft.com/content/cc3e3854-5f76-4422-a970-9010c3bc732b

Myers, A. (2021). *Rooting out anti-Muslim bias in popular language model GPT-3.* https://hai.stanford.edu/news/rooting-out-anti-muslim-bias-popular-language-model-gpt-3

NIST. (2021). *Post-quantum cryptography.* https://csrc.nist.gov/Projects/Post-Quantum-Cryptography/Post-Quantum-Cryptography-Standardization

Ozkaya, E. (2021). *Incident response in the age of cloud: Techniques and best practices to effectively respond to cybersecurity incidents.* Packt Publishing.

Page, C. (2021). *Cybersecurity V.C. funding surges to a record $11.5B in 2021.* https://techcrunch.com/2021/08/25/cybersecurity-vc-funding-surges-to-a-record-11-5b-in-2021/

Pease, A. (2021). *Threat hunting with elastic stack: Solve complex security challenges with integrated prevention, detection, and response.* Packt Publishing.

Pomerleau, P. L. (2019). *Countering the cyber threats against financial institutions in Canada: A qualitative study of a private and public partnership approach to critical infrastructure protection (Order No. 27540959).* Available from ProQuest Dissertations & Theses Global. (2320957957). https://about.proquest.com/products-services/pqdtglobal.html

Pomerleau, P. L., & Auger-Perreault, M. (2020). Fraud risk management: Using fraud analytics to combat external and insider threats. In L. Shapiro, & M. Maras (Eds.), *Encyclopedia of security and emergency management* (pp. 1–9). Springer. https://doi.org/10.1007/978-3-319-69891-5_296-1

Pomerleau, P. L., & Lowery, D. (2020). *Countering the cyber-threats to financial institutions.* Springer.

Poremba, S. (2021). *Data poisoning: When attackers turn AI and ML against you.* https://securityintelligence.com/articles/data-poisoning-ai-and-machine-learning/

Pratt, M. K. (2018). *What is zero trust? A model for more effective security.* https://www.csoonline.com/article/3247848/what-is-zero-trust-a-model-for-more-effective-security.html

Rose, S., Borchert, O., Mitchell, S., & Connelly, S. (2020). *Zero trust architecture.* NIST Special Publication 800–207. https://nvlpubs.nist.gov/nistpubs/SpecialPublications/NIST.SP.800-207.pdf

Samaniego, M., & Deters, R. (2018). Zero-trust hierarchical management in IoT. In *2018 IEEE International Congress on Internet of Things (ICIOT)* (pp. 88–95). https://doi.org/10.1109/ICIOT.2018.00019

Sauerwein, C., Fischer, D., Rubsamen, M., Rosenberger, G., Stelzer, D., & Breu, R. (2021). From threat data to actionable intelligence: An exploratory analysis of the intelligence cycle implementation in cyber threat intelligence sharing platforms. In *ARES 2021: The 16th International Conference on Availability, Reliability and Security* (pp. 1–9). https://doi.org/10.1145/3465481.3470048

Schneier, B. (2018). *Click here to kill everybody: Security and survival in a hyper-connected world.* W.W. Norton.

Senouci, S., Sedjelmaci, H., Liu, J., Rehmani, M., & Bou-Harb, E. (2020). AI-driven cybersecurity threats to future networks. *IEEE Vehicular Technology Magazine*, 15(3), 5–6. https://doi.org/10.1109/MVT.2020.3007981

Sharma, A. (2021). *$5.9 million ransomware attack on farming co-op may cause food shortage.* https://arstechnica.com/information-technology/2021/09/5-9-million-ransomware-attack-on-farming-co-op-may-cause-food-shortage/

Sibai, R. E., Challita, K., Abdo, J. B., & Demerjian, J. (2021). The impact of blockchain on cybersecurity management. In K. Daimi, & C. Peoples (Eds.), *Advances in cybersecurity management* (pp. 117–138). Springer. https://doi.org/10.1007/978-3-030-71381-2_7

Stanislav, M. (2015). *Two-factor authentication. [electronic resource]* (1st ed.). I.T. Governance Publishing.

Sullivan, M. (2021). *Tech-industry AI is getting dangerously homogenized, say Stanford experts.* https://www.fastcompany.com/90666920/ai-bias-stanford-percy-liang-fei-fei-li

Swathi, P., Modi, C., & Patel, D. (2019). Preventing Sybil attacks in blockchain using distributed behavior monitoring of miners. In *2019 10th International Conference on Computing, Communication and Networking Technologies (ICCCNT)* (pp. 1–6). https://doi.org/10.1109/ICCCNT45670.2019.8944507

Tao, F., Akhtar, M., & Jiayuan, S., Z. (2021). The future of artificial intelligence in cybersecurity: A comprehensive survey. *EAI Endorsed Transactions on Creative Technologies*, 2021, 1–15. https://doi.org/10.4108/eai.7-7-2021.170285

The Mitre Corporation. (2021). *ATT&CK matrix for enterprise.* https://attack.mitre.org/

Troia, V. (2020). *Hunting cyber criminals: A hacker's guide to online intelligence gathering tools and techniques.* Wiley.

Turton, W., & Mehrota, K. (2021). *Hackers breached Colonial Pipeline using compromised password.* https://www.bloomberg.com/news/articles/2021-06-04/hackers-breached-colonial-pipeline-using-compromised-password

University of Waterloo. (n.d.). *What is qubit? Institute of quantum computing.* https://uwaterloo.ca/institute-for-quantum-computing/quantum-101/quantum-information-science-and-technology/what-qubit#Spin

U.S. Cyberspace Solarium Commission. (2020). *United States of America Cyberspace Solarium Commission.* https://www.solarium.gov/report

United States District Court for the Central District of California. (2018). *United States v. Park Jin HYOK, also known as ("aka") "Jin Hyok Park," aka "Pak Jin Hek."* https://www.justice.gov/usao-cdca/press-release/file/1091951/download

Vidocq. (2021). *Compromised bank account trends in Canada.* https://vidocqgroup.com/cyber-intelligence-threat-assessment-report/

Walker, K. (2021). *Why we're committing $10 billion to advance cybersecurity.* https://blog.google/technology/safety-security/why-were-committing-10-billion-to-advance-cybersecurity/

Whelan, C., & Dupont, B. (2017). Taking stock of networks across the security field: A review, typology and research agenda. *Policing & Society*, 27(6), 671–687.

Wiggers, K. (2021). *Privacy-preserving data platform Duality Technologies raises $30M.* https://venturebeat.com/2021/10/05/privacy-preserving-data-platform-duality-technologies-raises-30m/

Woodie, A. (2021). *In homomorphic encryption we (must) trust.* https://www.datanami.com/2021/09/03/in-homomorphic-encryption-we-must-trust/

World Bank. (2017). *Combatting cybercrime: Tools and capacity building for emerging economies.* https://openknowledge.worldbank.org/handle/10986/30306?locale-attribute=fr

Zabierek, L., Bueno, F., Sady-Kennedy, A., Kanyeka, N., & Kennis, G. (2021). *Toward a collaborative cyber defense and enhanced threat intelligence structure.* Belfer Center Harvard Kennedy School. https://www.belfercenter.org/publication/toward-collaborative-cyber-defense-and-enhanced-threat-intelligence-structure

Zetter, K. (2014). *Countdown to zero day: Stuxnet and the launch of the world's first digital weapon.* Broadway Books.

Index

Note: Page numbers in **bold** refer to tables.

Printed in the United States
by Baker & Taylor Publisher Services